Holland

at its best

BY ROBERT S. KANE

The World At Its Best Travel Series
BRITAIN AT ITS BEST
FRANCE AT ITS BEST
SPAIN AT ITS BEST
GERMANY AT ITS BEST
ITALY AT ITS BEST
HAWAII AT ITS BEST
LONDON AT ITS BEST
PARIS AT ITS BEST
HOLLAND AT ITS BEST
SWITZERLAND AT ITS BEST

A to Z World Travel Guides
GRAND TOUR A TO Z: THE CAPITALS OF EUROPE
EASTERN EUROPE A TO Z
SOUTH PACIFIC A TO Z
CANADA A TO Z
ASIA A TO Z
SOUTH AMERICA A TO Z
AFRICA A TO Z

Robert S. Kane

Holland
at its best

Trade Imprint of National Textbook Company
Lincolnwood, Illinois U.S.A.

For Linda Gwinn

Published by Passport Books, Trade Imprint of National
Textbook Company, 4255 West Touhy Avenue,
Lincolnwood, Illinois 60646–1975.
© 1988 by Robert S. Kane. All rights reserved. No part of
this book may be reproduced, stored in a retrieval system,
or transmitted in any form, or by any means, electronic,
mechanical, photocopying or otherwise, without the prior
written permission of National Textbook Company.
Manufactured in the United States of America. Library of
Congress Catalog Card Number: 87-61079
7 8 9 0 ML 9 8 7 6 5 4 3 2 1

Contents

Foreword
Holland: Small but Special

Travel the length and breadth of Europe and you won't find a country that has so impacted the course of post-medieval history that is anywhere near as small as the Netherlands.

This remarkable little land—190 miles at its longest, 160 miles at its widest—is pint-sized in contrast not only to a giant like the United States (which knew Dutch colonists more than four centuries ago), but smaller, too, than such nations as England, Spain, and Portugal (whose Baroque-era fleets contended for New World hegemony).

Its uncanny knack at shipping and trading was responsible for a spate of Dutch development in the seventeenth century, which resulted in the evolution of a middle class so substantial that it might well have coined the term "disposable income" so in vogue today. With profits gained from Dutch seamen's skills as transoceanic mariners, Dutch merchants' flair for international commerce, and Dutch entrepreneurs' savvy with respect to overseas colonies as widely scattered as New York and Indonesia, the home folks spent wisely and well.

The while they nurtured egalitarian proclivities, the democratic Dutch—for long governed by *stadholders* rather than kings—enriched and educated themselves to the point where a powerful bourgeoisie built up a nationwide network of medium-sized cities to supplement showcase Amsterdam. Architects vied with each other in the design of civic centers— monumentally scaled churches, palatial city halls, splendidly embellished public weigh-houses flanking vast central squares from which radiated streets and canals lined by stone-and-brick mansions.

Cabinetmakers created the furniture—over-sized cabinets to hold extensive family wardrobes and treasures, sturdy chairs to surround generous-sized tables at which friends gathered to feast beneath the graceful brass chandeliers that to this day symbolize Holland's hospitality.

And a school of painters—proportionately more extensive than in any other country, in the course of the Baroque era—flourished not only in Amsterdam, but quite as brilliantly in provincial Dutch centers, recording for posterity a lifestyle based on a single word—*gezillig*, translating as cozy, comfortable, congenial—that, happily for those of us visiting Holland contemporarily, remains very much the criterion for the Dutch host or hostess.

What I attempt in the pages following is a hearty helping of Holland, opening with Amsterdam, not only because of its alphabetic precedence but because it is what I term, in the subheading of Chapter 2, "the great Dutch metropolis." Indeed, Amsterdam's magnetism—as manifested in the fine and performing arts, a capacious core blessedly devoid of high-rise buildings and with a facade essentially unchanged for several centuries, the kingdom's biggest concentration of hotels in all categories, and an immediately engaging populace—too often serves as a stumbling block. It's so easy to have a good time in the Big City that we short-change other Dutch destinations; I know of no country where more visitors are familiar with the capital at the expense of the provinces, not even Britain's London, France's Paris, or Italy's Rome.

Holland at Its Best will, I hope, remedy this situation. In Chapter 3, I offer the nitty-gritty on ten satisfying day-long excursions from Amsterdam, the range Aalsmeer (with its flower market) and Alkmaar (with its cheese market) through Haarlem (the city of the painter Hals) and Hoorn (contemporarily obscure and, perhaps for that reason, uncommonly beautiful).

Then follow seventeen tightly packed chapters on what I regard as non-excursion Holland, points where, for reasons

1

Holland
A Mini A to Z

ADDRESSES: *Netherlands Board of Tourism* (NBT) maintains offices in the United States at 355 Lexington Avenue, New York, NY 10017; 225 North Michigan Avenue, Chicago, IL 60601; and at 605 Market Street, San Francisco, CA 94105; as well as at 25 Adelaide Street East, Toronto, Ontario, Canada M5C1Y2; 25 Buckingham Gate, London, SW1; and 31 Avenue des Champs Élysées, Paris. These offices—whose function is to provide the prospective traveler in the Netherlands with gratis information and literature—are part of a worldwide network, whose headquarters are at Vlietweg 15, in Leidschendam, an eastern suburb of The Hague. Throughout Holland, the traveler's best information source is the local tourist office—identified by the initials VVV. These enterprises are multifunctional: They book hotel rooms, as well as seats for concerts, ballet, and the like; sell gifts with their logos; and very often change money. It is worth noting, though, that, by and large, they make a nominal charge for most printed materials. Ideally, you pick up as many of them as you can in advance of your trip and for free—from the Netherlands Board of Tourism.

BICYCLES: Everyone—Royal Family and ministers of the Crown included—rides them, in this mostly pancake-flat country. They are, quite sensibly, limited to well-defined bicycle lanes, and they're available for rental throughout the kingdom, should you want to give them a go. But I must caution you that, because they have no motors and are virtually noiseless (bikes are *supposed* to be horn equipped but are not always), you must be ever vigilant at intersections. Please heed my three-word warning: *Watch for bikes!*

BREAKFAST may—or may not—be included in hotel room rates. As a general rule, luxury-category hotels do *not* include it; hotels in lesser categories do. But there are exceptions; inquire when reserving. Included in your room rate or not, the first meal of the day is a generous buffet, usually including fruit juice and/or fresh fruit, sliced Dutch cheese and sliced Dutch ham, butter, jam, generally undistinguished breads (raisin bread is the best, and often there are self-service toasters) and possibly pastries, individual packets of cold cereals offered with the extraordinarily rich Dutch milk, boiled eggs, and sometimes scrambled and fried eggs, as well, in the company of ham or bacon. Coffee is good (the Dutch drink a lot of it), but it is served in oddly small cups. And, invariably, you have the option of room service, for which there may be a charge.

CASINOS: There are a limited number, as you will learn from chapters following. Foreigners must present passports. For gents, jacket and tie are usually required. You take your chances at blackjack and roulette, and slot machines await your shiny guilders.

CLIMATE: You are in a fairly damp, fairly cool, temperate-zone country. Long and lovely sunny spells are a possibility. (I have experienced them with great pleasure.) But you never want to travel without a raincoat and a collapsible umbrella. Averages, Fahrenheit:

of substantial size or, simply, geographical location, the traveler does well to settle in. The big cities—salty Rotterdam with its fabulous harbor, The Hague—connoting Netherlandish elegance—under-appreciated Utrecht, gastronomically superior Maastricht—each rate a major chapter. But I am quite as partial to smaller spots like Deventer and Giethoorn, Kampen and Zwolle. And the middle-sized cities are intriguing enough for me to zero in on a number of them—including Apeldoorn, the site of superbly restored Het Loo Palace; Arnhem, if only for the Van Goghs at its Kröller-Müller Museum; Delft—little changed since Vermeer painted it; treasure-laden Leeuwarden, in the isolated north; agreeably lively Den Bosch; quietly, almost shyly handsome Middelburg.

Although I do not neglect creature comforts—personally inhabited or carefully inspected hotels, and restaurants where I have eaten, categorized Luxury, First Class, and Moderate—in *Holland at Its Best* any more than in companion volumes of my *World at Its Best* series, I make a special point of calling to your attention this country's extraordinary cultural resources, far too little appreciated beyond metropolitan centers like Amsterdam where, understandably, we beeline for the Rijksmuseum's Rembrandts, and The Hague, whose Mauritshuis collection is not unknown to us. Still, we outlanders are as woefully ignorant of great art in teeming Rotterdam (where it is folly to neglect the Boymans-van Beuningen Museum) and vibrant Utrecht (where an aged onetime convent houses one of Europe's most memorable caches of Middle Ages art) as in smaller spots like Leiden and Gouda.

There remains Holland's not-so-secret touristic weapon: the Hollanders themselves. They are, all of them above the age of five or six, it would appear, incredibly fluent in English, the national No. 2 language, after their own. They are so well educated and international in outlook that you must not be surprised if they know the name of the governor of your state, and so well traveled that they may well have visited your home town—and more than once if it's a principal city. They are occasionally—but only occasionally—without senses of humor. It is not for nothing that their country has for centuries been known as the most tolerant in Europe; the Dutch do not shy away from divergent points of view. Nor are they, as a rule, bashful. Fear not: you will meet them as you move about their country. And like them. There are, to be sure, other stimulating Continental lands. But Holland stands out for us English speakers in this respect, because it, too, is English-speaking. In no country below the North Sea is it easier for us to get to know the resident populace, the better to appreciate their low but lovely land.

ROBERT S. KANE

	Maximum	Minimum
Winter (February)	41	31
Spring (May)	61	46
Summer (July)	69	55
Autumn (October)	57	45

CLOTHES: No question about it, the well-groomed, well-scrubbed Dutch are the most casually clad of Europeans. Jacket and tie are, of course, the business uniform for men, with business and professional women correspondingly conventionally attired. Otherwise, Hollanders tend to dispense with formality in their garb. Of course, visiting women will want a fairly dressy outfit or two; gents, a sport jacket or navy blazer and a tie or two. By and large, though, be as comfortable as you like.

CREDIT CARDS are accepted in many—but by no means all—restaurants, chain department stores, and shops. But they are not yet as widely accepted as in the United States. American Express, Diners Club, Visa, and MasterCard are all popular.

CURRENCY: Easy; you're comfortable with it in a day. The guilder (indicated, please note, by the symbol *f*—for florin, its old name) is divided into 100 cents and minted as 5-cent, 10-cent, 25-cent, *f*1 and *f*2.50 coins. There are, as well, *f*5, *f*10, *f*25, *f*50, *f*100, *f*250 and *f*1,000 notes. Your hotel will change money for you, but best rates are at banks and at the kingdomwide network of GWK (De Grenswisselkantoren) change offices in train stations and at border-crossing points, most of them are open evenings and on weekends; you need your passport. Take the bulk of your funds in traveler's checks—they're the safest—with plenty in 20-dollar denominations, as they are the most convenient.

CUSTOMS: *Entering the Netherlands:* You're allowed a couple of cartons of cigarettes and a couple of bottles of alcohol, as well as your personal effects, including of course cameras and a reasonable amount of film. Dutch immigration officers tend not to stamp passports, indicating dates of entry into and exit from Holland, unless you so request.

Returning to the United States: Each individual may bring back $400 worth of purchases duty free. That is allowable once every 30 days, provided you've been out of the country at least 48 hours. If you've spent more than $400, you'll be charged a flat 10 percent duty on the next $1,000 worth of purchases. Remember, too, that antiques, duly certified to be at least 100 years old, are admitted duty free and do not count as part of your $400 quota; neither do paintings, sculptures, and other works of art, of any date, if certified as originals. It's advisable that certification from the seller or other authority accompany them. Also exempt from duty but as part of the $400 quota: one quart of liquor. And—this is important—there is no restriction on how much one can bring in beyond the $400 quota, as long as the duty is paid.

DEPARTMENT STORES, SHOPS, AND SUPERMARKETS: Branches of two department-store chains—*Vroom & Dreesmann* (often with a supermarket in the basement) and budget-category *Hema* (invariably with packaged baked goods and candies)—blanket the country. *De Bijenkorf,* the premier chain, is to be found only in a few major cities. I make shopping suggestions in some detail, and by category, in Chapter 2 (Amsterdam) and in chapters on other important cities. The supermarket is happily ubiquitous and a source of grocery items, including wine, for hotel-room aperitifs.

DRIVING: All you need is your own home license—valid, of course. If you're a member of an automobile club that has reciprocal privileges with the Royal Dutch Touring Club (ANWB), you're eligible for help from the ANWB's road patrols, or you may join that organization for a temporary (one-month) period. For information on road conditions, phone ANWB at 070-31-31-31, day or night.

DUTCH DOGS are at least as spoiled as French dogs (see *Paris At Its Best* and *France At Its Best*) with a consequence fouled sidewalks the length and breadth of the kingdom. Would that Dutch footpaths were as clean as Dutch windows! Caveat: Wherever you walk, watch your step.

ELECTRIC CURRENT: 220 volts AC. Take along a transformer for your shaver or hair dryer and an adapter plug to be attached to the prongs of your appliance, so that it will fit into the holes of the Dutch outlet. American department stores sell kits containing a transformer and a variety of variously shaped adapters. The alternative is to buy a Dutch appliance on your arrival in Holland for use during your stay—counseled if your sojourn will be lengthy.

FLOWERS AND CANDLES: The nationals of no country that I know are more adept at floral arrangements than the Dutch—not surprising, of course, as they are preeminent growers. (See *Alsmeer* and *Keukenhof*, Chapter 3.) Still, credit where it is due: you'll enjoy the colorful displays on restaurant tables and in hotel lobbies throughout the country. And because the Dutch attach great importance to a *gezilig*, or cozy, ambience, they rarely wait until dark to light candles in restaurants and cafés; more often than not you'll have lunch, as well as dinner, by candlelight.

GEOGRAPHY: This is a small country—the size of a couple of New Jerseys or, if you prefer, Connecticut, Massachusetts, and tiny Rhode Island combined, with its length under 200 miles, its width 160 miles, a good portion reclaimed (thence called *polder*) with the aid of dikes and dams. About half of the territory of the Netherlands is below sea level, much of it gained in the last six decades, as a result of draining IJsselmeer, the lakelike inlet of the North Sea, which had been the Zuider Zee (see Delta Project, Chapter 16). Not surprisingly, Holland is, by and large, flat as a putting green, except in the south, near the Belgian border, where visitors from northerly provinces delight in hills as high as 300 feet. Three principal rivers—Maas (or Meuse), Rhine, and Schelde—flow through Holland, and besides the North Sea, it is bordered by Belgium to the south and West Germany to the west. There are an even dozen provinces; the twelfth—Flevoland—largely reclaimed land, or *polder*, came into being only in 1986. The others, for the record, are Drenthe, Friesland, Gelderland, Groningen (also the name of a city), Limburg, North Brabant (the "North" distinguishing it from Brabant proper, in Belgium, due south), North Holland, OverIjssel, South Holland, Utrecht (also the name of a city), and Zeeland.

This is one of the most densely populated countries in the world, so you're not surprised to learn, after traveling through a land where a substantial city pops up every 20 or 30 miles (17 have populations of 100,000-plus), that the population—14,500,000—is more than twice that of Switzerland, which has almost as large an area, and is but a million less than enormous-in-surface Australia.

HISTORY: The Romans, under no less august an emperor than Julius Caesar, vanquished resident Germanic tribes—the Frisians (who gave their name to a northerly province) and the Batavi (for whom the short-lived Batavian Republic was named, not to mention the city of Batavia, capital of the Dutch East Indies before the sovereign Indonesians changed it to Djakarta—not long before the start of the Christian era. Charlemagne ruled through the eighth and ninth centuries. In the course of the Middle Ages, the Counts of Holland—whose seat, 's Gravenhaage (The Count's Wood), evolved as The Hague and ultimately became the seat of government and of the States General, or Parliament—gained strength. But power passed from them to the Dukes of Burgundy and thence to the Holy Roman Emperor, Charles V. Trouble brewed under the repressive reign of Charles's son, the fanatic Philip II of Spain, a king so pious that the palace he built at El Escorial, outside Madrid (see *Spain At Its Best*), is as much monastery as royal residence.

Much-married Philip (one of whose wives was England's "Bloody" Mary I, Catholic half-sister of Elizabeth I) engendered Dutch opposition to the Inquisition-beset Spaniards. Anti-Spanish forces were led by a stadholder of the House of

Orange-Nassau (which was to become the Dutch royal house—see below), the very same Prince William of Orange whom history books dub William the Silent. Though no stranger to Philip, whom he had served as a diplomat, or to Philip's father, Charles V, of whom he was a special favorite, William raised an army that was successful in driving the Spaniards out. This resulted in the Union of Utrecht, which, in 1579, codified the federation of the seven northern provinces as the independent Republic of the United Netherlands.

Stadholders for most of the country's history were Princes of Orange. Of these, two stand out: William the Silent, to this day, hero of Dutch national unity; and, later, William III, who pulled off the neat trick of becoming king of a foreign country (England, of course, which he co-ruled with his wife Mary) at a time when his family had not yet ruled their *own* country, at least as monarchs. The Dutch Republic may have been rather oddball, what with descendants of Franco-German nobility—the House of Orange-Nassau—mostly serving as its hereditary heads. But it constituted the era of Holland's Golden Age.

Amsterdam became one of the centers of the world. Dutch explorers and mariners sailed tiny ships all over the globe. (If, like me, you grew up in Albany, New York, you had it drummed into your head, in the sixth grade, that Hendrik Hudson sailed his *Halve Maan* up the river now taking his name, reaching what is now the site of Albany on September 19, 1609; within a decade, Albany—called Fort Orange after the prince's house—came into being, the oldest continuous settlement of the original thirteen states, with the Hudson River itself long called Riviere van den Verst Mauritius, or River of Prince Maurice, after the descendant of William the Silent, who was then the Republic's stadholder.

Still another relatively obscure Dutch settlement—Nieuw Amsterdam—at the mouth of the river, became rather prominent; the English later renamed it New York. Additional Dutch ships went to the Caribbean (Willemstad, capital of Curaçao, remains Dutch in facade), to South America (the Dutch were briefly in Brazil; you see Frans Post's fine paintings of their settlements in museums throughout the kingdom), and to Asia, to what is now Indonesia, but had been for centuries the Dutch East Indies.

At home, the republican Dutch achieved an enviable reputation as the most tolerant people in Europe (indeed, they still are), welcoming diamond traders and other merchants from Antwerp, which remained under Spanish control. They opened their doors to religious refugees, as well—French Huguenots and Jews from Portugal and Spain, whom Philip II was persecuting. (Until World War II, Amsterdam's Jewish community was one of the most important in Europe.)

All these newcomers brought to Holland skills and ideas. Dutch commerce became the marvel of Europe. A substantial middle class developed, creating the market for the great art and architecture and artisanship that lure us to Dutch shores these many centuries later. (Holland, it might well be pointed out here, is the name of two provinces—North Holland and South Holland—of the Netherlands; in modern times, we call the entire country by that name, concurrently with the official designation, The Netherlands.)

The early eighteenth century saw the decline of the Golden Era. Before the century was out, the French-founded Batavian Republic was in, only to be followed some years later by a monarchy of Napoleon's devising, in which his brother Louis was made king. Louis surprised everyone, both his subjects and his brother. They had all expected him to be nothing more than a rubber stamp for Paris. But he attempted to reshape a Netherlands for the Netherlanders, to the point where Napoleon would have none of it, booted him off the throne, and took over himself in 1810, annexing the Netherlands to France.

The Congress of Vienna brought Holland, at long last, its first Dutch king. The Congress united the northern and southern Netherlands (read Holland and Belgium). But it didn't work. The Belgians revolted and formed their own kingdom, and the Dutch kings (the same Orange-Nassau dynasty that had provided the earlier princes) continued on as sovereigns of what had constituted the United Republic. They included a trio of unexciting Williams—I, II, and III, with Queen Wilhelmina following. The long reign of that no-nonsense lady embraced the two world wars. Holland remained neutral in the first and attempted a similar policy in the second. But the Nazis invaded in May 1940 without warning, quickly overcame Dutch resistance, and virtually destroyed the core and port of Rotterdam to the point where it is virtually a new city today. Wilhelmina, her family, and government set up exile in England and Canada, while Dutch forces fought alongside the Allies abroad: at home, the Dutch Underground so thwarted the Nazis that Hitler retaliated with mass executions and the deportation—to concentration camp ovens—of 104,000 of the 112,000 Dutch Jews. The waning years of the war were particularly cruel to Holland. In September 1944, the Dutch people united to rise against their captors in the premature conviction that Allied landings at nearby ports would lead to their immediate liberation. But only the extreme north of the country was freed; the rest suffered ferocious Nazi reprisals, mass starvation among them. In May 1945, with the demise of the Germans, Wilhelmina and the cabinet-in-exile returned. Post-World War II recovery (marked by Holland's originally uniting, for economic purposes, with neighboring Luxembourg and Belgium into the Benelux Union, which was the nucleus of the Common Market) was miraculously successful.

HOLIDAYS: Expect closed banks and offices, if not certain museums and restaurants, on New Year's Day, Good Friday, Easter Sunday and Monday and April 30th (Queen's Day), Ascension, Whit Sunday and Monday, and Christmas Day and the day following.

HOTELS: About the hotels in this book: I have lived in, dined in, and/or thoroughly inspected the hotels carefully selected for evaluation in these pages. I disregard the complexities of the star systems—that of the Dutch authorities has been replaced by all-Benelux ratings—and have divided hotels and restaurants into the same three price groups I use in all my books: *Luxury, First Class,* and *Moderate.* Bear in mind that I am fussy. In towns of any size and cities, I concentrate on *centrally sit-*

uated hotels, including country hotels only when they are exceptional and will be of interest to travelers with cars. All hotels in my *Luxury* and virtually all in my *First Class* categories have television and minibars (stocked with liquor, wine, soft drinks, and sometimes snacks, available for purchase) in all rooms, as well of course as private baths, often equipped, in the luxury hotels, with hair blower/driers. My *Moderate* category hotels are, by and large, *better* Moderate, very often with TV and/or mini-bars and with baths attached to most or all rooms. I indicate the proportion of baths in each case and make clear, as well, when showers replace tubs in bathrooms.

When a Dutch hotel is well operated, everything works well, reception to room service. I don't know of a hotel in the kingdom without fluently multilingual staffers (see Language, below) and in which housekeeping is not of an exceptional standard. Dutch hotels, by and large, are spotless; Dutch hotel managements, again by and large, are professional and cordial.

Hotels operated by crack United States-based international chains, such as *Hilton International* (heaviest represented, with three hotels), *Marriott*, *Inter-Continental*, and *Sonesta* are on scene; so, among other foreign-based chains, is the British-origin *Crest* group. There are a number of independently operated hotels, usually middle-category, associated with America's *Best Western*, and still others with a Holland-based group called *Golden Tulip*. There remain top rank hotels that have been voted membership in the blue chip *Relais et Châteaux* (represented by David B. Mitchell and Co., 200 Madison Avenue, New York, NY 10016) and, last but hardly least, still others, admitted by decision of their confrères, in the aptly titled *Leading Hotels of the World* (head office, 747 Third Avenue, New York, NY 10017).

KLM ROYAL DUTCH AIRLINES' beginnings were modest enough. What happened was that a young Dutch Army pilot, rarin' to go after World War I, conceived the idea of a commercial international air carrier. Albert Plesman, by name— he is recognized to this day as the airline's founder—he convinced enough backers to finance what the company has re-corded as the world's first scheduled air service. The year was 1920, the route was Amsterdam-London, the passenger load totaled two (each customer was provided with leather jacket, flying helmet, gloves, goggles, earplugs, and hot water bottle), and the cargo was a bundle of newspapers. Before long, Plesman was collaborating with a man whose name would later be given to aircraft he designed—Anthony Fok-ker—with the former flying and the latter creating what evolved into a transatlantic fleet.

No European airline made a quicker post-World War II re-covery. By May 1946, Plesman was back from the United States, where he had negotiated the purchase of a new fleet for KLM, in time for the airline to score another first: It be-came first on the Continent to operate flights between Europe and North America after the war. South America, Africa, and Australia followed, the while an intensive intra-European net-work developed.

Today KLM flies to 129 cities in 79 countries on six conti-nents, with six United States cities (New York, Atlanta, Chi-cago, Houston, Los Angeles, and Anchorage), as well as four Canadian gateways (Toronto, Montreal, Vancouver, and Cal-gary), linking North America and Schiphol, Holland's state-of-the-art intercontinental airport, with an enviable heart-of-Europe situation.

At Schiphol, KLM offers passengers—many of whom change planes there for onward routings—such facilities as a score of rooms for between-flight naps, fully equipped Con-ference-Seminar Center, nursery for baby feeding and bath-ing, spring-through-fall rooftop promenade deck; Aviodome, a museum of aviation history; nonsectarian meditation room; budget-tabbed, self-guided, four-hour tour of Amsterdam, with transportation to and from town on a KLM bus; and a fifty-store, duty-free shopping center, one of the world's largest.

KLM's Business Class has, in recent seasons, become one of the hottest tickets aloft, not only because of comfortable, wide seats but because you're fed so well. Aperitifs include young Dutch gin, or *genever* (I like it on the rocks), champagne, and the usual liquors; dinner wines are Bordeaux or Burgundies. The meal might be based on *tournedos Béarnaise*, duck, or perhaps roast hare, having opened with a shrimp or crayfish appetizer. If you're flying eastbound, expect a hearty pancake and scrambled egg breakfast prior to landing; westbound, the pre-North American touchdown is preceded by an elegant supper. Business Class's souvenirs have become collector's items; they're coaster-size Dutch tiles with three dozen different subjects. Frequent KLM flyers build up sets. (Alia, CP Air, El Al, Finnair, Martinair, Pan Am, Trans World and Wardair also link North America and Schiphol. NLM, a KLM subsidiary, provides domestic service to several cities within the Netherlands.)

LANGUAGE: Every Dutchman or Dutchwoman you meet will have studied English for six years in school—as well as French and/or German. Of the non-native English speakers in Europe, only Scandinavians rank with the Dutch in this respect. To state that English is Holland's No. 2 language is to understate. The fluency is extraordinary. You'll have not a whit of difficulty—anywhere. And if you know German, you'll find that you'll be able to read some Dutch—and even, after your ear becomes attuned, understand a bit.

MUSEUM CARD costs but a few bucks and is good for entry into some 300 museums throughout the Netherlands, Amsterdam's Rijksmuseum through Zwolle's Provincial Over-IJssels Museum. If you haven't had a chance to buy it from an office of the Netherlands Board of Tourism on home base, pick yours up at any of the city or town tourist offices (addresses in chapters following) or at many participating museums. And yes, you know which museums it's valid for; names of all 300 are printed on the two sides of this cleverly designed fold-up ducat.

OPEN HOURS: Many—but by no means all—*museums* are closed Mondays (some close other days), keeping decent hours on open days from 10:00 or 11:00 A.M. until 5:00 P.M. and not closing for lunch. Tourist offices and hotel desks are up to date on specifics. *Churches*—including top-ranking historic ones—often keep severely limited hours; again, ask at local tourist offices. *Shops* are generally open from 8:30 or 9:00 A.M. to 5:30 or 6:00 P.M., Monday through Friday, usually closing between 4:00 and 5:00 P.M. on Saturdays, in some instances for lunch, and, as well, for a full morning each week, which varies by city—as, indeed, do days of weekly open evenings. *Offices* open between 8:30 and 9:00 A.M., shutter for lunch at noon or 12:30 P.M. for an hour, and remain open in the afternoon until 5:00 P.M., Monday through Friday.

OPERA, BALLET, CONCERTS, MOVIES, FESTIVALS: This is a performing arts country of the top rank. Of course, you will want to consider taking in performances in the Big Four cities—Amsterdam (Chapter 1), The Hague (Chapter 10), Rotterdam (Chapter 15), and Utrecht (Chapter 19). But you're not limited to these. Holland is a country of medium-sized cities. In all of them and in many smaller towns, as well, you'll find a vibrant municipal theater with a wide range of performances. Local tourist offices have programs. Remember that movies are shown in their original version (with subtitles—they are not dubbed), so that you can be assured that British and American films will be in English. And bear in mind that the No. 1 performing arts festival, the annual Holland Festival, takes place over a three-week span every summer, in the Big Four cities, albeit with the bulk of performances in Amsterdam.

PASSPORTS: They are necessary for admittance to the Netherlands and must be presented to U.S. Immigration on your return. Apply at Department of State Passport Offices in a dozen-plus cities (look under U.S. Government in the phone book) or—in smaller towns—at the office of the clerk of a Federal Court and at certain post offices. Allow four weeks, especially for a first passport (valid for ten years), for which you'll need a pair of two-inch-square photos and birth certificate or other proof of citizenship. There's a $42 fee (subject to change) for first passports; renewals are cheaper. If you're in a hurry when you apply, say so; Uncle Sam will usually try to expedite if you can show documentation indicating imminent departure. Upon receipt of your passport sign your name where indicated, fill in the address of next of kin, and keep this valuable document with you—*not packed in a suitcase*—as you travel. In case of loss, contact local police, nearest U.S. Embassy or Consulate, or Passport Office, Department of State, Washington, D.C. 19524.

PROTECTED HISTORIC BUILDINGS are easily identified throughout Holland by a small shield—composed of two blue and two white triangles—affixed near the principal entrance. These buildings' pedigrees have been researched and vouched for, and their facades cannot be altered.

RATES for selected hotels (where I've stayed or which I've inspected) and restaurants (where I've eaten) are categorized as *Luxury, First Class,* or *Moderate;* these translate pretty much into what they would mean in the U.S., adjusted of course to the purchasing power of the dollar *with respect to the guilder* at the time of your visit.

RESTAURANTS/CUISINE: There are notable deviations from the rule—many selected in pages following. By and large, though, Dutch cuisine, as manifested in restaurants, is not a distinguished cuisine, except—and this is a major *except*—in those portions of the kingdom within, say, 20 or 25 miles of the Belgian frontier, close enough to the superior French-influenced fare of Belgium. Too often, Dutch portions can be gargantuan (ingredients are invariably excellent), but the cooking tends to lack subtlety. You will eat well enough in the Netherlands and on occasion—as I indicate in certain restaurant evaluations in succeeding chapters—very well, indeed. But a great cuisine is not part of the national culture, as is the case, say, in France or Italy. Nor can you expect the restaurant norm to be as consistently high as in such countries as Britain, Spain, Switzerland, Canada or the United States, not to mention the earlier-cited next-door neighbor, Belgium, and *its* neighbor, Luxembourg, or even, for that matter, also-adjacent Germany, whose national cuisine is infinitely more complex and varied than Holland's, if only to cite the single area of bread and pastries, where the Germans excel and the Dutch do not.

There are, of course, pluses. Dutch restaurants are at their best—other than at breakfast (above), a generally satisfying buffet in hotels—with simply prepared fish and seafood—Zeeland oysters on the half-shell, a decently sauced shrimp cocktail, grilled sole or other North Sea fish; with soups—the hearty pea soup is justifiably celebrated, but tomato and vegetable species are usually very good, too; and with fresh vegetables (quality is excellent in Holland). Omelets are usually a safe bet, as long as they're not gussied up with gloopy sauces. Sandwiches—*broodjes*—often sold in shops specializing in them—have okay fillings—the good Dutch cheese, sliced boiled ham—but rolls used are too often flabby and character-less. You may—or may not—enjoy *uit smijter*—ham or roast beef sandwiches topped with fried eggs. Typical *koffietafel* lunches are variations on ham-and-cheese-centered breakfasts. And many restaurants feature prix fixe Tourist Menus that are nutritious, filling, and reasonably priced.

In the restaurants of no western land that I know are cakes and pastries so rarely encountered as in Holland, where desserts usually are based on ice cream. ("It doesn't spoil, as cakes can if they're not eaten," restaurant people have told me.) If there is a baked sweet, inevitably it will be a heavy-crusted concoction, stuffed with apples and raisins. (There are, however, restaurants which specialize in pancakes (*pannekoeken*) and the little rolled and filled pancakes called *flensjes*—both tasty.)

Not surprisingly, restaurants with foreign—or foreign-accented—cuisines are increasingly popular with the widely traveled Dutch and their visitors. Restaurants that call themselves French (often with Dutch chefs who have trained in France) lead this category. Restaurants operated by born-in-Italy Italians (and invariably as reliable as they are authentic) follow. Indonesian restaurants are justifiably popular, and one finds, as well, restaurants wherein Indonesian and Chinese cuisine are peculiarly mixed to the Dutch taste.

Dutch beers (the big brands are Amstel and Heineken, as if you didn't know) are among the world's best. Young Dutch gin, or *genever,* is far to be preferred to the old and—when

combined with ice—somewhat approximates a dry martini
and makes an excellent aperitif. Of the cheeses, *aged* Gouda
comes close to being as wonderful as Italy's Parmesan; there
are good Dutch goat cheeses, too, in addition to the standard
Gouda and Edam.

Dutch chocolate—Droste is the leading brand—is excellent
too. And so is the rich Dutch milk and the even richer cream.

The restaurants in this book? I have selected a mix, typically
Dutch—seafood, French-accented, Italian, Indonesian, steak-
houses—which I believe for the most part to be among the
cream of the crop. As I have said already, you will eat well in
Holland, but you must not expect that every meal will be a
gustatory experience so long as you are north of the Belgian
border area embracing much of Limburg, North Brabant, and
Zeeland.

My favorite restaurants? I note in evaluations that follow in
succeeding chapters an even dozen restaurants that are, in
my estimation, based on my experience—cuisine, service,
and ambience are the criteria—among the best restaurants in
Holland. My honor list follows, alphabetically:

Auberge de Arent, Breda
Auberge de Koets, Den Bosch
Barbara, Zwolle
Le Chevalier, Delft
De Echoput, Appeldoorn
De Hoefslag, Bosch en Duin
Dorrius, Amsterdam
Kasteel Wittem, Wittem
Lorre, Utrecht
Sagittarius, Maastricht
't Schwarte Schoep, Amsterdam
Tout Court, Amsterdam

ROYAL FAMILY: Old Queen Wilhelmina abdicated—and
why not after a half-century, event-packed reign?—in 1948,
to be succeeded by her daughter, Juliana. Like Wilhelmina,
Juliana married a German (Prince Bernhard), bore only
daughters, and abdicated. The date was April 30, 1980, at the
Royal Palace in Amsterdam, and Juliana was succeeded the

very same day—the inauguration was, according to tradition, in the neighboring Nieuwe Kerk—by her eldest daughter, Crown Princess Beatrix. Like her grandmother and mother (the latter subsequently called Princess Juliana), Beatrix (born 1938) married a German (Prince Claus, born 1926), but, unlike her mother, she gave birth to three sons: Prince Willem-Alexander, the heir to the throne (born 1967), Prince Johan Friso (born 1968), and Prince Constantijn (born 1969).

Of the Queen's three sisters—Princess Irene (born 1939), Margriet (Canadian-born in 1943), and Maria Christina (born 1947)—it is Princess Margriet (married to Peter van Vollenhoven, a Dutch commoner, and the mother of four sons, all princes of the Royal House) who—like the Queen and Prince Claus—undertakes royal engagements: dedicating hospitals, welfare centers, and schools; ribbon breaking at factories and attending galas. Her husband, as a royal Aide-De-Camp, often represents the Queen at official functions.

TRAINS: In a word, super. *Nederlandse Spoorwegen/Dutch Railways* are among Europe's best, not as luxurious as those of France perhaps, but quite as punctual (you'll depart and arrive *on the minute*) and easily on a par with such top-ranking systems as those of Switzerland and Germany. Stations, to start. They have all been updated, and the key word is practicality. Signposting is excellent, station staffs are knowledgable, and scheduling is superior. By this last, I mean that if you just missed a train, chances are good that the next one will come along within a quarter-hour or twenty minutes; on main lines there are four to eight trains every hour, in both directions. Because you're in the Netherlands, personnel speak English—and well. More important trains have snack bars; on occasion, restaurant cars; and refreshment carts are invariably wheeled through. Bear in mind that Dutch Railways sells 1-, 3-, and 7-day Rover fares, allowing unlimited travel at reduced rates. And don't worry about being lonely. Every weekday some 4,300 trains transport between 500,000 and 600,000 passengers.

TOURS, TOUR OPERATORS, TRAVEL AGENTS: Agents first. Select one who is affiliated with the *American Society of Travel*

Agents (ASTA) and, ideally, who knows Holland firsthand. For a first trip, most travelers are happy with a package; tour operators making a specialty of Holland—whose packages may be booked through travel agents—include *American Express, Cartan Tours, Crown Line Tours, Extra Value Travel, Globus Gateway, Maupintour, Mill-Run Tours,* and *Unitours.* In studying brochures, note location of hotels—in cities, you want to be *central,* not out in the boonies; places *actually visited,* not simply passed by on the bus; free time at your disposal, especially in cities; and in the case of meals, whether they're prix fixe or à la carte. An introductory package behind you, you're ready for return visits on your own—to where *you* want to go, at *your* speed.

2

Amsterdam
The Great Dutch Metropolis

BACKGROUND BRIEFING

It is as though the Amsterdammers—lacking a pedigree that extends to Roman times, like so much else of urban Holland—wanted to make up for lost time. After all, a birthdate that goes back only to the thirteenth century—when a benevolent count signed a still extant document extending rights to a fishing hamlet that had sprung up around a dam spanning the Amstel River—is relatively recent, given the European norm.

The Amsterdam encountered contemporarily—with a population of three-quarters of a million, determinedly maintaining the essentially Baroque facade of a core blessedly devoid of skyscrapers, built on wooden and concrete piles, cut through by 40 canals crossed by a thousand bridges—is a consequence of a clever citizenry that, over long centuries, aided and abetted by strokes of luck and genius, exploited the city's geography to its advantage.

You have only to look at a map to see that Amsterdam's situation, embracing a complex of waterways linking the heartland of Europe with the North Sea and the Atlantic, was the impetus for what was to become commercial and cultural eminence. In the fourteenth century, the city had been accorded its first charter. By that time, the still-standing, Gothic-design Oude Kerk had gone up not far east of the historic central square called Dam. And Amsterdam had joined the German-led, mercantile-maritime Hanseatic League, growing as a port and a shipping entrepôt.

The fifteenth century saw it benefit by the attitude of tolerance it has never abandoned, wisely welcoming skilled merchants forced for political reasons to leave Antwerp and Jews expelled from Portugal in the course of the Inquisition, the while its mariners sailed to the New World and Asia, ultimately under the aegis of the powerful Amsterdam-based Dutch East and West India companies.

These last-mentioned enterprises were organized at the start of the seventeenth century, concurrently with the construction of the series of concentric canals—Herengracht, Keizersgracht, Prinsengracht—that to this day determine the contour of the city's core, and of the splendidly embellished canal houses, many of which still stand.

The Golden Age had flowered. Jacob Van Campen designed a city hall so opulent that it later became (and still is) a royal palace and along with other architects—Hendrick de Keyser, especially—transformed the facade of the city. Rembrandt van Rijn, greatest of the era's painters, came from Leiden (his Amsterdam home operates today as a museum) and—along with artists like Pieter de Hooch (celebrated for his intimate domestic interiors), Nicolaes Maes (influenced by his teacher, Rembrandt), Ferdinand Bol (a fine portraitist), and Paulus Potter (most skilled of the painters of animals)—gained Amsterdam an international reputation as an art center. Amsterdam had developed a substantial middle class, and more than that of any other European capital, it was portrait prone; solid burghers wanted their likenesses painted quite as often as the aristocracy did.

A rich banking-shipping-publishing patrician class thrived (with occasional overlapping, as, for example, P. C. Hooft—for whom Amsterdam's spiffiest shopping street is named—who was a to-the-manor-born literary light) as the seventeenth century became the eighteenth. The Rococo era saw Amsterdam capital, albeit briefly, of the French-founded Batavian Republic. Shortly thereafter, as a consequence of Napoleonic decree, Louis Bonaparte became king. Before Big Brother booted him out after a four-year reign—he was far too pro-Dutch to suit Paris—Louis had appropriated the Baroque-era Stadhuis as his Amsterdam seat and founded the Rijksmuseum.

The constitution of the subsequently established Kingdom of the Netherlands, promulgated in 1814, designated Amsterdam the capital. The Nieuwe Kerk is where sovereigns have been "inaugurated"—never "crowned" in the egalitarian Netherlands—ever since. And although the city hall-turned-Royal Palace is, on occasion, royally inhabited, Amsterdam has not, since the days of Louis Bonaparte, been the principal royal residence; sovereigns have lived either at Het Loo in Apeldoorn (Chapter 11), in the countryside near Utrecht (Chapter 13), or in The Hague (Chapter 10), for long the actual seat of government and of ambassadors accredited to the Crown.

The last quarter of the nineteenth century saw completion of a canal linking the city with the North Sea. By the time of World War II occupation by the Nazis beginning in 1940, Amsterdam had become a pan-European financial center. But the half-decade under the Germans was a period of bravery (resistance fighters were executed en masse), of privation (hunger was the rule, not the exception), and of deportation to concentration camps of the majority of the city's approximately 75,000 Jews. (All told, 104,000 Dutch Jews perished during World War II. Their plight is movingly portrayed in a small house where the child diarist Anne Frank lived with her family, now an always-packed museum.)

Today's Amsterdam is at once a world port, a center of commerce, a magnet as much for intellectuals and the politically conscious as for provincial Dutch who consider their easy-of-access capital a second home, and for transatlantic visitors, for whom the city is surely the most sought-out European capital after the Big Three—London, Paris, and Rome.

It is not, to be sure, the fastidious city it was, say, a decade or so back. There are dog droppings on pavements and gum wrappers in canals, and in no Western metropolis is dress so pointedly—almost aggressively—casual. Still, if sanitation departments gave cities brownie points, spotless Washington D.C. would be way ahead of New York in the popularity polls—but it isn't.

There are cities more elegant and more delicious than Amsterdam. None that I know, though, more successfully represents a marriage of the brash and the beautiful, wherein a beer at a noisy "brown" café is no less pleasurable than Beethoven at the Concertgebouw. Amsterdam's not-so-secret weapon is its own peculiar sense of style.

ON SCENE

Lay of the Land: Amsterdam is big and, it is well to make clear at the outset, *too* big to walk everywhere that you'll want to go. Learn to use public transport, bearing in mind that conductors—like virtually all of their compatriots—speak fluent English. The orange-colored map published by the tourist office (address below) could be easier to read, but it has the virtue of a street index on its reverse, wherein is also found the city's central area magnified in blessedly legible black and white. Generous dimensions notwithstanding, walk wherever you can, for a lot of what you pass by is eye-filling. Some 5,500 structures have been decreed protected monuments, and a substantial portion of these have been well restored. The center, in large part, is seventeenth and eighteenth century and, on occasion, older, to the extent that contemporary vistas—with people's clothes (not faces!) changed and some electric wires, signs, and modern vehicles deleted—are frequently as they were centuries back.

Central Amsterdam embraces an area that is largely ringed by the series of seventeenth-century canals to which I allude in earlier pages and which are almost concentric half-circles. Start at what is the beginning for many visitors: *Centraal Station*, an immense late-nineteenth-century pile—twin-towered like the Rijksmuseum (below) and designed by the same architect—with its situation near the IJ River, the harbor, and the Maritime Museum. The station fronts *Stationsplein* and the

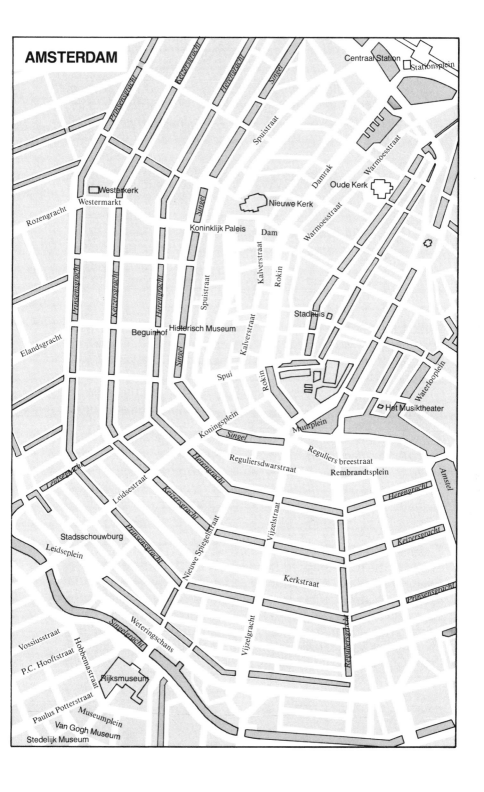

AMSTERDAM

Centraal Station
Stationsplein

Westerkerk
Westermarkt

Rozengracht

Prinsengracht
Keizersgracht
Herengracht
Singel

Spuistraat

Nieuwe Kerk

Koninklijk Paleis

Dam

Damrak

Warmoesstraat

Oude Kerk

Warmoesstraat

Warmoesstraat

Kalverstraat

Rokin

Prinsengracht
Keizersgracht
Herengracht

Singel

Spuistraat

Beguinhof   Histerisch Museum

Elandsgracht

Kalverstraat

Spui

Stadhuis

Rokin

Waterlooplein

Het Musiktheater

Koningsplein

Singel

Herengracht

Reguliersdwarstraat

Reguliers breestraat

Rembrandtsplein

Muntplein

Vijzelstraat

Amstel

Herengracht

Keizersgracht

Prinsengracht

Leidsegracht

Leidsestraat

Keizersgracht

Nieuwe Spiegelstraat

Stadsschouwburg

Leidseplein

Prinsengracht

Kerkstraat

Keizersgracht

Weteringschans

Singelgracht

Vossiusstraat

P.C. Hooftstraat

Hobbemastraat

Rijksmuseum

Vijzelgracht

Paulus Potterstraat   Museumplein

Van Gogh Museum

Stedelijk Museum

street perpendicular with it, called *Damrak*, which connects it with the city's principal square, known simply as the *Dam*, centered by the post-World War II *Nationaal Monument* and flanked by the Baroque *Koninklijk (Royal) Palace* and the Gothic *Nieuwe Kerk*, with Renaissance-era *Westerkerk* and neighboring *Anne Frank Huis* not far west along *Raadhuisstraat*, at *Westermarkt*, on *Prinsengracht*. Two parallel streets lead south from the Dam into the core of town; one is called *Rokin*; the other, more important, is the principal pedestrian-shopping thoroughfare, *Kalverstraat*. It's the site of the *Amsterdam Historisch Museum* and the *Begijnhof*, a tranquil cluster of venerable laynuns' houses. Kalverstraat and Rokin both pass the important street called *Spui* and terminate at *Muntplein*, named for the landmark fifteenth-century *Munttoren*, a one-time mint, with the city's celebrated *flower market* due east, fronting the canal called *Singel*—not difficult to confuse with the *Amstel River*, cutting eastward through the city at that point. Muntplein is but a few minutes' stroll east along *Reguliersbreestraat* to a hotel-café-bordered square called *Rembrandtsplein*. It is at Muntplein that the four principal concentric canals enter the scene; as you walk south, you pass one canal after another. I remember their sequence in this way: The first is *Singel* (think of one, the first); the next three are in alphabetical order: *Herengracht*, *Keizersgracht*, and finally *Prinsengracht*. Going farther into the city—along a major shopping street, *Leidsestraat*—one soon reaches *Leidseplein*, liveliest of the main squares, with its landmarks *Stadsschouwburg* (the municipal theater) and the *Amsterdam Marriott* and *American* hotels. Proceed east along *Stadhouderskade* a couple of blocks, passing *P.C. Hooftstraat* (with the city's swankest shops), and you've arrived at the twin-towered *Rijksmuseum* and its neighbors along *Museumstraat* to the south—the *Van Gogh Museum* and the *Stedelijk Museum*. This is the neighborhood, as well, of the *Concertgebouw*, a concert hall that gave its name to the principal Amsterdam symphony. Still another performing arts venue, *Het Musiektheater*, sharing a futuristic complex with the new *Stadhuis*, or city hall, is on *Waterlooplein*, due east, and the site also of the Baroque-era *Portuguees-Israelitsche Syn-*

agogue and classic-style *Mozes en Aaron Church*, with *Rembrandthuis* in the neighborhood and *Tropenmuseum*, an ethnographic museum, a fairish schlep east on *Mauritskade*.

SELECTED LANDMARKS

Amstelkring (a.k.a. Our Lord of The Attic—the English for *Ons Lieve Heer op Solder*; Oude Zijds Voorburgwal 40) is an Amsterdam oddity: a Roman Catholic chapel stretching across the top stories of three joined Baroque-era canal houses, the lower floors of which are handsomely furnished. The chapel is the last remaining of the so-called hidden churches that typified Dutch tolerance during the Reformation, when to be Catholic was out—but only sort of—and this form of worship was winked at by authorities.

Anne Frank Huis (Prinsengracht 263)—single most moving sightseeing experience in town—is where the globally celebrated Jewish girl, whose name the house takes, and her family hid from the Nazis during the World War II Nazi occupation, or at least until 1944, when they were discovered. Anne's father excepted, the entire family was exterminated in concentration camps. Most touching, at least to me, are the movie-magazine photos Anne had affixed to the wall of her attic bedroom—of Shirley Temple, Norma Shearer, Greta Garbo, David Niven, and Deanna Durbin, along with clips from newspapers of Britain's then Princess (now Queen) Elizabeth, and the then-in-exile Dutch Royal Family. But you see, as well, rooms where Mr. and Mrs. Frank and their daughter Margot slept, the bathroom (which was dangerous to use except at certain hours because of the noise), and rooms of the host Van Daan family. At the end of your self-guided tour, you pass an exhibit of the nonprofit Anne Frank Foundation, including foreign-language editions of Anne's Diary (they total 50, with sales of more than 13 million copies). *Note:* Unless hours change, it is worth noting that the house is open Sunday morning, when just about nothing else in Amsterdam is, churches and hotels excepted.

Begijnhof (Spui, off Kalverstraat) represents old Amsterdam at its most serene: an inner courtyard in the heart of town surrounded by a clutch of fifteenth- and sixteenth-century houses (some facades have been altered in succeeding centuries), an originally Catholic church that has been Scottish Presbyterian since not long after the Reformation, and a still-Catholic chapel wherein secret masses were celebrated, not unlike that in Amstelkrieg (above). Begijnhofs, still to be found throughout the Low Countries, are named for their inhabitants, *beguines*, or lay nuns. Amsterdam's was founded in 1346.

Canal houses: Herengracht has the loveliest houses (particularly in the choice area between Leidsestraat and Vijzelgracht). Keizersgracht follows, with Prinsengracht a by-no-means-inconsequential No. 3, and *Singel* is an interesting mix of churches, warehouses, and residences. *Prinsengracht's* houses were traditionally those of the lower-middle and middle-middle classes, and many of them today are meticulously maintained. *Keizersgracht's* standouts include No. 123 (House of the Heads, the heads being half a dozen Roman busts on the facade of this gabled brick mansion); Kooimans House at No. 125; and Nos. 778 through 786—a row of five strikingly matched structures. *Herengracht* has even more beauties of note: the Mayor's Mansion at No. 502, the eighteenth-century structure that houses the Willet-Holthuysen Museum (below) at No. 605, No. 465 with its Louis XIV facade, and the pair of early seventeenth-century warehouses at Nos. 43 and 45.

Visible everywhere is Amsterdam's coat of arms, surely the most easily identifiable in Europe, with its three X-shaped St. Andrew's crosses on a red-and-black shield above the Dutch words for "Heroic, Resolute, Compassionate"—officially added by decree of Queen Wilhelmina in 1947, in recognition of the citizens' bravery during the Nazi occupation of World War II.

Koninklijk Paleis (a.k.a. Paleis op de Dam, Dam): Amsterdam's cupola-topped Royal Palace—the classic-style landmark designed by the celebrated Golden Age architect Daniel

Van Campen as the city hall in the mid-seventeenth century—appeared so spectacular in the early eighteenth century to Napoleon's brother, King Louis Bonaparte, that he appropriated it for himself as the capital's royal residence. It has been just that ever since, even though it is rarely inhabited by Queen Beatrix and her family, who live principally at Paleis Huis den Bosch in The Hague (Chapter 10). The pity of this palace is that, even though it is empty so much of the year, the Royal Household opens it to the public only at Easter and in summer. Visitors in Amsterdam fall through spring—and there are not a few—should not be denied the opportunity to see Louis's throne room; the splendid Burgerzaal, with Eastern and Western hemispheres inlaid in the marble floor and sculptures representing the elements of earth, air, fire, and water in each corner; and the so-called Maid of Amsterdam, a sculptured female figure who symbolizes the city, at the entrance; as well as the onetime council chamber in which Queen Juliana abdicated in 1980. The Empire furniture, contemporary with the period of King Louis Bonaparte, was installed in the palace during his tenure and still is sat on by guests at royal receptions.

Nieuwe Kerk (Dam): Neighbor to the Royal Palace (above), this massively scaled Gothic church—called New (even though it went up as long ago as the fifteenth century) to distinguish it from the even older Oude (Old) Kerk (below)—is distinguished principally by monumental proportions, unusual clustered columns, a Baroque organ (used often for concerts); and tombs of a number of distinguished Hollanders. All of the kingdom's sovereigns, from William I in 1814 through Beatrix in 1980, have been sworn in at the New Church, which is now more meeting/exhibition/concert hall than place of worship, keeping regular open hours and maintaining a café (below).

Oude Kerk (Warmoesstraat)—appropriately named in that it is Amsterdam's oldest—embraces several centuries, from the fourteenth to the seventeenth. Its glory is a sixteenth-century spire, but the immense Gothic windows are exemplary, too, and so is the seventeenth-century pulpit. Rembrandt's wife, Saskia, is buried within, along with other noted Dutchmen, including the patroon Kilaen van Rensselaer, who in the seventeenth century founded Rensselaerwick, a colony along the Hudson River in what is now upstate New York, and for whom the present county and town of Rensselaer (across the river from my native Albany) are named.

Portugees Synagoge (Mr. Visserplein) bears the name of the country from which many Jews emigrated in the sixteenth century, some of them descendants of Spanish families who had fled to Portugal a century earlier during the Inquisition. Without, this red brick structure is graciously Baroque. The interior—its barrel vaults supported by stone columns surmounted by Ionic capitals—is high, handsome, and illuminated by several rows of the brass chandeliers typical of the era of construction.

Westerkerk (Westermarkt, facing Prinsengracht) is a Golden Age jewel designed by one of the period's leading architects, Hendrick de Keyser. Best perspectives are from the sides or even farther along Prinsengracht, when the telescopelike profile of the spire—highest in town—becomes apparent. Four massive chandeliers illuminate a severe interior (restored in the mid-1980s), which served as the burial place—on October 8, 1669—of Rembrandt; there's a bust of the painter, as well as a tomb plaque.

Universiteit van Amsterdam: Amsterdam's university, the Netherlands' largest, has seventeenth-century roots and buildings throughout the city. Surely none is more charming than the onetime *Oude Lutherse Kerk* (Singel at Spui)—once a Baroque church, red brick of facade, double galleried, still with floor tombs and its original organ—which has been deftly restored to serve as an *Aula*, or auditorium, of the university. Pop in. Still another onetime church, a fifteenth-century chapel at O. Z. Voorbuggwal 231, has been converted to house the university's *Historical Collection*—an absorbing mix of prints and drawings, photos and posters relating to the institution's past. The university's *Schriftmuseum*, located in the handsome library at Singel 425, has as its theme the unlikely but fascinating history of penmanship, ancient alphabets through to contemporary letters. And the thrust of the *Allard Pierson Museum* (Oude Turfmarkt, parallel with the street called Roken) is archeology. You will no doubt have seen more impressive such collections, but this one is worth perusing if you've a special interest in ancient Egypt (mostly from the later eras, close to and just after the birth of Christ) and the Middle East, including Persia (lovely pottery), Turkey, and classical Greece (a substantial cache of sculpture and ceramics).

SELECTED MUSEUMS

Amsterdam Jewish Historic Museum (Jonas Daniel Meyerplein 2)—the city's newest, and opened by Queen Beatrix in mid-1987—provides quarters for a vastly expanded half-century-old collection of antique ceremonial and art objects used in connection with worship at synagogues throughout Holland, with the striking setting—four imaginatively restored contiguous synagogues that had been pillaged by the Nazis during World War II—as noteworthy as the exhibits; the buildings, dating to the seventeenth and eighteenth centuries (and near the still-in-use Portuguese Synagogue, above) are joined by glass-enclosed walkways, with galleries for temporary exhibits as well as the permanent collection.

Amsterdam Historisch Museum (entered either at Kalverstraat 92, for which you must look carefully, or out back at St. Luciensteeg 27)—along with a Rotterdam counterpart similarly themed (Chapter 18)—is among the more beautiful and architecturally significant Dutch museums. Site is the originally fifteenth-century St. Lucia Convent, which had seen service from the sixteenth century all the way to 1969, as the Amsterdam Municipal Orphanage, and is partially the work of ranking Golden Age architect Hendrick de Keyser. Exhibits—superb paintings (many of Renaissance and Baroque-era Amsterdammers, others depicting the city in times past), aged maps and prints, Amsterdam applied arts, pewter through porcelain—are housed in a quadrangular-shaped structure, and the café-restaurant in the big courtyard is as busy with locals (location is just off the main shopping street) as with museum visitors. The Historisch is nicely combined with the neighboring Begijnhof (above).

Nederlandsch Scheepvaart Museum (Kattenburgenplein 1), the National Maritime Museum, makes its home in the seventeenth-century arsenal of the Amsterdam Admiralty, on the harbor, a short and scenic walk east from Centraal Station. Not unlike the Historisch Museum (above), environment is as compelling as exhibits on display. This is a dazzler of a Baroque building, elegantly pedimented and superbly sited at the water's edge. The thrust within is Dutch maritime history, early domestic vessels through sea battles with Spanish overlords in the sixteenth century, with heavy emphasis on high-seas commerce in the course of the seventeenth-century Golden Age. Special treat is the early-eighteenth-century Royal Barge, canopied, propelled by a score of oarsmen, and used as recently as 1962, on the occasion of the silver jubilee of Queen (now Princess) Juliana and Prince Bernhard. But the caliber of paintings—a Sir Peter Lely, for example, of seventeenth-century Admiral Cornelius Tromp—is extraordinary, no less so the centuries-old globes and maps. As for ships, models are only part of the Maritime's three floors of exhibits. Two full-scale towing barges of yore supplement the Royal Barge, within, and out front, permanently moored in the harbor, are a lifeboat, an icebreaker, and a honey of a sailing vessel. Café.

Rembrandthuis (Jodenbreestraat 4), Baroque-facaded, was the Leiden-born painter's home base between 1639 and 1660 and has operated as a museum—devoid of paintings but with well over 200 Rembrandt-printed etchings—since the early years of the present century, when it was infelicitously converted to its current use, sadly lacking little more than a trace of the ambience of Rembrandt's two-decade occupancy. For me, the most memorable works are two self-portraits (one of himself alone and wide-eyed, the other with his wife, Saskia), *The Three Crosses, Christ Presented to the People,* and *View of Amsterdam,* with a skyline of church towers and windmills.

Rijksmuseum (with the main entrance at Stadhouderskade 42 and another entrance out back at Hobbemastraat 19): Dutch Government-operated museums throughout the Netherlands are designated *Rijksmuseum.* Still, to foreigners, there is—understandably—but one Rijksmuseum, the massive, twin-towered, mock-Renaissance pile in Amsterdam that houses the kingdom's most widely reputed collection of the art of Holland's seventeenth-century Golden Age. In the course of an initial visit, you want to see Rembrandt's *The Night Watch*—correctly *The Company of Captain Frans Banning Cocq and Lieutenant Willemvan Ruytenbruch*—wherein the captain, red sash and white collar contrasting with his black garb, is ordering the lieutenant, modishly uniformed in tones of gold, to march off the guards under his command, with townspeople (including Saskia, Rembrandt's wife) and guardsmen in the background. This Rijksmuseum trademark occupies a place of honor in a gallery that takes its name. But relax, then, and take enough time to observe other works of art. (Three half-day visits in the immense Rijksmuseum are not too many.) Standouts? You'll find Frans Hals's joyous *Wedding Portrait,* Hendrik Avercamp's snowy *Winter Landscape with Ice Skaters,* Jan van Goyen's *Landscape with Two Oaks,* Paulus Potter's *Two Horses in a Meadow,* Adriaan van Ostade's *Peasants in an Interior,* Nicholaas Maes's *The Daydreamer,* Gerard ter Bosch's *The Paternal Admonition,* Johannes Vermeer's *The Kitchen Maid,* Jan Steen's *Woman at Her Toilet,* Pieter de Hooch's *Women beside a Linen Chest,* and Meindert Hobbema's *The Watermill.* You'll also see so much more of Rembrandt: an early portrait, *The Prophetess Anne, The Anatomy Lesson of Dr. Jean Deyman, Titus in a Monk's Habit, The Wardens of the Amsterdam Drapers' Guild* among many. And there are more Steens, more Hals, and more Vermeers, as well as works by less celebrated, if not necessarily less gifted, artists of the period and of later and earlier eras, as well. The Rijksmuseum's strength in the applied and decorative arts goes underappreciated. Look for fifteenth-century chests and silver-encrusted drinking horns, sixteenth-century goblets and jewels, Baroque silver and gold work, Delftware, and exceptionally fine furniture.

Paintings by foreign masters are nowhere in Holland as prevalent, save at Rotterdam's Boymans van Beuningen Museum (Chapter 18): Rubens and Van Dyck, among the Flemings; Goya and Murillo out of Spain; Guardi and Tiepolo, Veronese and Tintoretto, from Italy. The too-often-neglected Asian collections might well constitute a museum on their own. Treasures from Indonesia—for long the Dutch East Indies—are striking: gold jewelry and ivory, Javanese and Balinese ceremonial masks, quantites of the species of exquisitely worked wavy dagger called kris, with Chinese T'ang horses, Korean chests, Japanese kimonos, Siamese Buddhas, and Cambodian busts. Not to be missed either, in difficult-to-find ground-floor galleries, is the Dutch historical section—maps, prints, ship models, furnishings, and quite marvelous paintings of long-ago Dutch outposts in Indonesia, Cochin, and Brazil and of derring-do admirals and princes, invariably robust and rosy cheeked. Big, always jammed shop; disappointing, albeit convenient, cafeteria. And, I might add, knowledgable guards invariably happy to point you in the right direction.

Stedelijk Museum (Paulus Potterstraat 13), Amsterdam's Municipal Museum, is quartered in a connected, two-building complex—the older, mock-Renaissance and twin-towered; the newer, clean-lined post-World War II—and celebrates modern art, mid-nineteenth century and onward. A substantial portion of the extraordinary permanent collection is generally on view. Look for Cezanne's *Still Life with Fruit*, Van Gogh's *View of Montmartre*, Manet's *Bar at the Folies Bergère*, Monet's *Corniche de Monaco*, Vlaminck's *View of a Village*, Picasso's *Still Life with Guitar*, Chagall's *Fiddler on the Roof*, a Rouault clown, a Matisse Odalisque, a Beckmann self-portrait. There's a gallery devoted to Mondrian geometrics, and others concentrate on lesser-known Russian artist Kasimir Malewitch and works by contemporary Americans like Jasper Johns, Roy Lichtenstein, Barnett Newman, and Ellsworth Kelly. The garden is studded with sculpture by the likes of Renoir and Moore, Rodin and Arp, and a vast wall is surfaced with a brilliant Matisse abstract. The Stedelijk is very big on very good temporary exhibitions, takes photography seriously, stages concerts, shows movies, and operates a restaurant. Indeed, its multifaceted program more resembes that of New York's Museum of Modern Art than any other museum I know in Europe; a lot goes on here.

Tropenmuseum (Linneausstraat, east of the center): *Tropen* translates as *Tropical*, and this museum is one of a number throughout the Netherlands (in Leiden [Chapter 14] especially), that are ethnographic in content. The Tropen, though, focuses on Third World cultures thematically, with emphasis, in imaginative displays, on these peoples' occupations, habitations, religions, diversions, and clothes. Not surprisingly, Asia, as highlighted by Indonesia, the one-time Dutch East Indies, rates major emphasis (there are monthly concerts of Gamelan orchestras).

Van Gogh Museum (Paulus Potterstraat 7) is not only next door to the Stedelijk Museum (above), but an outgrowth of its world-class collection of works by the short-lived (1853–1890), Dutch-born Impressionist, Vincent van Gogh, who did his greatest work during a brief few years in France (for a period sharing a house in Arles with the painter Gauguin) before dying (two days after he shot himself) in the arms of his brother Theo.

It was Theo, Paris based and an art dealer, who formed the nucleus collection of Vincent's paintings. It was enlarged by Theo's widow and their son, from whom it passed to the foundation that loaned it to the Stedelijk, where it remained until this museum—ironically the best-designed contemporary museum in Holland, along with the Kröller-Müller in Arnhem (Chapter 4), itself the venue of a major Van Gogh collection—opened in 1973. Selections from among the 200 paintings, 500 drawings, and other Van Goghiana, including beautifully composed letters to brother Theo, are rotated for display on each of four levels, with the order chronological, starting with early Dutch days celebrated for portrayals of poor farmers, like *The Potato Eaters*, through the prolific Arles sojourn, and beyond to the final period of mental illness at hospitals in St.-Rémy and Auvers. You will decide for yourself whether you prefer the Kröller-Müller or the Amsterdam Van Gogh collections. Here the range is a white-capped *Head of a Peasant Woman*, painted before Vincent moved to France, and a Paris-wrought *Pair of Shoes*, through to *Vase with Sunflowers*, *The Artist's Bedroom*, *The Yellow House*, and *Harvest at La Crau* created at Arles; *Wheatfield with a Reaper*, done in the St. Rémy hospital; and *Farmhouse in Auvers*, painted not long before the artist's death.

Van Loon Museum (Kaisersgracht 672): Readers of my books know that I rarely accord precious space to museums or historic houses that keep severely limited hours. The Van Loon, traditionally open only on Monday from 10:00 A.M. to 5:00 P.M. and on no other day, is an exception. It's too good looking to omit; a pair of joined houses that went up in the late seventeenth century and long inhabited by the artist Ferdinand Bol (a pupil of Rembrandt). Decor is mostly eighteenth century. Principal salon is gilt chandeliered, with walls of pale gray damask and Dutch-made furniture in the style of Louis XV. The two-table dining room is no less appealing, nor are upstairs sitting- and bedrooms. As you move about, don't fail to note the fine paintings (alas, none are by Bol), and if the back door is open, stroll through the formal garden before taking your leave.

Verzetsmuseum (Lekstraat 63) translates as Resistance Museum, a commemoration of the Amsterdam-based underground that fought the Nazis during the World War II occupation, by means of documents and posters, secretly printed newspapers, maps, and photos, the lot focusing on a dark— but valiant—period in the city's history. Pay your respects.

Willet-Holthuysen Museum (Herengracht 605) occupies a stunner of a landmark canal house, double-width and elegantly detailed, that a patrician family built in the late seventeenth century. It constitutes a decorative arts museum of the first order, eighteenth-century basement kitchen through nineteenth-century main floor parlor, with a series of additional treasure-filled rooms, including a neo-Louis XV, mid-nineteenth century dining room, its table exquisitely set; a pair of street-floor parlors, their furniture Dutch interpretations of French eighteenth-century styles; an 1870 bedroom, hung with a pair of portraits by the Golden Age master, Nicholaes Maes; extraordinary collections of antique glass—Venetian and German, as well as Dutch; considerable Delft porcelain; and a honey of a formal French garden. (Interior buffs please note that still another Herengracht house, the *Tonel Theater) Museum* at No. 168, is at least as visible for its eighteenth-century decor as for its exhibits.)

SETTLING IN

SELECTED LUXURY HOTELS

Amstel Hotel (Professor Tulpplein 1; Phone 22-60-60): Leave it to the global, albeit New York-based, Inter-Continental chain to make historic additions to its group—the Willard in Washington, the Grand in Paris, the May Fair in London, the Carlton in Cannes, the Ritz in Lisbon are a handful. And the subject at hand, Amsterdam's Amstel, named for the river it overlooks, and—with a history of some 120 years—quite the *grande dame* hostelry of the Dutch capital. The inspiration of a mid-nineteenth-century physician named Sarphati, the Amstel's cornerstone was laid in 1866 by King William III. Within a decade, still another Amsterdam doctor opened a then-novel gym and massage parlor in the hotel, only to lure such guests as France's Empress Eugénie and Austria's Empress Elizabeth, not to mention Dutch royals and—through the reign of Juliana—their guests. Inter-Continental's stem-to-stern refurbishing has wisely left intact the hotel's atriumlike entrance-hall-cum-ceremonial-stairway, one of the city's more exemplary interiors. Those of the 111 rooms and suites I have either inhabited or inspected are handsomely Louis XV, with flawlessly selected textiles, furnishings, accessories—and top-notch baths. The terraced, picture-windowed bar-lounge gives onto the river; the subterranean restaurant is intimate and esteemed, the staff—long on-scene head concierge A. A. Wenskat, most especially—is skilled and smiling, and the location, a good quarter-hour's walk from the center, is scenic.

Amsterdam Hilton Hotel (Appollolaan 138; Phone 78-07-80): You appreciate the pioneering aspects of Hilton International—the first American-based chain to operate in Europe—when you learn on a long-delayed revisit to the Amsterdam Hilton that it only recently observed its quarter-century mark with a multimillion-dollar, stem-to-stern refurbishing. This is a handsome, canal-front hostelry, whose location in a smart residential quarter south of the center spurred construction of other area hotels (below). Those of the 274 rooms and suites I have inspected are generously proportioned, smartly styled in soft pastels, and with updated Yank-style baths with real showers—not European-style ones at the end of rubber tubes—over the tubs. The lobby, centered now as it was from the beginning with a circular copper fireplace that's lighted in chilly weather, hums with guests come to relax in the Half-Moon Bar, named for the ship Hendrik Hudson sailed up the river now bearing his name to Albany in 1609; enjoy Japanese fare (still quite a novelty in Amsterdam) in one of the restaurants or a Continental/American meal in the Terrace (later evaluated); have a go at roulette, blackjack, or the 120 slot machines in the casino; or indulge in late-hour disco dancing at Juliana's. And, hey! The general manager, congenial Amsterdammer Anne Shield, is, like her company, a pioneer: among the first female luxury-hotel directors in the Netherlands.

Amsterdam Marriott Hotel (Stadhouderskade 21; Phone 83-51-51): Don't let that multisyllable street address fool you; the Marriott faces heart-of-the-Amsterdam-action Leidseplein. Indeed, this central location—along with the alert service you know from Marriott back home or in other European capitals—is the Amsterdam Marriott's ace-in-the-hole. A favorite of mine since I covered its press opening in 1975, this house pulls off being big—there are 400 rooms (good sized, with super Yank-style baths, and some are balconied)—with being cozy. You get to know the staff—at the concierge's desk, in the pair of restaurants (one, dressy and later evaluated; the other, casual), and in the bars—within a day of your arrival. And you'll like being able to walk to major museums, the Concertgebouw, and shops, and to hop a tram right at the front door for longer excursions. Ask for high-up accommodations facing Leidseplein.

Amsterdam Sonesta Hotel (Kattegat 1; Phone 21-22-23) and the Amsterdam Marriott (above) have a birthdate—or at least year—in common; they both opened in 1975. I was as impressed than as I continue to be with the Sonesta—a modern, 425-room building, whose intentionally low-slung, deep-red-brick facade blends well into the profile of the historic quarter in which it is situated and an adjacent landmark of a domed Baroque church that had long been desanctified and is now put to sensible use as a conference center/concert hall. These two component parts of the Sonesta complex are linked by a tunnel cutting under Kattegat, and they edge the canal called Singel, site of the hotel's own pier for sightseeing boats. The hotel proper is contemporary in look, its walls hung with some 900 original graphics, lithographs, and paintings. Accommodations to aim for are those facing the ex-church's superb dome. Amsterdammers, as well as hotel guests, populate the Sonesta's public places, which include a sleek restaurant, coffee shop wherein is served the hotel's generous buffet breakfasts, a "brown" café (later evaluated), spacious cocktail lounge, and dense and dark disco, as well as a fitness center. Staff? It's young, cordial, and professional—none nicer in town.

Apollo Hotel (Apollolaan 2; Phone 73-59-22) is a near neighbor of the Amsterdam Hilton (above) in the area south of the center made popular by the early-bird Hilton. This is a gracious contemporary house, with inviting public spaces and 220 generously proportioned rooms, the lot of them either twins or doubles (if you're alone, you get a double but at a single rate), and those I have inspected smartly traditional, with fine baths. The bar-lounge has picture windows giving onto the adjacent canal. There are formal and casual restaurants (the latter is reviewed in a later paragraph), and staff is crackerjack, not surprising when one considers that this is a unit of Britain-based Trusthouse Forte, whose hotels include Paris's George V and London's Hyde Park.

De l'Europe Hotel (Nieuwe Doelenstraat 2; Phone 23-48-36) represents Amsterdam hotelkeeping at its most charming. This is a turn-of-century house (it went up in 1895), gabled and turreted in delightful mock-Renaissance style, with a room count low enough to allow for personal service. There are just under 100 rooms and suites, including 16 spiffy junior suites in two recently converted adjacent houses. Decor is quietly traditional Louis XVI, with baths intelligently updated and views—from two sides of the hotel, which means many of the rooms—of the Amstel River and historic Munttoren, the Middle Ages mint on Muntplein. There's a fitness center with a small swimming pool, and there are three restaurants. The riverview Excelsior warrants comment on a later page; it is complemented by Le Relais (smartly casual and worth knowing about, even if you're not a house guest, given its traidtional open hours—noon through midnight), and La Terrasse, for alfresco, warm-weather meals and drinks at the water's edge. I save location for last; you may walk everywhere from the De l'Europe; Kalverstraat shops are immediately north, restaurants of Regulierdwarstraat and café-dotted Rembrandtplein are due east, while Leidsestraat (another major shopping street) leads south to busy Leidseplein, with the Concertgebouw, major museums, and trendy P. C. Hooftstraat not far distant. This is Amsterdam's best-located luxury hotel. Member, Leading Hotels of the World.

Garden Hotel (Dijsselhofplantsoen 7; Phone 64-21-21) is a relatively recent neighbor of the Amsterdam Hilton and Apollo hotels (above) in the residential area south of the center. The lobby is a flashy mass of white-leather chairs, with pricey restaurant (there is no coffee shop) and bar leading from it, and a hundred rooms (those I have inspected are smallish and unexceptional) on upper floors. Disappointing.

Krasnapolsky Hotel (Dam 9; Phone 55-49-111): There is no escaping the Krasnapolsky's illustrious past as an Amsterdam institution—and, for that matter, an across-the-Dam neighbor of both the Royal Palace and the church in which Dutch sovereigns are inaugurated. Stop for a cuppa in the Krasserie café, and you see blown-up photos, snapped long ago, of the founding Krasnapolskys, newcomers from Poland in the 1860s, but popular Amsterdammers by the time they expanded their restaurant into a hotel in 1883—with a hundred parquet-floored, centrally heated, electrically illuminated rooms that were the talk of the town. The hotel—long since known as the "Kras"—has been expanded, enlarged, and of course refurbished over the years. There are now 300 rooms and suites in a multibuilding complex, a range of restaurants (two are reviewed on later pages) and bars, with a humming lobby, staff with more than its share of knowing old-timers, and remarkable mix of accommodations—the range, suites and traditional-style superior rooms through to a group of original-building accommodations still without private baths.

Okura Hotel (Ferdinand Bolstraat 333; Phone 78-71-11): Fans of the "mother house" Okura in Tokyo—and I am a devoted one—will recognize the Okura look of this Amsterdam outpost: contemporarily styled but with unmistakable Japanese-decor emphasis and admirable Japanese attention to detail. This is the highest rise of the contemporary Amsterdam hostelries, with a vast lobby, 400 spacious, modern-design rooms with excellent baths (and from up-high ones excellent views), mix of restaurants—Japanese of course, but classic French and Continental, as well—and a south-of-the-center location near the RAI Congress Center, which makes the hotel especially attractive to conventioneers. Member, Leading Hotels of the World.

Pulitzer Hotel (Prinsengracht 315; Phone 22-83-33): Even when you explain the Pulitzer's geography to friends—and geography *is* the word—you're greeted with skeptical reactions. But it's true: This modern hotel comprises a clutch of no less than 19 seventeenth- and eighteenth-century houses. The bulk of them face Prinsengracht, one of the classic Amsterdam canals, with others abutting also-lovely Keizersgracht, and the remainder on historic streets running perpendicular with the canals. Facades remain original (all these houses are designated landmarks), but the hotel's designers have created new interiors (retaining original beams and other architectural details) and joined the buildings by means of walkways, both indoors and through sculpture-centered garden courtyards that are among the prettier in town. Accommodations are contemporary in look—the Pulitzer is partial to plaids and rattan—with modern baths, of course, and utterly idyllic views from canal-front rooms. There are a pair of restaurants—one, a perky coffee shop; the other, intimate, French accented, and later evaluated; a bar with at least as many Amsterdammers as hotel guests among clients (and with not easy to find *aged* Gouda cheese accompanying drinks); a staff, not one of whose members, in my experience, is not enthusiastic, friendly, or professional; and a location as central as it is romantic.

SELECTED FIRST CLASS HOTELS

Acca Hotel (Van der Veldestraat 3; Phone 62-52-62), a hop and a skip from both the Stedelijk Museum and the shops of P. C. Hooftstraat, is small (there are but 25 ever so sleek, peachy-pastel rooms with brass-edged furniture and good baths—but smart (the little lobby is a symphony in clean-lined black and white, and the bar-breakfast room is brown-accented). Breakfast only.

Alexander Hotel (Prinsengracht 444: Phone 26-77-21) is superbly situated—at the intersection of a major canal and Leidsestraat, a major shopping street. Its three restaurants—the long celebrated Dikker & Thijs and the less grand Prinsenkelder (both evaluated on a later page), as well as the convenient Café du Centre and a fancy food deli are at least as well known as the hotel part of this operation. There are just 25 rooms; ask for one with a view of the canal. Those I have either inhabited or inspected are spacious, with big, modern baths and tasteful, modern furnishings. And the staff is kindly.

Ambassade Hotel (Herengracht 341; Phone 26-23-33) occupies seven canal houses, three of them connected, the others independently entered. There are 42 no-two-alike rooms, their look an agreeable mix of the traditional and the contemporary; and very attractive public spaces, which center on an antiques-furnished lobby-lounge, and a breakfast room that may well be the smartest looking such in town. There's no restaurant, but rather, 24-hour room service for snacks. Delightful staff.

American Hotel (Leidsekade 97, at Leidseplein; Phone 24-53-22) has, ever since it opened in 1882, been a Leidseplein landmark—as how could this masterful specimen of Art Nouveau architecture, with its solitary brick tower and intricately patterned brick facade, be otherwise? The Forum Hotels division of New York-based Inter-Continental Hotels took over some years back and has thoroughly refurbished this 185-room house. Rooms I have inspected are generously proportioned, some decorated in plaids (duplexes among them), some in small-patterned fabrics. There's a congenial bar, and Café Américain—still with priceless original museum-caliber decor and outdoor tables, as well—is so special that I review it on another page. Friendly.

Ascot Hotel (Damrak 95; Phone 26-00-66) is among the newer links in the constantly expanding—and exemplary—Swissôtel chain, a group I became familiar with in the course of researching *Switzerland At Its Best*. Just off the Dam, the Ascot occupies a pair of joined and aged buildings whose interiors it has replaced with 110 carefully planned rooms, in tones of gray and blue, with super marble baths. You want to aim for those with unforgettable views of the Dam's Royal Palace and Nieuw Kerk. And you want to have a Swiss-accented meal in the hotel's Bistro, fin de siécle in look, where *bundnerfleisch*— paper-thin, air-dried-beef—is among appetizers, and classically Swiss veal in cream and mushroom sauce is always a featured entrée.

Capitool Hotel (N. Z. Voorburgwaal 67; Phone 27-59-00) is, to be sure, nineteenth-century mock-Renaissance of facade. But the interior has been smartly restyled by PLM-Etap, a France-based chain. Those of the 150 rooms and suites I have inspected are attractive—plum and gray are among color schemes—and have good baths. And the plush Pullman Bar, which could be out of the old Orient Express, serves bistro-type food in the evening. Nice.

Caransa Crest Hotel (Rembrandtsplein 19; Phone 22-94-55) is well situated on one of Amsterdam's pleasanter squares. This is a modern house, with agreeable public spaces that include a good-value restaurant-café, as well as 66 quietly attractive rooms; aim for one looking out on Rembrandtsplein. A link of the Britain-based Crest chain.

Carlton Hotel (Vijzelstraat 2; Phone 22-22-66)—imposingly Art Nouveau from without and enviably central, with the Muntplein adjacent—has been taken over by Jolly Hotels, an admirable Italian chain I have come to admire in the course of travels researching *Italy At Its Best*. By the time of your visit, Jolly's multimillion-guilder refurbishment program may well have been completed. The 156-room Carlton, where I headquartered with pleasure on an Amsterdam visit some years back, is worthy of a Jolly facelift. Staff is hospitable; rooms, good size; bar, relaxing; and the Jolly breakfast buffet—esteemed throughout Italy—copious.

Doelen Crest Hotel (Nieuwe Doelenstraat 24; Phone 22-07-22) was, when I first knew it, on an early Amsterdam visit, an all-city leader, built in the monumental style typical of the late nineteenth century and strategically situated on the Amstel

River. Newer hotels came along, though, and the Doelen took a back seat for a period, until the British Crest chain refurbished it—keeping its historic ambience uppermost in the decor scheme. It is, today, an 86-room house (with modern baths throughout), a restaurant whose picture windows afford it one of the truly sublime Amsterdam views while dining, and a pub-café.

Jan Luyken Hotel (Jan Luykenstraat 58; Phone 76-41-11; and pronounced *Lowken*) occupies three joined houses. Those of the 65 rooms I have inspected are nicely equipped (a corner double, especially); lobby and bar are welcoming; and management—which has a loyal following—is cordial. Between P. C. Hoofstraat and the Concertgebouw/Museums quarter.

Memphis Hotel (De Lairessestraat 87; Phone 73-31-41) edges the southerly quarter dominated by the Amsterdam Hilton, in a relatively nondescript area, just opposite the Amsterdam outpost of Christie's auction gallery. There are 81 full-facility rooms, bar, and restaurant. So-so.

Park Hotel (Stadthouderskade 25; Phone 71-74-74) has the best of both worlds, with respect to location, about midway between fleshpots of Leidseplein and major museums of Museumplein. This is a substantial, nicely maintained house with a pair of restaurants and a bar, as well as 186 full-facility rooms, some of course bigger—and affording better vistas—than others. Operated by the Britain-based Ladbrooke chain.

Port van Cleve Hotel (N. Z. Voorburgwal 178; Phone 14-48-60) brings back memories of an early Amsterdam visit when, with colleagues, I had a good time sampling the numbered steaks of its long-respected restaurant. Well, the steaks still are numbered, but the hotel has spruced itself up. Those of the 109 rooms I have looked at are up to the minute, staff is alert, and location, as always—not far from the Dam —is central.

Victoria Hotel (Damrak 1; Phone 23-42-55): We are, I suspect, invariably partial to personal "firsts." The Victoria, on a long-ago visit, was my very first Amsterdam hotel. I had stepped off a train, come south from Copenhagen, crossed Station-splein, *et voila*! There was the indubitably Victorian facade of the Victoria. I stepped in, registered, and ever since have been both a Victoria *and* an Amsterdam aficionado. Relatively recently emerged from a meticulous refurbishing, the hotel (which dates to 1886) welcomes you in an inviting lobby, feeds you at either of a pair of reliable restaurants (one has a fabulous fireplace, lighted when weather warrants), relaxes you at its bar, makes a sportsman (or sportswoman) of you in the casino, and pleases you with its rooms. Those of the lot I have inspected are humdingers—handsomely traditional and with good baths. And the staff smiles.

SELECTED MODERATE-CATEGORY HOTELS

Agora Hotel (Singel 462; Phone 27-22-00): Either Giorgio Campeggi or Pierre Giauque—the Italo-Swiss owning-team—is on hand to welcome guests to this delightful, centrally located, early-eighteenth-century canal house-turned-hostelry. Ground floor is given over to an attractive lounge and antiques-accented breakfast room. Upstairs (mind, there is no elevator), 11 of the 14 rooms have baths; no two are alike, but those I have inspected are charming. Congenial.

Atlas Hotel (Van Eeghenstraat 64; Phone 76-63-36) appears quite as the English-language part of its brochure rather quaintly describes it: "Old-fashioned from the outside but completely modern at the inside and applicable to all the wishes of the modern traveler and businessman." The red-brick, white-trim, gabled facade is in sharp contrast to the lounge, all sleek, black-leather chairs and vases of fresh flowers set against stark white walls. Those of the two dozen mod-look rooms I've inspected are small but well equipped. And there's a small but reliable restaurant-cum-bar. Near major museums.

Canal House Hotel (Keizersgracht 148) is accurately titled, occupying a Baroque mansion on a principal Amsterdam waterway. The ground floor embraces an antiques-accented lounge-cum-bar and a crystal-chandeliered breakfast room giving onto the garden. The 17 rooms are no two alike (canalview ones are the most preferable), but all have baths with either tub or shower. Note that there is neither restaurant nor elevator.

Eden Hotel (Amstel 144; Phone 26-62-43) is a friendly house with a situation both scenic (it's on the Amstel River) and strategic (it's near Het Musiektheater and Rembrandtplein). The look is neat-as-a-pin functional, and all 17 rooms have either tubs or showers in their baths; those I have inspected are plain and small. Breakfast only.

Esthéria Hotel (Singel 303; Phone 24-51-46) is well located and welcoming and offers private facilities in most of its 70 rooms, some considerably smaller than others, but spotless and with good beds. There's an elevator—rare in canal-house hotels—and a restaurant.

Gouden Kettingh Hotel (Keizersgracht 2681; Phone 24-82-87) is centrally situated, a seventeenth-century canal house that has been converted into a small and modest hotel, with cordial owner-management and 20 no-two-alike rooms (doubles with canal views are the nicest), the majority of which have private baths or showers. Breakfast only.

Holland Hotel (P. C. Hooftstraat 162; Phone 76-42-53) is a find: a budget hotel on the most exclusive shopping street in town. Accommodations—there are 70 bath- or shower-equipped rooms—are more functional than opulent. But management is cordial; housekeeping, exemplary; and the bar, inviting. Breakfast only.

Museum Hotel (P. C. Hooftstraat 2; Phone 62-14-02) suggests, by its name, proximity to a museum, and the Rijksmuseum is indeed a hop and a skip distant. This is an agreeable hostelry with 120 rooms (those I have seen are neat and functional), all with bath or shower, plus a reliable restaurant-café.

Owl Hotel (Roemer Visscherstraat 1; Phone 18-94-84) has the virtues of being well situated and cheerful. All of the 34 rooms I have inspected, though not necessarily generous in space, are bright and inviting and bath equipped; there is, moreover, an elevator, and the breakfast room (there is no restaurant) overlooks the garden.

Smits Hotel (P. C. Hooftstraat 24; Phone 71-47-85) meets my requirements for comfort and convenience at a fair fee. Forty-three of the 48 rooms are bath or shower equipped; by the time you arrive, a dozen more rooms are likely to have been added. And management is welcoming. Breakfast only.

Trianon Hotel (J. W. Brouwerstraat 2; Phone 73-20-73): You may tumble out of bed and right into the Concertgebouw from the Trianon, and major museums are near neighbors, too. This is an attractive, essentially contemporary house with half a hundred comfortable bath- or shower-equipped rooms, as well as restaurant and bar.

Zandbergen Hotel (Willemsparkweg 205; Phone 76-93-21): The smart black and white facade of this centrally positioned townhouse turned hotel lures you in, and you like what you encounter: a cordial welcome at reception and 17 inelegant but spotless rooms, all with either bath or shower.

STAYING AT SCHIPHOL

Hilton International Schiphol Hotel (Schiphol International Airport; Phone 511-59-11) is an all-Netherlands surprise package, a snappy 282-room house a hop and a skip from the terminals (the hotel's gratis shuttle buses make the run in two minutes), with a lobby at once rambling and inviting, a kicky cocktail lounge edging it, a pair of restaurants leading from it (smart, copper-chandeliered Dutch oven with a Continental menu; Delft Sandwich Shoppe) that are ideal for lunch when you're touring in this east-of-Amsterdam area, and 282 rooms and suites. Accommodations are a Schiphol Hilton highlight; the 204 main-building rooms, relatively recently updated, are decorated in restful pastels. Even newer—and even handsomer—are the 78 rooms of the Executive Wing, as smart as they are rich in amenities and with their own concierge, as well as complimentary breakfast and cocktails in the wing's own lounge. And there are other facilities, including meeting rooms and business comforts for execs who fly in for conferences, and a swimming pool. Bravo, Hilton International. *Luxury*.

DAILY BREAD

CAFÉS AND "BROWN" CAFÉS

Café Américain (American Hotel, Leidsekade 97; Phone 24-53-22) is the landmark restaurant of a landmark Art Nouveau hotel (above) with its original turn-of-century decor intact—furniture and leaded windows, carved decorative elements and sculptures, paintings and chandeliers—from the twenties. There are two menu cards. One is à la carte, with Dutch and international dishes—onion soup and Dutch shrimps through minute steak and porkchops, with the all-inclusive buffet as an option. The other menu features snacks (*quiche Lorraine*, veal *croquettes*), sandwiches, sweets, and drinks. And there are outdoor tables. *Moderate/First Class*.

Beems Brasserie (Rokin 9; Phone 34-58-90) is a good looker—pale hued and contemporary, with caned chairs of pale oak around its tables. Steaks and salads, ice cream and coffee. *Moderate*.

Divertimento (Corner of Singel and Konigsplein; Phone 36-79-56) is just the spot for resting tired tootsies in the course of a stroll through town; snacks, drinks, and the passing parade. Attractive. *Moderate*.

Koepel Café (Amsterdam Sonesta Hotel, Kattengat 1; Phone 21-22-33) doubles as a typically Amsterdam "brown" café (have a beer at the bar) and as a source of sustenance, with such standbys as club and grilled ham and cheese sandwiches, the typical nibblies called *bitterballen* (tiny and tasty *croquettes*), and Indonesian-origin *saté*—grilled skewered meat cubes, spicily sauced. Lots of neighborhood regulars. *Moderate.*

Krasserie (Krasnapolsky Hotel, Dam; Phone 554-91-11) is the Kras's café, with picture windows giving onto the Dam and a well-organized international menu—the options, hamburgers and omelets through gooey ice-cream desserts. Tip: This is among the relatively few spots in the neighborhood that's open for Sunday lunch. *Moderate.*

La Ruche (Bijenkorf department store, Dam): Up you go on the escalator for morning coffee, a casual lunch, or afternoon tea. *Moderate.*

Maison de Bonneterie (Rokin entrance) is quite the poshest of the big chain specialty shops (see Shopper's Amsterdam, below) and is called to your attention here because its street-level coffee shop serves what I consider to be just about the best pastry in town, not to mention milkshakes, sandwiches on French-style *baguettes*, and *cappuccino*. *Moderate.*

Nieuwe Kafé (in Nieuwe Kerk, Dam): Kudos to the Nieuwe Kerk for operating this splendidly sited café, at its best in fair weather, when tables are set on the square. Coffee, snacks, light lunches. *Moderate.*

L'Opéra (Rembrandtsplein 27; Phone 27-52-32): The sun is shining, and you could do with coffee or a beer and a view of the Rembrandtsplein action. An alfresco table at L'Opéra fills the bill; if it's packed, consider the competition: *Café Monaco, Café Rhapsody,* and *Café Hof van Holland.* All are *Moderate.*

Smits Koffiehuis (Stationsplein 10) is a source of sustenance opposite Centraal Station, on the harbor, at its best when you've an outdoor table, so that you can minimize the substandard quality of the pastries, coffee, and service. *Moderate.*

"Brown" cafés —English for *Bruine Kroegen*, and so called because of the overall brown tones of their heavy woodwork—are to Amsterdammers what neighborhood pubs, or "locals," are to Londoners. Pop into any that seem congenial or consider choosing from among these favorites: *Drie Fleschjes* (Gravenstraat 8), with a big choice of Dutch gins and seventeenth-century ambience; *Gollem* (Raamsteeg 4), with its ace-in-the-hole 100 species of beer; *Frascati* (Nes 59), with pronounced Art Nouveau decor; *Het Gebed* (Gebed Zonder End 5), originally a stable; *Hoppe* (Spui 18), invariably packed, so that you must look hard to note the traditionally sand-covered floor; *De Reiger* (Neuwe Leliestraat 34), mid-nineteenth century and with good grub; *Pieper* (Prinsengracht 121), which draws a smart crowd; and *Café Nol* (Westerstraat 109), in the trendy Jordaan quarter.

DUTCH

Admiraal (Herengracht 319; Phone 25-43-34) qualifies as a "brown" café (see above) but is brought to your attention at this point because it's a convenient choice for a casual omelet or salad lunch. Atmospheric, aged, and *Moderate.*

Pannekoeken Beckvelt (Stadhouderskade 21; Phone 27-46-98): Dutch pancake houses invariably resemble carousels. Mr. Beckvelt's, next door to the Amsterdam Marriott, is no exception. The pancakes come in limitless varieties, including such savory choices as ham, cheese, and bacon and such sweet choices as rum, brandy, pineapple, and Grand Marnier. Or opt for the standard butter and sugar. *Moderate.*

Dorrius (Spuistraat 285; Phone 23-52-45) opened its doors in 1890 and has—with good reason—been a favorite of Amsterdammers ever since. If you experience a single Dutch-cuisine restaurant, this should be it. Look is agreeably old-fashioned; waiters, these many years, have worn Dorrius's own design, long white aprons—and could not be more kindly. And nowhere that I know are typical national dishes tastier. Order from the extensive á la carte—Dutch herring, Dutch smoked eel, Dutch shrimps in a brandy-spiked sauce, and Dutch soups are among starters. Zeeland codfish teamed with mussel and shrimp and tossed with sauce Hollandaise is a seafood specialty, while braised beef served with red cabbage and boiled potatoes is among traditional meat entrées. Best buys are daily specials. One sticks in my mind—and stuck to my ribs—*erwtensoep complet*, the celebrated Dutch pea soup (nowhere in Holland, in my experience, any tastier) served with smoked sausage, bacon, pork, and rye bread. And *mosselen*, mussels, cooked in white wine and served Belgian style with french fries and a choice of sauces, is another Dorrius winner. A selection of Dutch cheeses makes a good dessert substitute, although the house's hot apple pie blanketed with thick cream is hardly to be despised. In my experience, one of Holland's best restaurants. *First Class.*

Haesje Claes (Spuistraat 27; Phone 24-99-98), which claims on its card to have originated *Anno 1520*, looks better than it, tastes. There is no faulting the decor—paneled walls, green silk-shaded lighting fixtures, oaken chairs, candles and flowers at the tables. But such typical Dutch dishes as *hutspot*—which we translate as hotchpotch with good reason—can disappoint (better, though, when based on grilled sausages and sauerkraut than with endive and meatballs). You're better off with an omelet. *Moderate.*

Keyzer (Van Baerlestraat 96; Phone 62-07-78), a next-door neighbor of the Concertgebouw, must look today quite as it did when it opened in 1906—Persian rugs covering tables at the front-of-house café and gilded leather surfacing the walls of the restaurant section to the rear, with tables centered with red roses and illuminated by candles in silver sticks. Clientele—mostly solid, well-dressed, and fed Amsterdammers—is at least as absorbing as the decor. Prix-fixe menus are hearty and tasty. You might open with mussel *croquettes*, continue with veal *schnitzel*—accompanied by several vegetables—as an entrée, and conclude with raisin pudding or pistachio ice cream. Or order a somewhat lighter meal—grilled filet of sole, with home fried potatoes and a salad—from the á la carte. Portions are huge, service is cordial but formal. *First Class*.

FRENCH-ACCENTED

L'Entrée (Reguliersdwarsstraat 42; Phone 26-94-97), once gained by means of a flight of stairs from the street, attempts an air of grandeur, what with high ceilings, an entire mirrored wall, and Louis XV-style chairs covered in the same blue fabric that drapes windows. Problems commence with what the French call *accueil*: The welcome is distinctly cool. Service at table—by a bored and inept waitress—is hardly an improvement. And the proof of the pudding, L'Entrée's fare, is no compensation, starting with frozen rolls that have been underheated and continuing through the course for which the restaurant is named (two lamb choices, each meager and with neither flavor nor texture). Even wine by the glass—an advertised specialty—is disappointing, given the tiny quantities. *First Class*.

Excelsior (Hotel de l'Europe, Nieuwe Doelenstraat 2; Phone 23-48-36)—its picture windows giving on to the Amstel River—is a looker, framed by crystal chandeliers, its tables widely spaced, candlelit, and centered by bowls of flowers quite obviously arranged by professionals. The à la carte melds classic and *nouvelle* French—oysters on the half-shell with a squirt of lemon in the traditional Gallic manner and marinated salmon with snail eggs (a contemporary presentation) are among starters. *Entrecôte de boeuf Charolais*—an old-fashioned entrée—contrasts with the more modern *blanc de pintadeau au melon et jus de gingembre* (guinea hen in a melon and ginger sauce). Order either á la carte or select one of the two prix-fixe menus. The cellar is extensive, and the extraordinary digestif selection includes no less than 15 cognacs, as many liquers, half a dozen fine ports, and both Swiss and French *eaux-de-vie. Luxury.*

Dikker & Thijs (Prinsengracht 444, at the corner of Leidsestraat; Phone 26-77-21) is a long-on-scene Amsterdam institution, where for some 70 years locals have celebrated special occasions or gone for a gala supper after a weekend opera performance. This up-a-flight restaurant (in the building housing the same management's Alexander Hotel [above]) is quietly classic, in tones of green and gold, with three-stick candelabra at dinner tables. But the menu has *nouvelle* overtones, as, for example, in a first-course salad of truffle-sauced sweetbreads, double *consommé* with a *quenelle* of spinach, roast quail with a mushroom stuffing, or filet of sole served in tandem with salmon *mousse*, watercress sauced. Wines are choice; service, skilled. *Luxury.* (The same firm's *Prinsenkelder*—occupying the cellar of an adjacent eighteenth-century canal house—is less formal, less pricey, and less *nouvelle*; a meal might consist of three kinds of ham from the Dikker & Thijs on-premises deli as an opener, grilled veal steak or thyme-sauced roast lamb as entrées, with assorted *petits-fours* as dessert. *First Class.*)

De Goudsbloem (Pulitzer Hotel, Prinsengracht 232; Phone 25-32-88) is smart—colors are green and coral—and small, and its fare, either traditional or contemporary French, is ordered from a pair of prix-fixe menus or á la carte. Openers are mostly *nouvelle*—seafood salads served warm, or *tiède*, or cream of corn soup flecked with morsels of smoked salmon. *Waterzooi*, Belgium's chicken soup-stew, is among entrées, along with roast lamb and veal medallions combined with fresh figs. Wines have been well selected, and service is a pleasure. *Luxury.*

Der Kerstentuin (Garden Hotel, Dijsselhofplantsoen 7; Phone 64-21-21) is the glitzy restaurant—heavily lacquered, fussily mirrored and trellised, top-heavy with tall plants and oversized floral arrangements—of a glossy hotel (above). The service is pretentious—an oversolicitous waiter with a frozen smile pours your mineral water (the half-pint bottle is kept on a detached table) two sips at a time, as though it were a rare Pauillac. And the fare is the most expensive I have encountered in the Netherlands. House drink—cherry-flavored champagne, presented in vulgarly oversized hollow-stem flutes—is pricey and predictable. *Bouillabaisse*, served as an appetizer, arrives lukewarm. And such entrées as grilled sole and roast lamb are well enough prepared, but so they should be, given their cost. *Luxury.*

Petit Culinair (P. C. Hooftstraat 87; Phone 93-89-56) is just the ticket for a Gallic-influenced lunch after a morning in the shops of this smart street. Open with *carpaccio*, shrimp salad, or onion soup. Consider *cassoulet* or *lasagne* as an entrée, and conclude with a frozen sweet. Decor is smartly contemporary. *Moderate.*

Le Reflet d'Or (Krasnapolsky Hotel, Dam 9; Phone 554-91-91) is a step back to Belle Époque Amsterdam—graceful columns, tall arched windows, original woodwork elaborately detailed, and tailcoated waiters. Open with Parma ham or duck breast salads. Precede your entrée with cream of tomato soup, a Dutch favorite. Fish—trout, turbot, sole, halibut—is creatively prepared. Filet of pork and sirloin steak are favored meat entrées. Sweets include pastries, the wine list is exemplary, and hours are noteworthy, noon through 11:00 P.M., nonstop. *Luxury.*

La Rive (Amstel Hotel, Prof. Tulpplein 1; Phone 22-60-60): If you go back far enough as an Amstel customer, you remember when its restaurant had a place of honor in a sumptuous, high-ceilinged room, riverview and off the lobby. The hotel's handsome cocktail lounge still has that type of location, and if you're lucky enough to be present on a Sunday, you do well to book the champagne buffet brunch, served in a crystal-chandeliered, off-lobby space. The name of La Rive's game, however, is intimacy; setting is a down-a-flight, lower-level room, as luxuriously traditional in look as the fare is *nouvelle*. Open with duck liver terrine or grilled oysters on a bed of watercress, accented with lemon *mousse*, or a seafood-flecked potato soup. Broiled tuna with caviar and *créme fraîche* is among fish entrees. Lamb is also a good choice, with a sauce made from diced green olives, pistachios, and basil. Cheeses are paid attention, and, if you're up to dessert, go for the strawberry-banana *clafoutis*, buried under strawberry sauce. Excellent wines (you are, after all, in an Inter-Continental hotel) and service. *Luxury.*

De Silveren Spiegel (Kattegat 4, opposite Amsterdam Sonesta Hotel; Phone 24-65-89) occupies a honey of a seventeenth-century house (take a table either downstairs or up; both are attractive) and is delightfully staffed (your welcome is warm). But you can't eat ambience. Stick to simpler things—cream of leek soup or smoked salmon as starters (snails are best avoided), roast chicken or filet of beef as entrées; (skip *paillard* of veal). *First Class.*

't Swarte Schaep (Korte Leidsedwarsstraat 24, up a flight and overlooking Leidseplein; Phone 22-30-21) has the engaging look of the English countryside—quite marvelously carved oaken details, a ceiling accented by antique beams, and brightly polished brass chandeliers. Flower-centered tables are immaculately set with beige linen. Tuxedoed staff is warm in its welcome and, you come to learn, professionally skilled. The single prix-fixe menu is indicated here, at what translates as the Black Sheep. You might open with an unusual—and unusually delicious—quail *pâté* studded with shaved truffle or *bisque de homard*, generous with chunks of lobster. Select from among such entrées as grilled salmon sautéed with a delicate *vinaigrette des tomates*—again unusual, again successful. Or opt for roast pigeon or the day's fish prepared to your taste. The dessert specialty, a trio of the house's own sherbets (conceivably melon, pear, and raspberry), is a sweet way to end, but consider also the cheese platter—one of the finest such I have encountered in Holland and with the estimable *aged* Gouda among its offerings. Fine wines. In my experience, one of Holland's best restaurants. *First Class.*

Tout Court (Runstraat 17; Phone 25-86-37) represents the handiwork of owner-chef John Fagel, one of an extraordinary family of eight brothers who own (usually doubling as chefs in) some of the best restaurants in the kingdom. (Another in Amsterdam is L'Entrecôte, below, and still others brought to your attention in this book are De Hoefslag in Bosch en Duin and Café de Paris in Utrecht (both Chapter 19). Tout Court, brother John's labor of love, is small (book a few days in advance) and smart—the look is an unlikely but winning mix of wicker chairs and marble-topped tables—but by no means pretentious. Somehow or other, John Fagel manages to duck out of his small, partially open kitchen to greet virtually every guest. He offers five sensibly priced prix-fixe menus if you eschew the à la carte. Fagel fare is solidly French, albeit with his own touches. You might open with a bowl of celeriac soup, seafood aspic on a bed of cabbage leaves, or simply Zeeland oysters on the half-shell with a squirt of lemon. Roast chicken, so rarely encountered in Dutch restaurants, is masterfully prepared, in tandem with *sauce armoricaine*. So are both sweetbreads and kidneys, not to mention *entrecôte* served with an authentic *sauce bordelaise*, and roast lamb, in tandem with *sauce béarnaise*. John Fagel's French-style tarts are surpassed by no confection that I know in Holland. And he takes both cheese (Dutch, as well as French) and wine (predominantly Bordeaux and Burgundies) seriously. Dinner only. In my experience, one of Holland's best restaurants. *Luxury*.

De Trechter (Hobbemakade 63, in the neighborhood of the Concertgebouw; Phone 71-26-23) is intimate but charmless. Tables are so close that you overhear conversations of neighbors in all directions. Service, in my experience, is extended by a single unsmiling waiter working under the somber-visaged boss's direction. The menu is one of less than a handful that I have come across in the Netherlands that is published only in the Dutch language, which means that the solitary waiter must rattle off an *in toto* translation for most foreigners. By the time he finishes, you've forgotten a lot, and must ask for at least partial repetition. A meal—finally selected from an extremely expensive à la carte (there is no prix-fixe menu)—might consist of sliced goose breast or onion-flecked oxtail soup, *tournedos* with an olive oil-based sauce or roast pork with leeks in white wine sauce, each accompanied by tiny dabs of *nouvelle* vegetables. Good French wines help somewhat to dispel the chilly atmosphere—but not enough. *Luxury.*

Yves (Utrechtsestraat 28; Phone 25-13-92): Francophiles who are partial to the French institution of the friendly, no-frills bistro are in for a treat at Yves—which bears the name of its congenial, French-born *patron*, who greets customers, takes orders, supervises the kitchen with an eagle eye, and helps an agile staff serve whenever necessary. The consequence is a humming, happy environment, in large part thanks to the delicious—in part classic, in part *nouvelle*—fare ordered from a reasonably priced à la carte. A meal might open with fennel soup, smoked trout, or the house *pâté*. Broiled tuna steak or seafood stew are among fish entrées; superbly sauced *grenadin* of veal and filet of pork *à l'orange*, among meat courses. Well-priced wines. *First Class.*

INDONESIAN

Indonesia (Singel 550, at Muntplein, upstairs; Phone 23-29-35) is a beloved old-timer—high ceilinged and ballroom sized, with a staff of friendly, Indonesian-origin waiters, happy to explain the extraordinary range of piquant dishes—10 to 20, depending on which all-inclusive typically Indonesian *rijsttafel* feast you order. They come to table virtually en masse; you center your plate with a helping of plain boiled rice, picking and choosing accompaniments from among servings of such favorites as beef in curry sauce, pork scallops in soy sauce, vegetables in peanut sauce or coconut milk, and favorite of the lot—*saté*—grilled skewered meat that you dip in a hot *sambal* sauce. Beer or, failing that, dry white wine, is the indicated accompaniment. Fun. *First Class.*

Kowloon (Singel 498, opposite the alfresco flower market, near Muntplein; Phone 25-32-64) does indeed sound Chinese (Kowloon is, of course, a sector of Hong Kong). But this long, narrow space, accented by red-silk draperies and illuminated by indisputably Chinese-style lanterns, is the genuine Indonesian article, serving up a tasty *rijsttafel* to the satisfaction of many loyal Amsterdammers. *First Class.*

Sama Sebo (P. C. Hooftstraat 27; Phone 62-81-46) offers a location on the city's fanciest shopping street and an intimate setting ("cramped" might be a better adjective)—there are but a dozen tables—in lieu of the more bourgeois ambience of Kowloon or Indonesia (above). But this is hardly to say that the quality of the fare or the warmth of one's welcome is less than satisfactory. *First Class.*

INTERNATIONAL

D'Vijff Vlieghen (a.k.a. The Five Flies, Spuistraat 294; Phone 24-83-69) can thank its advanced age and extraordinary good looks—it is quartered in a contiguous quintet of still-splendid seventeenth-century houses—for the reputation it has achieved. Nary a foreign visitor to Amsterdam dares leave without having experienced a meal here. The fare, which had deteriorated in recent seasons, has gone into forward gear of late, thanks to special efforts by a team of experts—chefs as well as out-front staff—engaged by the owning Krasnapolsky Hotel management. A consequence is that you may now lunch or dine satisfactorily. A meal might embrace a cocktail of Dutch shrimps or bean soup as openers; filet of sole in lobster sauce, mushroom-sauced breast of chicken, or *steak au poivre* as entrées. Select ice cream sundaes or cheese to conclude. There is no charge for a don't-miss tour of the wonderfully antiques-accented premises—arms and helmets in the Knight's Hall, drawn-from-life etchings of the painter for whom the Rembrandt Room is named, centuries-old crystal in the Glass Room, venerable artifacts in the Bridal Room, and a veritable museum of aged Amsterdam art in the Print Room. Special. *First Class.*

Terrace (Amsterdam Hilton Hotel, Apollolaan 138; Phone 78-07-80)—recently emerged from a stylish refurbishing—has become one of the city's handsomest restaurants, with the menu an inspired mix of Dutch, American, and French favorites. This means you may have a cheeseburger with fries quite the equal of any back home, a bowl of Holland's esteemed pea soup, or either of two three-course, prix-fixe menus, opening, for example, with Madeira-spiked oxtail soup, continuing with *paillards* of veal served with wild mushrooms or filet of turbot with saffron-accented mussels, and concluding with a choice of desserts (the Hilton's *pâtissiers* are skilled) from the sweets trolley. *First Class.*

Pavilijoen Brasserie (Apollo Hotel, Apollolaan 2; Phone 73-59-22)—a symphony, bright and inviting, in Dutch tile—is as tasty as it is good looking. It offers considerable options, including Holland's own herring, smoked eel, *croquettes* and *uitsmijters* (open ham sandwiches topped with fried eggs), France's onion soup, Switzerland's cream-sauced veal, Italy's *lasagne*. *First Class.*

ITALIAN

Il Giardino (Herengracht 413; Phone 25-45-68): Unlike so many restaurants labeled French in Holland—but actually operated by Dutchmen—Italian restaurants invariably are run by owner-chefs born on the Italian peninsula, serving the genuine Italian article. Il Giardino, in a lovely old canal house, is typical. Select an authentically sauced pasta as an opener—*lasagne, paglia a fieno, orecchiette,* spaghetti *puttanesca,* for example—following with any number of veal entrées—such as *scaloppine al limone*—and concluding with a rich *zabaglione.* Italian wines. *First Class.*

Mirafiori (Hobbemastraat 2; Phone 62-30-13, near the Rijksmuseum) is perhaps the smartest of the Italian eateries, with white tiebacks at its windows, a light-look interior, and reliable fare—the range, *antipasto* based on imported salamis, the eggdrop soup called *stracciatella,* pastas in abundance, and

Florentine-style beefsteak, as well as veal among entrées. *First Class.*

Pico Bello (Spuistraat 1; Phone 27-12-82, opposite Amsterdam Sonesta Hotel) is compact, congenial, and, like most Italian restaurants in Holland, outside of Amsterdam, as much pizzeria as *ristorante.* The individual cheese pizzas—called *margherita*, as indeed they are in Naples—are excellent. *Moderate.*

Raffaello (Spuistraat 90: Phone 26-95-82), though plain and simple, offers kindly service and adequate pastas—*penne all'Arabiata* and *spaghetti all'Amatriciana*—if less successful salads and entrées. Italian wines are inexpensive. *Moderate.*

SEAFOOD

De Oesterbar (Leidseplein 10; Phone 23-29-88) is a Leidseplein fixture of considerable longevity, extending from a tile-walled, main-floor dining room up a flight to a more formal environment, no less inviting. The oysters of the title—from Zeeland and at their best on the half-shell, served with lemon—make a good opener, as indeed do Dutch shrimps as the basis of a nicely sauced cocktail, or fish soup. There is no better grilled filet of sole in town, but other fish, including trout, are excellent, too. And service is kindly and caring. *First Class.*

Le Pecheur (Reguliersdwarsstraat 32; Phone 24-31-21)—a glossily got-up, compact space on Amsterdam's Restaurant Row—attempts grandeur without special success, at least at lunch, when, in my experience, service has been in the hands of a solitary, upsupervised waiter. At tables set with green linen, the while you are seated in white caned chairs, you're served from a pricey à la carte. Tomato soup flecked with mussels is a satisfactory starter. Sole is but one of a number of species of fish offered as entrées. But I prefer seafood in a less pretentious setting and with sprightlier service. *First Class/Luxury.*

STEAKS

L'Entrecôte (P. C. Hooftstraat 70; Phone 73-77-76), operated by one of the restaurant-owning Fagel brothers (see Tout Court, above), occupies an absolute smasher of a black-and-white Art Deco space. The little bar is on the ground floor; the dining room is upstairs, and the menu is based on the kind of steak whose name the restaurant takes. It's deliciously sauced and accompanied by a mound of crispy *frites*. Veal steak may be substituted at a price, and you're urged to conclude with *profiteroles au chocolat* or *tarte maison*. Super. *First Class*.

Gaucho (Korte Leidsedwarsstraat 45, Phone 23-80-87; Damstraat 5, Phone 23-96-32; and other locations) has a winning formula: grilled Argentine beef in a number of cuts and sizes, variously sauced, with french fries as principal accompaniment, and a sensibly limited choice of appetizers, soups, salads, and sweets, along with Argentine wine, by glass or bottle. Good value. *Moderate*.

Henri Brouvin (Gravenstraat 20; Phone 23-93-33) is as much traditional-style "brown" café as steakhouse, and a core-of-town neighbor of Nieuwe Kerk. Steak and roast beef are favored entrées, with sound-value wine by the glass. Open nonstop, noon through 8:30 P.M. *Moderate*.

Port o' Amsterdam (Amsterdam Marriott Hotel, Stadhouderskade 21; Phone 83-51-51): Brick-walled, with windows giving onto the always-busy Leidseplein, Port o' Amsterdam lures Amsterdammers, as well as Americans, with imported-from-the-U.S. Angus beef. Choose either tenderloin or strip steaks; they're grilled on mesquite, dotted with globs of herb-flavored butter, and accompanied by a salad to which you help yourself from a counter, Stateside style. Roast prime rib is an entrée option—one of a number. You do well to open with avocado-shrimp salad or onion soup, concluding with a minimasterwork baked by the Marriott's master *pâtissier*. Wine list is exceptional; service, a pleasure. *Luxury*.

Die Port van Cleve (in the hotel of the same name, Nieuwe Zijds Voorburgwal 178; Phone 24-48-60) has served, according to its careful count, more than five and a half million steaks since 1870. Your waiter places the order by shouting it into the kitchen, just as his illiterate predecessors, several generations removed, did, and it comes to you numbered, to what advantage no one seems to know. If the weather is brisk, open with *erwtensoep*—pea soup—and conclude with *poire Belle Hélène*—poached pear mated with vanilla ice cream under an umbrella of hot chocolate sauce. *First Class.*

AFTER DARK

Het Muziektheater (Waterlooplein): What it lacks in grace, style, and beauty, the 1600-seat, curved-front, brick, glass, and marble Muziektheater—which opened toward the end of 1986 as part of a controversial and massive complex housing also the new Stadhuis, or City Hall—compensates for with state-of-the-art technology, excellent acoustics, and plenty of lobby space for intermission promenades, drinks, and coffee. It is the home of two globally celebrated companies. *De Nederlandse Operastichting/Netherlands Opera*, founded in 1964, has both Dutch and foreign soloists and a 56-voice chorus. It presents a hundred performances of a dozen productions each year—contemporary works like Otto Ketting's *Ithaka* and Philip Glass's *Satlagraha* through to Verdi's *Falstaff*, Tchaikovsky's *Eugene Onegin*, Strauss's *Die Fliedermaus*, and Rossini's *Barber of Seville*. *Het Nationale Ballet/Dutch National Ballet* is no less exemplary. On scene since 1961, its repertory is a delightful mix of the classic—*Giselle* and *Swan Lake*, *The Sleeping Beauty* and *Petrushka*—and the contemporary, as evidenced by performances of works by George Balanchine, Antony Tudor, and Kurt Jooss, not to mention such noted Dutch choreographers as Rudi van Dantzig, Hans van Manen, and Toer van Schayk. The company, 88 dancers strong and accompanied by the top-ranked *Nederlands Balletorkest/Netherlands Ballet Orchestra*, dances some 76 performances of seven distinctive programs per year on home base and another 30 on tour throughout Holland. Het Muziektheater is also the Amsterdam venue of Holland's other leading company, *Nederlands*

Dans Theater/Netherlands Dance Theater, a modern dance group headed by Jiri Kylian, which has performed extensively abroad, including at New York's Metropolitan Opera House.

Concertgebouw (Van Baerlestraat 98) is the name both of a capacious concert hall (built in 1888) and of a world-renowned symphony; the latter makes its home in the former. The orchestra gained an international reputation during the half-century conductorship of Wilhelm Mengelberg, which terminated after World War II. Bernard Haitink assumed the orchestra's baton thereafter, with Riccardo Chailly his principal co-conductor in recent seasons. The Concertgebouw is the venue, as well, of frequent free lunch-hour concerts, and of appearances by the *Netherlands Philharmonic, Radio Philharmonic, Netherlands Chamber Orchestra*, and *Amsterdam Baroque Orchestra*, among others; some of these perform in the building's second—and smaller—*Kleine Zaal*.

Church concerts —in *Nieuwe Kerk* (Dam), *Oude Kerk* (Oudeksersplein), and *Westerkerk* (Westermarkt)—take place regularly. And the onetime church, Baroque and domed, that is now part of the *Amsterdam Sonesta Hotel* (Kattegat), is the site of concerts (pop, as well as classical) every Sunday at 11:00 A.M., with the service of coffee commencing a half-hour in advance.

Stadsschouwburg (Leidseplein) is the turn-of-century Municipal Theater, with a range of offerings, Dutch-language plays and operetta among them.

Theater Carré (Amstel 115)—refurbished for its centennial in 1987—is musical comedy headquarters; there are often U.S. imports.

Imported films are shown in their original version with Dutch subtitles; dubbing isn't necessary in this kingdom of extraordinarily gifted linguists. Thus, if you pass by a marquee with an American or British film playing, go right in; the language will be English.

The Holland Festival hasn't missed an annual three-week season since the first—in 1947. This star-studded melange of music, ballet, movies, and assorted additional entertainment takes place in the four biggest cities of the kingdom—The Hague (Chapter 10), Rotterdam (Chapter 18), Utrecht (Chapter 19), and, not surprisingly, Amsterdam, traditionally with the bulk of performances. The month, again traditionally, is June.

Rosse Buurt —Amsterdam's red-light district, adjacent to the sailors' quarter called Zeedijk, is Ladies of the Night territory, and quite as celebrated, in its way, as its Reeperbahn counterpart in Hamburg (see *Germany At Its Best*). Gents stroll about, selecting companions seated on display in the manner of department store mannequins—in open, lighted windows.

Gay scene: The Netherlands has long led the world with progressive homosexual-rights legislation. Amsterdam has gay hotels, restaurants, dancehalls, saunas, and "brown" cafés—all perfectly legal and non-eyebrow raising among the populace at large. Among gay "brown" cafés are *Chez Manfred*, *Amstel Taverne*, and *Monopol* on Halve Maansteeg, off Rembrandtsplein.

Television: You will not be watching it over breakfast in your hotel room as in, say, France or Britain. Dutch TV is a 7:00 P.M.-to-midnight proposition. But there are compensations in this land of linguists: German, French, and English stations from neighboring countries are available. Simply flip the channel selector.

This Week in Amsterdam is a gratis what's on weekly, with museum open hours and concert and ballet schedules; ask your hotel concierge or the tourist office (below) for a copy.

SHOPPER'S AMSTERDAM
Hours first: They're generally 9:00 A.M. to 6:00 P.M., except on Saturday, when closing time is 5:00 P.M. Thursday, most shops stay open until 9:00 P.M., and Monday finds most stores

closed in the morning. *Bijenjorf* (Dam), the No. 1 department store, has luggage and menswear on Main, women's clothing on 1, children's wear, toys, and a restaurant (above) on 2, and housewares on 3—along with Mister Minit, for shoe repairs. *Vroom & Dreesmann* has opposite-each-other buildings on Kalverstraat and Rokin; there's an excellent supermarket in the Kalverstraat building, along with books (including English language), while chocolates and menswear are on Main in the Rokin building, which also houses women's clothing and a post office on 1, souvenirs and housewares on 3, and De Munt Restaurant on 4.

Hema (Reguliersbreestraat, and not unlike Vroom & Dreesmann, with branches throughout Holland) is the Netherlands' answer to Britain-based Marks & Spencer—with bargain-priced clothing, accessories, toothpaste and shaving cream-type necessities, and—important this—absolutely delicious packaged chocolates, cookies, and cocktail snacks. *Peek & Cloppermann* (Dam) is a moderate-priced clothing house (men's, women's, and children's wear on two floors) that's part of a chain. *Maison de Bonneterie* (with entrances on Kalverstraat and Rokin) is the mother house of a three-city chain—crystal chandeliers illuminating its main floors are a trademark—that vends smart, albeit essentially conservative, men's and women's clothing, much of it imported from Britain, France, Italy, and America, and that has a commendable café (above).

Players (Vijzelstraat, near Muntplein) is among the city's more impressive men's shops. *Berntsen* (P. C. Hooftstraat 97) is for splurge purchases of their own and Belgian chocolates. *Warmolts* (P. C. Hooftstraat 81) has a selection of Dutch cheeses (including aged Gouda) unsurpassed in the kingdom—and they let you taste. *Hans Douglas* has reliable unisex hair and beauty salons at Nieuwe Doelenstraat 3 (opposite De l'Europe Hotel), Dam 9, and on the first floor of Bijenkorf department store; *Boendi* (P. C. Hooftstraat 23) is a good hairdresser, too.

A. H. Abels en Zoon is among the kinder and more knowledgable bulb and flower merchants in the massive, open-air flower stalls on Singel near Muntplein; many of the bulbs in these stalls have the necessary "health certificate" allowing import into the United States—but not all. À la Carte (Spui 25) is a bookstore specializing in travel books, many in the English language. Diamond merchants are dotted about in this long preeminent diamond-cutting city. Bigger ones make arrangements with tour operators and even hotels to lure groups in; gimmick is being able to watch cutters at work, and then you find yourself in the sales area en route to the exit. When a saleswoman in Coster (Paulus Potterstraat 2) quoted me prices in dollars rather than guilders, I asked why. Her reason (insulting, I thought) was that "tourists have never heard of guilders." I walked out. The sales staff at Amsterdam Diamond Center (Rokin 1) quoted tabs in the national currency and was more polite. But I am not an expert in diamonds, and I suggest you do a bit of homework in this area, if you are not and if you contemplate purchasing.

And this brings us to principal shopping streets. On Kalverstraat, in addition to stores recommended above, note Fiorucci (way-out clothing and accessories by way of Italy); Foto Optik, an optician, should you need one; Bata (men's and women's shoes out of Switzerland); American Book Center (discount titles); and Folke & Meltzer—porcelain, including Delft, and crystal.

Leidsestraat's shops include Laura Ashley (women's clothes), Liberty at Metz & Co. (British imported fabrics, women's clothing, glass, and kitchenware), the earlier mentioned Dikker & Thijs fancy food store (with Dutch cheeses), and—on Leidseplein—Thomas Cook (travel agency-change office) and Tesselschade (elder craftsmen's outlet for dolls, toys, crafts).

I've already mentioned what I consider key P. C. Hooftstraat shops; others of note on this smartest of Amsterdam's shopping streets include Azzurro and Edgar Voss (women's clothing), Barbas, McGregor, and Cool Cat (all men's clothing), Gianni Versace (women's and men's), La Culotte (lingerie), Scarabo (women's bags), Douglas (perfumes), Stéphane Kelian (men's and women's shoes out of Paris), Speel Goed (toys), Schlichte (antique sculpture and paintings), A. van der Meer (antique prints and etchings), and Van Muyden (an utterly irresistible bakery).

Van Baerlestraat—site of the Concertgebouw—is trendy, with such shops as *Van Geldern* (china and crystal), *Hobbit* (costly kids' clothes), *A. J. Bakker* (pricey men's and women's shoes), *Kenzo* (a branch of the Paris-based women's shop), *Mod Man* (men's duds), and the Amsterdam office of *American Express*.

Nieuwe Spiegelstraat—Antiques Row—rarely yields anything approaching a bargain; you go for quality to such shops as *Frans Leidelmeijer* (Art Nouveau and Art Deco), *Benjamin Stein* (Oriental pottery), *H. F. Hill* (eighteenth- and nineteenth-century furniture), *Stender* (clocks), *Het Spiegeltje* (silver and doodads), *Degenaar & Bijleveld* (globes, small clocks, telescopes), and *Anne Paul Brinkman* (Chinese porcelain, eighteenth- and nineteenth-century furniture).

The street called *Rokin* has fine antiques shops, too: *Salomon Stodel* (seventeenth-century furniture and Delft porcelain), *Gebr. Douwes* (antique paintings of high caliber), *Vecht* (tapestries, glass, porcelain and bronzes), and—should you be auction minded—the Amsterdam outlet of *Sotheby's*.

INCIDENTAL INTELLIGENCE

There are frequent, quick and inexpensive trains between Schiphol International Airport and Amsterdam's Centraal Station. *KLM Royal Dutch Airlines* is at Leidseplein 1; phone 43-42-42. Taxis are expensive. Ask the tourist office (below) for the gratis leaflet *Tram/Bus/Metro Amsterdam*, with routes and a multilingual breakdown of the transit system. *Further information*: VVV Amsterdam, Stationsplein 10—the principal information office, with others at Leidsestraat 106, and on Rijksweg (Highway) AZ, edging the city.

3

Amsterdam

Ten Excursions from the Capital

Aalsmeer	Haarlem
Alkmaar	Hoorn
Edam	Keukenhof
Enkhuisen	Marken and Monnickendam
Gouda	Volendam

BACKGROUND BRIEFING

In a country that is 190 miles at its longest, day-long excursions may be made—and effortlessly—to any point you care to choose, with combinations to several places convenient, in the case of shorter trips. Withal, the way to know a country is to travel about, bedding down in the course of a substantial journey; that, of course, is what this 20-chapter book is all about.

Still, certain points lend themselves well to day-long excursions from Amsterdam. Depart either by rented car or by train—invariably there are frequent departures—from Amsterdam's Centraal Station. Six of these ten excursions are to points north or northeast of town; the others are to the west and south. The most distant town, Gouda, is 34 miles. (It is about midway between Rotterdam [Chapter 18] and Utrecht

[Chapter 19], should you want to visit it from either of those cities.) But the other points are all closer to Amsterdam; five of them are under 20 miles.

I suggest stopping first, on arrival, for a map at the local tourist office, which is usually near the train station; I provide addresses below. Make a plan of attack for the morning and afternoon, allowing time for a lunch break—I make restaurant suggestions—and ascertaining in advance (if you are traveling by train) departure times of return trains toward the end of the afternoon.

AALSMEER (12 miles south of Amsterdam): You don't have to be a confirmed—or even a budding—gardener or flower buff to appreciate the world's largest flower auction; don't let me frighten you away when I give you its Dutch name: *Verenigde Bloemenveilingen Aalsmeer.* This is a Monday-through-Friday proposition, mornings only. You want to arrive between 8:00 and 9:00 AM., when the market is at its busiest. There is, to be sure, an entrance fee, but you're taken through with a guide.

Aalsmeer is contained within a 75-acre shed, an area whose size is that of 50 football fields. Its management claims it's the largest single-roofed building in the world, and I believe them. Every day some 50,000 transactions take place, in the course of which some eight and a half million cut flowers, as well as around 700,000 plants—coming from more than 4,000 owners—are sold, departing the shed by air for transcontinental points like America and Japan and by truck within Europe.

The tour begins with visits to a few of the half-dozen glass-enclosed auction rooms, where you watch batches of flowers and plants rolled onto a platform—as, indeed, are antique furniture and paintings at art-auction galleries—with bidding (in the Dutch language only) and sales recorded by sophisticated computers. Moving along, you gain a bird's eye view of the vast sheds from an elevated walkway, later descending to the floor. More than a thousand species of flowers, all of them Holland-grown, are auctioned off each day. Roses—80 varieties—are by far the most popular, totaling 900 million per year, with tulips, the flower most associated with Holland by us foreigners, a low-down second (150 million per year); carnations and chrysanthemums follow.

You're so close to Amsterdam that you can return there for lunch, but if you're going on to other destinations in this general area, consider a midday meal at the nearby *Schiphol Hilton International Schiphol Hotel*, but a couple of miles distant, with a choice of casual (*Moderate*-category) and more formal (*First-Class*) restaurants and a congenial bar-lounge where you might enjoy a premeal aperitif.

ALKMAAR (14 miles north of Amsterdam) is to cheese what Aalsmeer is to flowers: the preeminent market. But with a difference. Aalsmeer is a product of the computer age, whereas Alkmaar is an essentially Renaissance-Baroque town where the ritual of its *cheese auction* has not changed for three and half centuries. Timing is everything in this case: Friday mornings *only,* late April through mid-September. If you arrive by train, make your way from the terminal on Stationstraat, a fair distance northwest of the center, to *Waagplein*—named for the Waag, or weigh house, essentially late sixteenth century and before which the proceedings take place. Arrive by 10:00 A.M., starting time for the market, to watch wholesale buyers taste samples from immense piles of round Edam cheeses, covered either a familiar-to-us-foreigners red (for export), or yellow (for sale within Holland). Utilizing special scoops, buyers extract substantial chunks from each cheese tested, then smell (to determine age), crumble (to determine texture), and taste (of course, for flavor), with bargaining over price the next step, and—when a sale is effected—a handshake.

The ceremony you've come to witness begins only when the cheese has been sold. It's then that the so-called cheese-carriers—members of a guild founded in the seventeenth century—set to work. They're divided into four sections, with the provost, or leader, of each designated by a miniature silver cheese barrow suspended from a ribbon in the color—red, green, blue, or yellow—of his group. He directs activities of his men, the lot of them uniformed according to tradition, in spotless white, topped by lacquered straw hats the color of their section. In teams of two, they load 80 four-pound

cheeses on traditionally crafted barrows, painted in their section's colors—one chap grasping front handles and one at the
rear (as would carriers of the Baroque-era's sedan chairs) and
transport them, on the double, to scales at the Waag. There,
the cheeses are weighed, their weights sounded out by the
weighmaster and recorded on a blackboard. Only then do the
carriers, or porters, take the cheese to buyers' warehouses.
After the auction, pop into the Waag and take in the *Cheese
Museum* before proceeding to lunch. A number of restaurants
serve the cheese-based, so-called Cheese-carrier's lunch, including *Dinosaurus* on Waagplein; Phone 15-56-55; *First Class*
and that in *Vroom & Dreesmann* department store (Laat 143:
Moderate) are among them.

Midday meal concluded, take in Alkmaar's *Stedelijk Museum*
(Doelenstraat), in a lovely sixteenth-century building, with
antique toys and a wealth of local lore; *Stadhuis* (Langestraat),
the sixteenth-century town hall, with its interior—council
chamber, mayor's salon, antiques-furnished Nieropkamer—
open to visitors; and spectacular *Grote Kerk* (Kerkplein), like
so many of its counterparts elsewhere in Holland, the biggest
building in town, an essentially fifteenth-century Gothic masterwork, high, wide, and handsome, with a noted Baroque
organ and a disproportionately small and also-Baroque tower.

EDAM —15 miles northeast of Amsterdam—is, despite the
global celebrity of the cheese bearing its name, delightfully
small and tranquil. It is also, I might add, charming, in pleasant contrast to brash Volendam (below), a near-neighbor to
the south; the two, in tandem perhaps with Marken (below),
are conveniently combined in a day. There has not been a
cheese market on the order of Alkmaar's (above) since 1922.
But the eighteenth-century *Kaaswaag*, or weigh house, is a
reminder of earlier and grander Edam eras and opens up
April through September, so that you may see an exhibition
detailing Edam cheese's history.

There are, alas, no trains to Edam; if you've no car, go by
bus. From the station at the southeastern edge of the core,
it's a short walk to the Dam, the handsome main square,
seventeenth century mostly, a major exception being the el-

egantly facaded eighteenth-century *Stadhuis,* or town hall, whose council chamber, beautifully antique wallpapered, warrants inspection, as, indeed, does the *Gemeente Museum,* brimming with municipal historical lore and with an oddball "floating" cellar, which gives the impression of being waterborne.

Save the best for last: *Grote Kerk*—fifteenth-century Gothic and monumentally scaled, with a finely detailed choir and no less than 30 seventeenth-century stained-glass windows. Have a Gallic-accented lunch at *Rotisserie Étoile* (Blekerssingel 1; Phone 12253; *First Class*), overnighting, if your schedule will allow, in charming breakfast-only *De Fortuna Hotel* (Spuistraat 1; Phone 71171)—occupying five seventeenth-century houses, with a cozy lounge and baths in most of the nearly 30 rooms. And be sure to visit the VVV; it's quartered in *Speeltoren,* a carillon-equipped tower of a no longer standing Gothic church.

ENKHUISEN (38 miles northeast of Amsterdam and ideally combined with Hoorn, below): When, half a century back, the Zuiderzee, an outlet of the North Sea, was dammed off— to be no longer open to the larger body of water, becoming a lake called IJsselmeer—the way of life that had evolved around a centuries-old deep-sea fishing industry disappeared. The point of the Dutch Government-operated *Rijksmuseum Zuiderzee,* long in the making and finally opened in 1983, is to portray the old Zuiderzee culture.

The only means of arrival—and of departure—is by the museum's boats. If you've come by train, simply proceed to the rear of the station and you'll see the pier; departures are quarter-hourly. If you've arrived by car, you may board from the pier edging the parking area alongside the road between Enkhuisen and Lelystad.

Once at the museum, you've plenty to keep you busy: 130 houses in a village setting—fronting canals, as well as lining streets—which interpret Zuiderzee life in the half-century span between the 1880s and the 1930s, with dwellings of fishing families through those of farmers. But there's more—a detached pavilion sheltering a dozen sailing ships of yore, as

well as historic interiors and costumes. If you've time, consider a stroll along Enkhuisen's Westerstraat, the principal
street, and visits to its Gothic *Zuiderkerk*, as well as the *Gemeente Museum*, whose exhibits relate the town's history, its
setting the Waag, or Weighhouse, built in the sixteenth century. Have lunch either at a restaurant in the museum complex (*Moderate*) or in town at *Die Drie Haringhe* (Dijk 28; Phone
18610; *First Class*) in an atmospheric and aged warehouse.

GOUDA —34 miles south of Amsterdam and pronounced
Howda—is, like Edam (above) the site of a weekly *cheese market*. Gouda's is on Thursday morning. You want to be there
from between 9:00 and 10:00 A.M. If you've arrived by train,
it's a pleasant walk south from the railway station on Stationsplein, along Vredebest and Kleiweg (the principal pedestrian
street) to the enormous square called *Markt*, which is, at one
and the same time, site of the utterly beautiful, veritable pin-
nacle of a Gothic *Stadhuis*, or town hall, a mid-fifteenth-cen-
tury treasure with a mechanical clock whose characters enact
a little pageant every half-hour; site of the *Waag*, or cheese
weigh house, like the Stadhuis a treasure, albeit of the seventeenth century; and site of the weekly cheese market. The
cheese is delivered in horse-drawn carriages that have long
been traditional, and after the cheeses (some of which weigh
close to 20 pounds) have been sampled by buyers, the age-
old ritual of purchase takes place and is concluded with a
uniquely Gouda-style clap—or better yet—slap of the hands.
     A day or even overnight in this town, one of the more
unspoiled of the smaller Dutch cities, is not too long. Pause,
after the market, with lunch in the restaurant of *De Zalm Hotel*
(Markt 54; Phone 12344; *First Class)* or in *De Zes Starren* (Achter de Kerk 14; Phone 16095; *First Class*). The latter is a part
of *Stedelijk Museum Het Catherina Gasthuis*, one of the finest
small-city museums in the Netherlands, built as a hospice for
travelers in the fourteenth century and largely rebuilt as a
hospital in the seventeenth century, which it remained until
1910. The quartet of period rooms—recreating seventeenth-,
eighteenth-, and nineteenth-century interiors—is superb.
There are memorable paintings by such artists as Nicolaes

Maes, Ferdinand Bol, and Thomas de Keyser, medieval polychrome sculpture of great beauty, extraordinary Renaissance triptychs (most especially, a sixteenth-century *Flight into
Egypt*), and exceptional silver, glass, and church vestments.
Requisite too, is *St. Janskerk* (Markt)—massive and magnifi-
cent Gothic, essentially sixteenth century, with its ace-in-the-
hole a group of 70 stained-glass windows, some from final
years of a Catholic era, others from early years of the Protestant Reformation, with, for example, windows that were
gifts of both Catholic King Philip II of Spain, and Protestant
Prince William the Silent.

HAARLEM , 16 miles west of Amsterdam, is the city that
gave its name to that section of Manhattan in New York City,
where it is spelled with but one *a*. The Dutch Haarlem is of
respectable size—some 150,000. I mention this so that you
will not be surprised at the area you'll cover as you walk
about. Arrive by train, and you're at the far northern edge of
the center, on Stationsplein. To gain the heart of the city
means a 10- to 15-minute walk south along Kruisweg, which
becomes Kruistraat and then changes its name again —gain-
ing status as the principal pedestrian shopping street—to *Bar-
teljoristraat*, before it leads you to *Grotemarkt,* the imposing
main square. You're ready, perhaps, for coffee at *Kron*, a café
on the square. Cross over then to *Grote Kerk* (a.k.a. St. Ba-
vokerk), the only sanctified church in Holland I know of that
charges an admission fee. Withal, you're glad you went; this
is a Gothic masterwork out of the fourteenth and fifteenth
centuries (originally of course Catholic, now Protestant and
reopened in 1985 after closing for a five-year restoration), with
a nave so long that it is illuminated by no less than nine
enormous brass chandeliers, beautifully vaulted wooden ceiling, eighteenth-century organ on which Mozart played,
splendidly embellished pulpit, and—in the floor of the nave—
the tomb of the painter Frans Hals (1580–1666) who, though
born in Antwerp, spent most of his life in Haarlem, much of
it as a poor man.

   The essentially seventeenth-century *Stadhuis,* or town hall,
another Grotemarkt landmark, is among Holland's hand-

somest; pop in to see the beamed ceiling Gravenzaal, the mayor's parlor, and the library. Amble through the eighteenth-century structure housing *Teylers Museum* (Spaarne), hoping the day is sunny, for, by terms of the founder, no artificial illumination is permitted. Have a look at paneling of the Teylers' accurately named Oval Room, ignoring the fossils in favor of the drawings—by the likes of Michelangelo, Rembrandt, and Claude Lorrain.

Take a lunch break, ideally at *Restaurant Peter Cuyper* (Kleine Houtstraat 70; Phone 32-08-35; *First Class)*; it's in a smartly updated Renaissance house, and its good-value prix-fixe menu nicely blends classic and *nouvelle* aspects of French cuisine. You're not far, now, from Haarlem's *Frans Hals Museum* (at the extreme southern tip of the center, on the street called Groot Heiligland). It occupies a good-looking building that opened as a home for aged men in the seventeenth century, later became an orphanage, and was rebuilt and expanded in advance of its opening, in 1913, as a museum. You'll enjoy the Hals so long as you don't expect a collection of Hals's portraits. What you see of Haarlem's favorite son are mostly large civic groups, excellent, to be sure, but surpassed by the kind of incisive studies of individuals that have made Hals a household word and that are to be seen in larger museums elsewhere in Holland—and abroad. There is much else, though—fine work by Steen, Brouwer, van Scorel, van Goyen, van Ostade, van Ruysdael, and under-appreciated Frans Post (who worked in Brazil when it was briefly Dutch). There are authentically decorated seventeenth-century rooms—a leather-walled one with a painted ceiling and Queen Anne-style furniture stands out. Karel Appel is perhaps the best known of the contemporary painters represented. The garden of the courtyard is tranquil. And there's a simple café. If you must overnight in Haarlem, the best hotel is the *Moderate*-category *Lion d'Or* (Kruisweg 34; Phone 32-17-50), so-so, with just under 40 bath-equipped rooms, restaurant, and bar.

HOORN —30 miles north of Amsterdam and nicely visited in tandem with Enkhuisen (above)—was a Zuiderzee port of consequence well into the Golden Age of the seventeenth century, and it remains, possibly in part because of its out-of-the-way situation—handsome, monument filled, history laden (a Hoorn explorer, Willem Schouten, named the southern tip of South America Cape Horn—for his native village—after he was the first to sail around it), and a pleasure to stroll. Arrive by train, and you're in the northwest edge of town, on Spoorsingel. Gain the center by means of an agreeable walk (Hoorn facades are noteworthy), south on *Kleine Noord*, a principal shopping street that changes names to *Grote Noord* and concludes at the square called *Rode Steen*—just where you want to be to inspect the *Westfries Museum*, with the setting, a gracious Baroque building, as exceptional as the exhibits. Thrust is West Friesland historical lore—medieval weapons and household implements; official portraits and dazzling uniforms; weathered maps and proclamations; and lovely small objects like model ships and toys. The various galleries are museum pieces in and of themselves—beamed and paneled and superbly furnished. And you'll note paintings by such masters as Jan van Goyen and Ferdinand Bol. Pause for a hearty lunch at *Oude Rosmullen* (Duinsteeg 1, just off Grote Nord; Phone 14752; *First Class*), later taking in the *Stadhuis*, or town hall (Nieuwstraat), dating to the seventeenth century and with impressive interiors. Note facades of such monumental buildings as the *Waag*, or weigh house (Rode Steen), *De Boterhao* (Kerkstraat), and *Ooster Kerk* (Gravenstraat), as you work your way southeast to the landmark Baroque tower, *Hoofdtoren*, edging the horn-shaped port that gave the town its name.

KEUKENHOF —in Lisse, 25 miles southwest of Amsterdam—immodestly but accurately dubs itself the greatest flower show on earth. Occupying a 70-acre site—cut through by canals flowing into a westerly lake, with 10 miles of walking paths, 15,000 square-foot indoor garden, pair of special-exhibition halls, and trio of cafeterias—it lures some 500,000 visitors annually. This is not a bad figure when you consider the season: but seven or eight spring weeks, usually late March through late May, with such traditionally generous open hours—8:00 A.M. to 6:30 P.M.—that I make mention of them.

As Dutch history goes, Keukenhof is young. Situated on grounds of a long-razed castle, inhabited during the fifteenth century by a countess whose four husbands (one at a time) included a Dauphin of France and a Duke of Gloucester, it was opened a few years after the end of World War II by a group of bulb-growers intent on exhibiting the splendor of Dutch flowers. Did they ever succeed. Keukenhof had become prestigious enough by 1962 for Queen Juliana and Prince Bernhard to have celebrated their twenty-eighth wedding anniversary on the grounds, with imported royals and heads of state topping the guest list.

Rare is the springtime visitor in Holland who does not visit Keukenhof. Hope for a sunny day, but remember that the covered pavilions are compensation in case of rain. Some gardens make a specialty of tulips in extraordinary variety. Others present almost the whole family of daffodils and narcissi. An approximate time table:

Tulips (often mid-April to middle or end of May)
Daffodils and narcissi (beginning to end of April)
Hyacinths (second half of April)

You may, of course, drive (there are parking lots at the gate), and Keukenhof is nicely combined with Aalsmeer (above). Many railway stations sell special tickets that include rail fare to Haarlem (above) or Leiden (Chapter 14) and bus fare (via the NZH line) from either of those cities to the bus stop at Keukenhof's main entrance.

MARKEN AND MONNICKENDAM, 11 miles northeast of Amsterdam, are (along with neighboring Volendam) so conveniently close to the capital that they have come to be known among foreign visitors as prototypical Dutch villages. They were just that, in pre-tour group days. But contemporarily, despite the persistence of residents in wearing traditional costumes and environments hardly without historic structures, they are, alas, too tourist trod. In a country like Holland— with so many pleasanter, smaller towns and villages—I can't imagine anyone on a limited schedule wanting to take time for them. Still, *Monnickendam* has an undisputably fine Gothic-origin *Grote Kerk* that keeps decent summer open hours (the choir is lovely and the scale impressive); a Baroque *Speeltoren*, or clock tower, sheltering a small museum of local archeological finds; and an eighteenth-century *Stadhuis*, or town hall, whose interior is worth a peek.

Marken—an island in what had been the Zuiderzee, which has been connected with the mainland by a causeway for a quarter-century—is filled with cutesy-pie frame houses painted primary colors and offers two worthwhile interiors: that of the Baroque-origin *Reformed Church*, with brass chandeliers illuminating a clutch of model ships and that of the *Marken Museum*, based on a cluster of four contiguous—and very typical—houses, wherein one of the kindly Dutch-speaking attendants explains the house's Marken-origin furnishings. Monnickendam and Marken are traditionally combined with Volendam (below). Should you wish to have lunch before moving along, consider *Posthoorn* (Noordeinde 41; Phone 1471), in Monnickendam. Its interior is authentically aged, its fish is reliable, and it's *First Class*.

VOLENDAM —14 miles northeast of Amsterdam and accessible also by boat from Marken (above)—is bigger than Marken, with proportionately larger crowds, and, for this visitor at least, is proportionately less appealing. You'll stroll the tacky shop- and café-lined waterfront, visit the *fish market* (at least if you're in town before 11:00 A.M., when it closes), pop into the *Volendam Museum* (Klosterbuurt 5) for an idea of what the town was like before the hordes arrived, and—if it's open—visit the mid-seventeenth-century *Reformed Church*, like the museum, a reminder of the Volendam of yore. The restaurant of the *Spaander Hotel* (Haven 15; Phone 63595; *Moderate*) will serve you a fairly decent fish lunch; the dining room (also *Moderate*) of the *Van Diepen Hotel* (Haven 35; Phone 63705) is an alternative.

4

Arnhem
Great Art at the Kröller-Müller

BACKGROUND BRIEFING
Travelers of a certain age—or, for that matter, of any age, if they have studied World War II—associate the eastern city of Arnhem with the tragic battle taking its name, in the course of which a daring 1944 landing by a force of British and Polish parachutists set off a battle in which 7,000 Allied troops were killed and Arnhem was leveled.

Come upon Arnhem today, though, and you find that its beloved Gothic Grote Kerk has been meticulously rebuilt (the task took two full decades) in the center of an otherwise contemporary core.

Moreover, this Rhine River city, dubbed *Arnacum* by the Romans and the Middle Ages seat of Dukes of Gelderland, is the lively capital of Gelderland Province and the site of three extraordinary museums: an exurban repository of modern art that is one of the greatest such in Europe, a remarkable complex to whose grounds 75 historic structures have been transported from all over the Netherlands, and a museum whose subject is the Battle of Arnhem, with its site the onetime hotel that served as headquarters of the British troops' commanding general.

ON SCENE

Lay of the Land: The Rhine—more properly the Lower (or *Neder*) Rhine—serves as southern border of the city. *Markt* and *Kerkplein*, two contiguous squares constituting the heart of town, are just north of the river at the point where the twin conical towers of *Sabelspoort*, the only remaining medieval gate (1440), pierce the sky. Site of historic *Grote Kerk* (below), this is also the neighborhood of the fifteenth-century city hall, *Oude Raadhuis* (a.k.a. *Duivelshuis)*, where you want to take in the plethora of sculpted heads embellishing its facade, all representations of Renaissance-era locals, except for the ogreish figures on the corner of the building, which give the structure its nickname, Devil's House. *John FrostBrug*, at the southeastern corner of the core, is a bridge bearing the name of the British colonel whose troops held it for four days in the course of the September 1944 battle, when it was taken by the Germans. The second city bridge, *Roermonds PleinBrug*, is up-river to the west and strikingly futuristic. *Jeansplaats*, inland from it, is the center of the shopping district, with *Jeanstraat* the principal pedestrian street, along with nearby *Roggestraat* (site of Vroom & Dreesmann department store) and *Bakkerstraat* (with antiques shops). *Korenmarkt*—just below the railway station, on Stationsplein, in the northwest corner of the city—is where Arnhem relaxes, at any of a host of cafés, all with tables outdoors in fine weather. And, saving most significant for last, both *Kröller-Müller* and *Openlucht* museums are northwest of town.

Grote Kerk (a.k.a. Eusebiuskerk, on Kerkplein) celebrates the Golden Age of Arnhem, the medieval period of the Dukes of Gelderland, with the mausoleum of Duke Charles of Egmont—a mid-sixteenth century masterwork—the dominant feature of its soaring Gothic interior. The 270-foot tower houses a 54-bell carillon (there are concerts every Friday at 10:00 A.M.) and is visible for miles around. (The also-Gothic, still-Catholic *St. Walburgiskerk* and the eighteenth-century *Waag*, or weigh house, are near neighbors.)

Gemeentemuseum (west of the center, at Utrechtseweg 87), distinguished by the rotunda of its late-nineteenth-century, garden-enclosed quarters, combines Gelderland art with Gelderland history. There are evocative paintings of the city and provinces over the centuries. Decorative arts sections (silver and glass, furniture and clocks, Delft and Oriental porcelains) are lovely. There are exhibits of Roman and medieval Gelderland, and if you are curious about the state of contemporary painting in Holland, the Gemeentemuseum will bring you up to date; it is strong—and striking—in this area.

Airborne Museum (west of the center, at Utrechtseweg 232, in suburban Oosterbeek) recounts—by means of well-executed dioramas, scale models, photographs, and other audiovisual material—the course of the tragic World War II Battle of Arnhem, envisioned by Allied planners as a victory that would pave the way to capturing the German Ruhr, due east, and ultimate victory. The Nijmegen and Eindhoven segments of Operation Market Garden, the operation's code name, were successful, but the key Arnhem portion of the campaign—which involved taking its Rhine River bridge—was not. The Allies lost the Battle of Arnhem, necessitating evacuation of the city. For western Holland, defeat meant another long winter of suffering and near starvation before the advent of peace.

Nederlands Openluchtmuseum (Hoeferlaan, north of town): Danes, Swedes, Swiss, Canadians, and Americans, all are experts at creating and operating open-air museums. But the Dutch are proud of the Netherlands Open Air Museum with good reason. They haven't stopped working at expanding and refining its operation since its doors opened in 1918, with half a dozen houses. Today the museum embraces 75 buildings from throughout the kingdom. The idea is to provide visitors with a graphic picture of the way Dutch people lived in the not-too-distant past. To tour the museum is not simply to pass by facades. You go inside, and "inside" is authentic, with respect as much to furnishings and equipment as to inhabitants and lifestyles. Once you pay your admission, you're on your own. Buy a booklet that offers a trio of routings—short, middling, and longish in duration. Or poke your head into whatever seems appealing. Simpler places, a late-nineteenth century eelmonger's hut from Amsterdam or a South Limburg outhouse, for instance, are more sociologically significant than they are amusing. But the multiroom Krawinkel farmstead, the A-frame dwelling from Beltrum, the farmhouse from Veluwe (pure Little Red Riding Hood!), the Hanekamp Inn from Zwolle, and the castlelike squire's seat from Koog are delightful. So are the windmills and the laundry, the bakery and the paper mill, the boatyard and the brewery. And there are two restaurants (below).

Rijksmuseum Kröller-Müller (four miles north of Arnhem, in the midst of *Nationaal Park Hoge Veluwe*, with the entrance nearest to Arnhem at Schaarsbergen and other gates at Otterlo and Hoenderloo): A world-class art collection housed in a contemporary pavilion of exceptional grace set in a 13,500-acre national park—alive with buzzards and badgers, red deer and wild boar—proves nothing less than an all-Netherlands phenomenon. How did it come about? A young German woman, Helen Müller—at once attractive and determined, in early photos—married a Rotterdammer named Anthony G. Kröller before the turn of the century. When his father-in-law, a shipping tycoon, died, young Kröller moved the business from Germany to Holland and became so rich that he bought the acreage that is now Hoge Veluwe, so that he could have a place of his very own in which to hunt.

While Mr. Kröller expanded his business and hunted, Helene Kröller-Müller, aided and abetted by the gifted art critic H. P. Bremmer, began buying paintings. She started with a trio of Van Goghs (there are now 278 of that master's works in the museum), and continued to collect, with the dominant periods pre-Impressionists like Courbet and Corot, through Impressionists and post-Impressionists, beyond to the Art Nouveau period, later masters like Picasso and Léger, and Dutch abstractionists including Mondriaan and van Der Leck.

The collection's greatest expansion occurred between the two world wars. In 1935, it was substantial enough for the

Dutch Government to have accepted it as a gift for the nation, with the proviso that it build a museum—in the Kröller-Müller's vast and verdant Hoge Veluwe tract—to house and display the art. The original building, designed by Belgian architect Henri van der Velde, opened in 1938 and was supplemented by a similarly light and airy addition designed by W. G. Quist, completed in 1977, concurrent with the accession of a group of sculptures exhibited in what is now Europe's largest sculpture garden.

Chances are you will have wandered through the Van Gogh Museum in Amsterdam (Chapter 2) in advance of your arrival at Kröller-Müller. No matter. You will be dazzled with this immense selection of Van Goghs. Mrs. Kröller-Müller began with *Still Life with Lemons, The Sower,* and *Dying Sunflowers.* To these, there have been so many, many additions— a hardly flattering 1887 self-portrait; the flower-filled interior of a Paris restaurant that may have been where Vincent dined regularly with his brother Theo, who figures heavily in his much-published correspondence; a view of Saintes-Maries, a still-heavily visited village in the Camargue outside Arles. (See *France At Its Best.*) But so much besides Van Gogh attracts: A Fantin-Latour still life with fruit; a rare portrait by Courbet; beach scenes by the Dutch Impressionist Jongkind, who worked in the Norman port of Honfleur as part of the so-called St. Siméon School; an unusual Renoir clown; an unsmiling Seurat family at breakfast; a considerable clutch of works by Gris, as well as by Léger; and the likes of Maillol, Rodin, Lipschitz, Arp, Hepworth, Marini, Nevelson, Moore, Oldenburg, and Dubuffet in the sculpture galleries and garden. The surprise of older works are special treats: Avercamp ice-skaters, a Cranach stag hunt, a Gerard David *Pietà,* and Baldung-Grien's *Venus and Cupid.*

You want to make a day of the Kröller-Müller (its restaurant-cum-terrace edges the sculpture garden, and there are two others of note, below evaluated), taking time out to scoot through the national park on one of its gratis white bicycles, perhaps taking in the original Kröller-Müller hunting lodge and game-viewing from Wildkansel, a principal observation point, near the park's Visitor Center.

SETTLING IN

Haarhuis Hotel (Sationsplein; Phone 42-74-41) rates pride of place because it is central (opposite the station and an easy walk to the core), with an agreeable contemporary ambience, 85 functional rooms with bath, rambling lobby-lounge, and reliable restaurant-café that draws locals, as well as visitors. Friendly. *Moderate.*

Rijn Hotel (Onderlangs 10; Phone 43-46-42) has the disadvantage of being away from the center (you want a car), but with a Rhine River situation that affords nice views from those of the 48 rooms (33 in a relatively recent addition) that are riverfront, a welcoming bar, and a restaurant worthy of review in a later paragraph. *First Class.*

Bilderberg Hotel (Itrechtseweg 261, in suburban Osterbeek; Phone 34-08-43)—rambling and set in a big garden—is an elderly house that has been contemporarily refurbished, comfortably enough, with 146 rooms (those I have inspected are satisfactory), pair of restaurants, cocktail lounge, and big indoor pool with a glass wall that opens to the garden in summer. Okay, if you have a car. *First Class.*

Postiljon Hotel (Europaweg 25; Phone 45-37-41) is a link of a Dutch chain offering good contemporary facilities at a good price and with good service. There are 28 doubles and a reliable restaurant-café with an umbrella-covered summer terrace. Away from the center; you need a car. *Moderate.*

DAILY BREAD

Begijnemolen (Zijpendaalseweg 28; Phone 43-39-63; a five-minute drive from the center) is set in a seventeenth-century water mill centered in a pretty park. Tables are surrounded by ladderback chairs in a room hung with red-velvet draperies and dotted with antique accents. The menu is French accented, with hearty soups among starters, such tasty entrées as roast chicken and trout meunière, nicely prepared vegetables, and typically Dutch desserts based on ice cream and sherbert. Service is delightful. *First Class.*

Klein Hartenstein (Utrechtseweg 226; Phone 34-21-21) occupies a former coach house, white walled and white-wicker furnished, adjacent to the Airborne Museum and convenient for visitors to that museum or the Gemeentemuseum (above). Why management—the owner is fluent in English and with United States experience—prints the bill of fare exclusively in the Dutch language is difficult to understand, but the food (seafood salads, vegetable soup, a hot oyster appetizer, among starters; veal chops and *entrecôte* steak, among entrées; and chocolate *mousse*, among sweets) is satisfactory. *First Class.*

La Lampara (Stationsplein 40; Phone 42-65-80), with outdoor tables on the station square that make it pleasant for a summer lunch, makes a specialty of pizza and deliciously sauced pasta—in variety. Italian wines. *Moderate.*

Surabaya (Korenmarkt 19; Phone 51-37-77), located on the square whose outdoor restaurant and café tables draw crowds in balmy weather, is as good a place as any for a multi-course *rijsttafel* feast; let your waiter explain the piquant Indonesian cuisine, as he brings it on, course after course after course. Order beer to accompany. *First Class.*

Le Saumon (Rijn Hotel, Onderlangs 10; Phone 43-46-42): Request a table by the picture windows, the better for panoramic view of the Rhine, and opt for the prix-fixe menu. A meal might open with shrimp and mussel soup, continue with fresh salmon and *buerre-blanc* sauce, and conclude with *profiteroles* (tiny cream puffs, ice-cream filled), buried by hot chocolate or caramel sauce. Smart service. *First Class.*

Café Wampie (Korenmarkt): Given a bit of sunshine, you want to head for Korenmarkt and something to eat or drink, the while crowd watching from this, one of its plethora of cafés. *Moderate.*

De Oude Bijenkorf (Nederlands Openluchtmuseum; Phone 42-06-57)—thatch roofed and authentically aged, not unlike other structures of the Netherlands Open Air Museum (above) serves nourishing fare (prix-fixe menus are good bets) both in its big, dark-beamed dining room and on a cheerful terrace, from where you may take in the crowds. *First Class.* (Note, also, the museum's *Hanecamp*, also terraced, with pancakes and *pofertjes* the specialties and the category *Moderate.*)

Rijzenburg (National Park Hoge Veluwe, near the Schaarsbergen gate; Phone 43-67-33) is a felicitously proportioned farmhouse of advanced age that has been deftly converted to restaurant use. The look is smart; the fare, Franco-Dutch; and the prix-fixe menu—a hearty soup or *pâté*, among starters; entrées of fish and veal; elaborate desserts—a good bet. Consider Rijzenburg as an alternative to the Kröller-Müller Museum café or De Koperen Kop (below) in the course of a park/museum visit. *First Class.*

De Koperen Kop (National Park Hoge Veluwe, near the Visitor Center; Phone 1289) is rustic looking in keeping with its park setting, and makes a specialty of pancakes but serves more substantial fare, as well. *Moderate.*

Rijksmuseum Kröller-Müller Restaurant (National Park Hoge Veluwe) is white walled, with white chairs surrounding white tables and a terrace giving onto the museum's splendid sculpture garden. Self-service, salads through sweets. *Moderate.*

SOUND OF MUSIC
Music Sacrum (Jansbinnensingel), dating to the late nineteenth century, is topped with a pair of cupolas and is the venue of concerts by Het Gelders Orkest, the provincial symphony, and other groups, both classical and pop.

Stadsschouwburg (Jansbinnensingel) is Music Sacrum's near neighbor and home to the Oost Nederland Opera; dance and other presentations, too. The tourist office (below) has schedules for both theaters.

INCIDENTAL INTELLIGENCE ═══════════════

Apeldoorn (Chapter 11) and Nijmegen (Chapter 17) are Arnhem's near neighbors. *Further information:* VVV Arnhem, Stationsplein 45.

5

Breda

Town of the Treaties

BACKGROUND BRIEFING

One way or another, assuming you're either a history or an art buff, the name Breda rings a bell. No less a master than Velásquez portrayed the surrender of a bowing, contrite-appearing Dutch governor to a Spanish general—resplendent in black, gold, and flowing scarlet sash—after the decisive Battle of Breda in 1625; the painting hangs in Madrid's Prado Museum (see *Spain At Its Best*). But even if you haven't observed it, chances are good that, in one classroom or another, you will have encountered the Compromise of Breda (wherein, in 1566, Dutch nobles recorded collective antipathy toward Spanish overlords and the Inquisition), the Declaration of Breda (wherein, in 1660, the exiled English king-in-residence, Charles II, stated conditions necessary for his effecting the post-Cromwell Restoration); and the 1667 Treaty of Breda.

It was the last mentioned that, among much else, decreed the transfer of the colony of New Netherland to the English, who promptly renamed it after the then-Duke of York, and replaced the Dutch language with their own. (Were it not for that long-ago treaty, would those of us who now live in New York be Dutch speaking?)

ON SCENE

Lay of the Land: Breda is southerly; the Belgian port of Antwerp is less than 30 miles away. From the railway station, fronting *Stationplein* at the northern edge of town, it's an easy walk south along *Willemstraat* or *Emmastraat* and through pretty *Valkenburg Park* to a pair of adjacent historic landmarks—*Spanjaardsgat*, the so-called Spaniards' Gate, a felicitous pair of hectagonal towers formidably enclosing a fortification and fronted by the water, which figured in a late-sixteenth-century battle of consequence; and *Kasteel van Breda* (below), for long a home to ruling nobles and now put to sensible use as Holland's military academy. From the castle, dominating *Kasteelplein*, stroll south onto Breda's ebullient main square, *Grote Markt* which, with contiguous *Havermarkt*, appears as a veritable sea of outdoor restaurant tables, constituting in toto one of Europe's biggest alfresco cafés. It is dominated by towering *Grote Kerk* (below) and the site of the eighteenth-century *Gemeentehuis*, or town hall, within which is a reproduction of the Velásquez painting (to which I refer above) depicting the Dutch surrender following the 1625 Battle of Breda. Neighboring *Torenstraat*, principal shopping street, is the site of department stores like *Vroom & Dreesmann* and *Hema*. Antiques stores blanket this quarter (its *Sint Annastraat's* Renaissance facades are notable), and *Veemarktstraat*, east of Grote Kerk, is shop lined too.

Grote Kerk (Grote Markt): Forget about the Baroque tip of Grote Kerk's tower and its also-Baroque organ. It is otherwise consistently Gothic, worthy of a walk around its exterior, past a quite splendid apse, all the way back to the main entrance, and a view along the nave to a fine choir with exceptional carved-wood folding seats, or misericords; a range of sixteenth-century frescoes—including a lovely *Annunciation*—surfacing vaults; a plethora of exquisitely wrought tombs of Breda counts, whose descendants were the princes of Orange who came to constitute Holland's Orange-Nassau dynasty; and a triptych by sixteenth-century painter Jan van Scorel, its theme at once military and spiritual.

Kasteel van Breda (Kasteelplein, and, since 1828, dubbed *Koninklijke Militaire Academie*—a counterpart of America's West Point or Britain's Sandhurst) is visitable only by means of the town tourist office's organized expeditions. Alas—despite historic eminence as seat of the Breda *Heren*, or Counts of Nassau, ancestors of the reigning Royal House of Orange-Nassau—the essentially sixteenth- and seventeenth-century castle today compensates with utility (you see the Royal Military Academy's cadets' plain quarters and mess hall) for what it lacks in atmosphere.

Begijnhof (Catharinastraat) is a charming throwback to the early sixteenth century when it was built to accommodate a community of lay nuns in semidetached brick houses occupying a pair of wings that enclose an herb-planted garden, with a classic-style, still-Catholic chapel at the rear. Ties with the Royal Family remain; its members continue to be received by the Begijnhof's Mother Superior on visits to Breda.

Stedelijk Museum (Grote Markt 19) has its quarters in a seventeeth-century building with a graceful eighteenth-century facade, whose narrow dimensions belie its size. Exhibits relate as much to secular Breda—a Baroque canopied bed, Renaissance armor, Rococo silver, paintings of city scenes and city fathers—as to the pre-Reformation period when the town was the seat of a Catholic bishop. A triptych, or altar piece, painted in 1500—its subject the *Pietà*, with Christ in his mother's arms, following the Crucifixion—is quite possibly the loveliest specimen of religious art, but there is a sixteenth-century oil of the Holy Family, an eighteenth-century sculpture of St. Theresa of Ávila, a number of paintings originally hung in the Grote Kerk, as well as silver monstrances and elaborately embroidered vestments.

Rijksmuseum voor Volkenkunde Justinus van Nassau (Kasteelplein 55) is a long way of saying "ethnographic museum," with a variety of exhibits from the onetime Dutch East Indies—Indonesian shadow puppets, batik fabrics, and decidedly unferocious temple lions and lion masks, as well as artifacts from points as disparate as Japan (a traditional house with *shoji* screen and tatami floor mats) and the western United States (a diorama of a Sioux village).

SETTLING IN

Motel Breda (Roskam 20, a couple of miles southwest of the center; Phone 22-21-27) is a nicely operated, nicely equipped house, with 120 good-sized rooms (including a Business Floor with superior accommodations), pair of restaurants (one casual, one more formal), indoor pool with glass walls giving onto the garden, sauna, and welcoming cocktail lounge. Friendly. *First Class.*

Novotel Breda (Dr. Batenburglaan 74; Phone 65-92-20) is, like its neighbor, Motel Breda (above), a couple of miles southwest of the center. It's a link in the French-origin Novotel chain, with 81 rooms (plain looking, as is typical of the chain, but with all of the basics), restaurant worthy of evaluation on a later page, bar-lounge, and outdoor pool. Congenial. *Moderate.*

Mastbosch Hotel (Burgemeester Kerstanlaan 20; Phone 65-00-50), edging an out-of-town forest, is, apparently, so successful as a venue for conferences that it has not undertaken the wide-scale refurbishing that seemed necessary in the course of my inspection. There are 40 rooms with white-painted furnishings; pair of restaurants, with meals served as well on a terrace in warm weather; bar; game room; and unprepossessing lobby. Disappointing. *Moderate.*

De Klok Hotel's (Grote Markt 24; Phone 13-40-82) prime lure is a heart-of-town situation on the principal square, where it occupies a pair of contiguous, albeit unpretentious, buildings. You want to aim for one of the 23 bath- or shower-equipped rooms facing Grote Markt. Bar-café. *Moderate.*

DAILY BREAD

Auberge de Arent (Schoolstraat 2; Phone 14-46-01): Setting first: The Auberge makes its home in a landmark Renaissance house, elegantly gabled, with views from the tall windows of Grote Kerk, just opposite. There are private-party rooms upstairs, and the restaurant proper occupies a high-ceilinged, ground-level space, with a painted ceiling and beautiful Baroque fireplace. Tables, set with white linen accented by floral bouquets, are widely spaced on a checkerboard marble floor. Owner-manager Roger van Bommel smiles a welcome, explains specials of the day, and takes orders from the à la carte or either of several prix-fixe menus, the best value being that served at midday. Cream of tomato is a standout, but other openers—crayfish salad and *foie gras de canard* (duck liver sautéed Alsatian style)—are good, too. Nowhere in Holland have I had more delicious grilled salmon, but veal steaks are super, as well. Cheeses, often neglected in Dutch restaurants, appear in profusion on a platter, and desserts include pastries that, like cheeses, are rarely encountered in the Netherlands. The wine list is exceptional, and there's a wide choice of mostly French digestifs. In my experience, one of Holland's best restaurants. *Luxury.*

Mirabelle (Dr. Batenburglaan 76; Phone 65-66-50)—in a low-slung, white-stucco pavilion a couple of miles outside of town, next door to Novotel Breda (above)—greets you with wide smiles. You're ushered into a capacious lounge, where you sink into gray-leather easy chairs, to linger over a drink until your table—in either of the pair of dining rooms—is called. The à la carte is a pleasure; Ardennes ham with melon, shrimp salad, and lobster bisque are among first courses. *Langue de veau*—calf's tongue, tarragon flavored—is among entrées, along with a reputed *sole meunière*. *Crêpes Suzette*, prepared at table, is a festive dessert. Wine list is lengthy; service, super. *Luxury.*

Da Atilio (Grote Markt 35; Phone 14-39-00) is Italian staffed and serves Italian favorites. *Antipasto* or *minestrone* are opening choices to start a meal, as is pasta; there's a good selection. Veal entrées so typical of Italy are reliable. Dinner only. Congenial. *First Class.*

In the Mood (Grote Markt 46; Phone 13-79-75)—its pink-linen-set tables inviting, its steaks and mixed grill invariably tasty—is a Grote Markt leader. *First Class.*

Walliser Stube (Grote Markt 44; Phone 13-50-27) is the genuine Swiss article. By that I mean fondue—the definitive hot cheese dip—is indicated for you and your party. And if you opt for a meat entrée, insist that it be accompanied by the potato masterwork called *rosti*. *First Class.*

Le Grill (Novotel Breda, Dr. Batenburglaan 74; Phone 65-92-20): Given the French roots of the Novotel chain, this Gallic-accented restaurant comes as no surprise. You may open with *escargots Bourguignons* or *soupe à l'oignon*. *Filet de volaille*—breast of chicken—is always available, and you've a choice of such beef dishes as *entrecôte* with garlic butter, *filet de boeuf* with Bordelaise sauce, and tournedos with *sauce Béarnaise*. *First Class.*

Café Franciskaner (Grote Markt 23) is the traditional Grote Markt source of coffee and cake, mid-morning or mid-afternoon. *Moderate.*

Café De Toren (Havermarkt) is right for casual lunch or coffee. *Moderate.*

SOUND OF MUSIC
Concordia Stadsschouwburg (Van Coothplein 37, somewhat south of the core) is Breda's municipal theater; the tourist office (below) has schedules of what's playing—with performances of Het Brabant Orkest (the regional symphony) and pop and rock groups. Ballet and opera, too.

Breda Jazz Festival is an annual August event, with a range of imported soloists and ensembles, and Grote Kerk the principal venue.

INCIDENTAL INTELLIGENCE

Den Bosch (Chapter 8) is but 30 miles from Breda; the two cities are linked by frequent trains. *Further information:* VVV Breda, Willemstraat 17 (opposite the railway station).

6

Delft

As Painted by Vermeer

BACKGROUND BRIEFING

It is not unusual for great artists to go unrepresented in the art museums of their birthplace, especially if they come from smaller cities. Still, it would be nice—and so appropriate—if *View of Delft*, one of the rare cityscapes painted by Johannes Vermeer, born in 1632 in Delft's Nieuwe Kerk and buried only 43 years later in Delft's Oude Kerk, were to hang in the master's hometown Prisenhof Museum rather than in The Hague's Mauritshuis.

Still, there can be advantages to such a situation. It was a first viewing of the Vermeer in the bigger city and Holland's seat of government that first drew me to Delft. And I am sure there have been many others like me, curious to see if it is recognizable today from the profile of its skyline as delineated more than four centuries ago by the most celebrated of its natives.

It is, indeed. Remarkably so. The irony of Delft is that in the half a millennium between the time when it was founded, in the eleventh century, and the Baroque era when Vermeer painted it—in the seventeenth—it had (especially after becoming officially chartered in 1246) evolved as an increasingly wealthy *entrepôt*. But Rotterdam, only a dozen miles south on a river whose mouth is nearby on the North Sea, began to develop as a port, eventually becoming the world's largest, with a contemporary population exceeding half a million, which dwarfs Delft's 90,000.

Not even eminence as the source, beginning in the mid-seventeenth century, of the globally admired ceramics—named Delftware, in its honor—was sufficient to foster anything like the growth of neighboring Rotterdam. The Delft we visit today—associated not only with Vermeer, but with William the Silent, the father of Dutch unity, who was assassinated in the very building that now houses the art museum—conveys, at least as much as any smaller city, an impression of the fabric of urban Holland as it must have been in its heyday.

Arrive today and Vermeer's images are recalled: the slim steeple of the Nieuw Kerk and turrets of the city's monumental gates (*View of Delft*), step-gabled facades of its middle class's brick houses (*A Street in Delft*), and its beamed, tapestried and brass-chandelier-hung interiors (*A Painter in His Studio*). When the sun reflects itself in the waters of its canals, traversed by a veritable network of little bridges, no small city in Holland more evokes its Golden Age.

ON SCENE
Lay of the Land: Stop in at the lobby shop of the Municipal Archives (below), and you'll see postcards on which are reproduced maps of Delft in earlier centuries, which you can follow today, by and large, to get around the town—changed relatively little in its historic core. Arrive by train, and by the time you've walked from the station (on *Van Leeuwenhoeksingel*, near the western edge of town) to the center, you've become a fan. Simply cross the canal called *Westsingel* to the principal north-south, canal-bordering thoroughfare called *Oude Delft*, walking north to *Oude Lengendijk*, where you turn west to find yourself in the principal square, *Markt*, lined with cafés and dominated by a pair of masterful monuments, the *Nieuwe Kerk*, with its landmark tower, and *Stadhuis*, or town hall (both below). *Hippolytusbuurt* is the site of *Vroom & Dreesmann* and other big stores. *Oostpoort*, only survivor of eight fourteenth-century gates and with a pair of conical towers, flanks the

eastern edge of the center, at the terminus of the canal called *Oost Einde*. Streets of that portion of the center lying between *Vrouwenregt*, *Voldersgracht*, *Lange Geer*—to name a trio—are eminently walkable.

Nieuwe Kerk (Markt) is a Gothic treasure. Its 130-foot-high tower is as pleasing to behold as to listen to (there are regularly scheduled morning carillon concerts), and its nave (almost as long as the tower is high) impresses with dazzling scale, superb twentieth-century stained glass, a masterful nineteenth-century organ, tombs (32, all told, and not open to public view) of virtually all members of the long-reigning House of Orange (principal exceptions are Stadholder William III and his wife, Mary Stuart, who, as King and Queen of England, are buried in London's Westminster Abbey), and— not to be missed—the mausoleum, designed by Hendrik de Keyser, of William the Silent (Prince William of Orange), the sixteenth-century father of Dutch unity, who was assassinated in Delft (below). An effigy of the prince, in white marble, reposes in a black-marble casket, framed by a canopy of the same material and supported by two elegant columns. Built in the decades that saw the fourteenth century become the fifteenth, this originally Catholic church became Dutch Reformed in 1572. A quite marvelous mix of noble architecture, extraordinary art, and significant history, it is an all-Dutch ranker, No. 2 of the kingdom's churches, in my view, after St. Janskathedraal in Den Bosch (Chapter 7).

Stadhuis (Markt) embraces the original fifteenth-century Town Hall tower—all that remains after a fire that impelled a seventeenth-century rebuilding, with the same Hendrik de Keyser who designed William the Silent's mausoleum (above) its creator. Exuberantly Baroque of facade, the Stadhuis warrants interior inspection; you want especially to see the wedding hall, its walls brilliant with seventeenth-century paintings.

Oude Kerk (entered from Heilige Geest Kerkhof), though with mid-thirteenth-century origins, is essentially early-fifteenth-century Gothic, more felicitous architecturally, to this viewer, at least, from without—thanks to its fat tower surmounted by five turrets—than from within, where walls partially separate its three naves. Of the two dozen modern stained-glass windows, the one whose central panels depict the late Queen Wilhelmina's return to Holland after World War II exile in England is the most moving and the most observed. The carved-wood, sixteenth-century pulpit is notable, and there are a number of well-sculpted memorials, but the most sought after, at least by foreigners, is a small tomb with the inscription "Johannes Vermeer 1632–1675."

Stedelijk Museum Het Prinsenhof (St. Agathaplein): What it lacks in paintings by superstar masters, this onetime fifteenth-century convent—red-brick Gothic with a serene garden, in the shadow of the Oude Kerk's high tower—compensates for with its setting, the felicitous consequence of a skilled World War II restoration in the style of the sixteenth century. You will not be disappointed with the artistic contents of the Prinsenhof, but you are in a historic spot: You climb the very stairway on which the architect of Dutch unity—the stadholder-prince of Orange known as William the Silent, who made his home in the building after the nuns departed in 1572—was murdered on July 10, 1584. The assassin was Balthasar Gerards, a French Catholic fanatic. Bullet holes remain on walls of the stairwell. You see what had been the dining room William had exited just before his death, with adjacent exhibits relating to it. A onetime hall for formal receptions brims with official portraits of stadholders and their ladies. A kitchen is resplendent with Delft tile walls, complementing a gallery of Delft china and fine paintings, one of which portrays Prince William as he lay dying.

Volkenkundig Museum Nusantara (St. Agathaplein, a near neighbor of the Prinsenhof, above), and conveniently taken in tandem with it, is one of a number of museums throughout the Netherlands reflecting the long Dutch colonial period in Indonesia, which ended with World War II—by which time settlers had brought home rich caches of Indonesian art and artifacts. The range here is extensive—shadow puppets, ceremonial masks, spears, and the textiles at which Indonesians excel.

Museum Huis Lambert van Meerten (Oude Delft 199) occupies a late-nineteenth-century house of considerable interest, fronting Delft's handsomest canalside street. It's not your everyday museum. The builder, a wealthy industrialist whose house the name takes, erected it expressly to exhibit the art and artifacts—china, tiles, glass, and fragments of aged houses—he had collected over a sustained period, using certain of his collected fragments in the construction. Five years after opening the house, he went bankrupt. His collection was dispersed, but friends banded together as a society, bought the building and presented it to the Dutch Government with the proviso that it be operated as a museum of the decorative arts. And so it is, with its *chef d'oeuvre* a portrait of an unknown woman by a late-seventeenth-century French painter, Nicholas Largillière, and a superb tile collection. Atmospheric.

Paul Tétar van Elven Museum (Koornmarkt 67): You may or may not esteem the nineteenth-century paintings of the artist whose house this name takes, but there is no denying the solid good looks of the structure itself—eighteenth century, canalview, and interestingly decorated, the range ceiling frescoes through wall-hung pottery.

Armamentarium (Korte Geer 1) is Delft's newest museum— a generously proportioned seventeenth-century warehouse that has been imaginatively converted into what translates as the Royal Armor and Weapons Museum. Lesson to be learned from a visit is that a great deal of taste, skill, and imagination has gone into the design of objects used by armies and navies to destroy their enemies— stylishly fashioned helmets, magnificently embellished shooting arms, and suits of armor, with a bonus: veritable armies of toy soldiers.

SETTLING IN
Delft Museumhotel (Oude Delft 189; Phone 14-09-30) is Delft's newest—as a hotel, that is. Actually, the two contiguous houses comprising it date to the seventeenth century. The facade retains its period look, but public rooms—lobby, bar-lounge, café wherein breakfast and snacks are served—are agreeably contemporary, and so are the 30 no-two-alike rooms (many with original ceiling beams and including two junior suites). The staff is hospitable. *Moderate/First Class.*

De Ark Hotel (Koornmarkt 65; Phone 14-05-32) occupies a nicely restored house on one of the more atmospheric canals. There are 16 no-two-alike rooms, all with baths; cozy bar; and inviting, brick-walled restaurant. And there are nine one-bed-room suites in an across-the-street annex. Friendly. *Moderate.*

Leeuwenbrug Hotel (Koornmarkt 16; Phone 12-30-62): Most of the 33 rooms in this canal house—some contemporary, some more traditional in look—have showers rather than tubs in their bathrooms. Bar-lounge and breakfast but no restaurant. *Moderate.*

De Flaming Hotel (Vlamingstraat 52; Phone 13-21-27), in a converted canal house and centrally situated, has baths in its ten functional rooms. Breakfast only. *Moderate.*

Juliana Hotel (Maarten Trompstraat 33; Phone 56-76-12) occupies a relatively contemporary converted house away from the center (you want a car). Most, but not all, of the more than 20 rooms have shower-equipped bathrooms. Breakfast only. *Moderate.*

DAILY BREAD
Le Chevalier (Oude Delft 125; Phone 12-46-21) is a charmer—and a delicious one, at that. Proprietors Margriet and Hans Bakx (he is the skilled chef; she, the hostess) have turned a fine old Oude Delft house into a sleek, contemporary restaurant. Open with a drink in the bar-lounge to the rear,

returning forward for a deftly served meal—the three-course menu is a good bet—*nouvelle* influenced but sensibly so. Start with thin slices of sautéed goose liver and lobster as the basis of a delicious salad or a well-seasoned crayfish bisque, continuing with grilled salmon in a basil-tomato sauce, perfectly roasted suckling pig, or filet of beef, with a hint of garlic in the accompanying sauce. Desserts rate a card of their own, wines have been well selected, and service is skilled. In my experience, one of Holland's best restaurants. *Luxury.*

De Prinsenkelder (Schoolstraat 11; Phone 12-28-93) just has to be the most atmospheric eatery in town. Setting is a subterranean space—white walled and gracefully vaulted—beneath what had been the refectory of the convent of Franciscan nuns that became the Prinsenhof, residence of the murdered William the Silent and now a museum (above). Manager Willem Moers greets guests, and his staff serves up tasty Gallic-influenced fare. A meal from the à la carte might begin with smoked salmon, snails Burgundy style, a platter of two distinctive house *pâtés*, onion soup, or shrimp bisque. Entrées run to filet of sole, grilled tournedos, or *boeuf Stroganoff*. And *crêpes Suzette*, prepared at table, are among desserts. Good wines. *First Class.*

Le Vieux Jean (Heilige Geestkerkhof 3; Phone 13-04-33) looks good—white chairs surround tables set with white linen in an aged core-of-town house. Devotées of French cuisine should be content here. Open with soup or a salad, concentrate on such hearty main courses as *boeuf Bourguignon, entrecôte* served with *frites,* or filet of veal. *First Class.*

Salvatore (Oude Delft 88; Phone 14-56-87): To partake of an authentic Italian meal served in an authentic Oude Delft canal house with a centuries-old pedigree is indeed to be blessed with the best of two worlds. You've a nice selection of pastas to choose as first courses—*primi,* as they say in Italy—continuing with an entrée of veal *scaloppine* or *bistecca Fiorentina,* as close as Delft can come to a grilled steak in the classic style of Florence. Italian wines. *First Class.*

Monopole (Markt 48): Take a table on the square, ordering a snack or light lunch or simply opt for coffee or a cold drink. Big crowds, big views. *Moderate.*

Expresso (Oude Delft 143): I can't imagine a lovelier spot on which to relax on a balmy day than the terrace—the scheme is black and white—of this welcoming café, bordering the city's premier canal. *Moderate.*

SHOPPER'S DELFT

For many visitors—cost notwithstanding, and believe me, it is very, but *very* costly—shopping in Delft means one thing: Delftware. In the early seventeenth century, after Dutch merchant ships had brought porcelain from China, there were 30 potteries in Delft and others in such towns as Makkum (Chapter 14) and Haarlem (Chapter 3). Originally, Delftware was heavily imitative of the work of the Chinese, but a peculiarly Dutch Delft decor developed, and although there are only three potteries today, there appears to be no dearth of takers for their products, exorbitant prices notwithstanding. The factory called *De Porcelayne Flies* (Rotterdamsweg 196)—biggest, best known and most aggressive at marketing—is a ten-minute drive from the center; has artisans demonstrating their work during the summer; and, needless to say, a shop (with a section for seconds, 25 percent to 40 percent cheaper than unflawed pieces) wherein is vended the traditional blue-and-white Delftware; the Polychrome (decorated in green, yellow, and red), with Baroque-era Majolica as its inspiration; Pynacker (in red, blue, and gold, based on Japanese Imari porcelain); and Black Delft, black grounded and based on seventeenth-century patterns. This factory has two shops on the Markt square in town (at Nos. 36 and 62, also with seconds departments). The other factories are *De Delftse Pau* (Delftweg 133, with tours and a retail shop) and *Atelier de Candelaer* (Kerkstraat 13, also with tours and a shop). Worth noting too:

Gemeentelijke Archiefdienst—the Municipal Archives shop (for reproductions of old paintings, drawings, and maps, available as post- and note-cards), on the main floor of a honey of a sixteenth-century house at Oude Delft 169.

SOUND OF MUSIC

Stadedoelen (Verwersdijk 44) is the *Schouwburg*, or theater of the municipality, offering classic and pop concerts, ballet, and opera. The tourist office (below) has schedules.

Waagtheater (Wijnhaven 24, but with the entrance at Markt 11) is located in the eighteenth-century municipal weigh house; it's compact and with an upstairs café.

INCIDENTAL INTELLIGENCE

Despite its proximity to Rotterdam (Chapter 18), a quarter-hour by train, with very frequent departures in either direction, Delft is deserving of more than a day's excursion; it wants to be savored by means of at least an overnight stay. *Further information:* VVV Delft, Markt 85.

7

Den Bosch/ 's Hertogenbosch

The Duke's Domain

BACKGROUND BRIEFING

The French propensity for translating foreign place names into their own tongue—a practice we adhere to relatively rarely in English—has the virtue of making immediately clear to Gallic visitors the significance of this city's official Dutch name: 's Hertogenbosch (which the Dutch and we English speakers shorten to the easier Den Bosch). The French *Bois-le-Duc* means, quite simply, the Duke's Wood and connotes Den Bosch's origin—as a village that gradually grew up around a hunting lodge built by a medieval Duke of Brabant as a retreat from palace life in Brussels, not far to the south.

The period embraced the closing decades of the twelfth century and the early years of the thirteenth. Not long after his original house—built of wood—went up, Duke Henry I gave Den Bosch its first charter, in 1185. At the turn of the thirteenth century, he replaced his original lodge with a second, impressively gabled and with a solitary corner turret. Eight centuries later, City Fathers wisely took advantage of that still-standing structure's rich history and exemplary location, smack on the main square, and after a 1960s refurbishing it became the seat of the VVV, Den Bosch's municipal tourist office. When you step up to the counter for information, remember that you're where it all began.

ON SCENE

Lay of the Land: Given its population (in the neighborhood of 90,000), this perky southern city—because of a relatively compact core virtually surrounded by one body of water or another—seems smaller than it is. Walking about is a distinct pleasure. The railway station edges the western edge of town, on *Stationsweg*. From it, proceed directly east to *Visstraat*, working your way from it via *Hogesteenweg* to the enormous principal square, called *Markt* and with landmarks including not only the historically significant building housing the VVV (above), but the *Stadhuis*, or town hall (below), and with a contemporary central statue of the city's favorite son, the Renaissance artist Hieronymus Bosch, whose busily detailed paintings, populated by macabre figures and grotesque animals, are familiar to museumgoers. Shops are all about; both *Vroom & Dreesmann* and *C & A* department stores are directly on Markt (along with produce stalls); *Hema* and *Peek & Cloppenburg* are just off Markt on the busy street called *Pensmarkt*. Nearby *Ververstraat* is the site of the onetime Rococo palace that is now *Noordbrabants Museum* (below) and abounds in antiques shops and art galleries. *Hinthamerstraat*—the city's favorite thoroughfare for promenades—leads east from Markt to the monumental square called *Parade*, dominated by a Gothic structure that is arguably the Netherlands' greatest cathedral (below) and the eighteenth-century Bishop's Palace. North of the core, on *Citadelaan*, the moated *Citadel*—with four of its five-centuries-old bastions renovated in the early 1980s—stands guard over the city (doubling as a repository of Provincial records). To the south, a sixteenth-century cannon remains embedded in a bastion, *Orange* by name, of the city wall.

St. Janskathedraal (Parade): Cathedrals that were erected as ordinary parish churches are not all that uncommon in England, where not a few became seats of Anglican bishops some centuries after their construction (see *Britain at Its Best*). On the continent, though, it is rare to come upon a Gothic cathedral that was not created as such. Den Bosch's St. Jan's is an exception. Work began in 1380, the while artisans plied their skills throughout the fifteenth century, completing the building in 1552, to the delight of the faithful of an increasingly wealthy town—but under aegis of the Bishop of Liège, to the south. Only in 1559 did 's Hertogenbosch become an independent diocese.

Shortly thereafter, though, in 1566, post-Reformation Protestants took it over—but briefly. In 1579, Catholics came to the fore for the succeeding half-century. St. Jan's became Protestant once again, with the advent of the early seventeenth-century Dutch Republic, remaining so into the early nineteenth century, when Napoleon declared that predominantly Catholic Den Bosch once again deserved a Catholic cathedral.

Much-needed restoration began in 1859, continuing for something like half a century, albeit according to the fanciful *neo*-Gothic—rather than recreated original Gothic—taste of the era. Only relatively recently, a fruitful ten-year period concluding in 1984, was the cathedral set to rights, restored, renewed, and refurbished in the spirit of its early designers, with the consequence an all-Europe ranker of its kind.

Pause before going in. The tower is as old as the cathedral's nearly eight centuries: lowest part, Romanesque; center, Gothic; slim spire, seventeenth-century Baroque. You want to walk all the way around before entering. Not even the flying buttresses of Paris's Notre Dame have the power of those of St. Jan. And these are embellished with sculpted figures—nearly a hundred, all told, surrounded by no-two-alike gargoyles—beneath a network of delicate pinnacles, foil for the massive windows typical of Perpendicular Gothic.

Once inside—you hold your breath with the vista of the long nave joining the west front with the choir and high altar—concentrate on specifics. In no other church have I seen floor tombs so beautifully restored, and they are all about. Baroque organs are commonplace in Holland, but none is more impressive than St. Jan's, seventeenth century and restored over a recent two-year period. Nor is contemporary stained glass anywhere more pleasing: Note especially the 1966 North Transept window. Take in, as well, carved-wood reliefs of the fifteenth-sixteenth century pulpit (*The Sermon on the Mount* especially); detail of the fifteenth-century choir stalls; the half-dozen exquisitely wrought brass figures atop the also-brass baptismal font, a medieval masterwork; Sakraments Kapelle, a Gothic treasure that is the finest of a network of chapels; and, most sublime of the cathedral's art, Altar of the Passion, a fifteenth-century triptych, its central portions gilt-accented sculptures of great beauty depicting *Christ Carrying the Cross*, the *Crucifixion*, and the *Descent from the Cross*, with half a dozen paintings (surfacing shutters which, when closed, protect the altar) at its extremities.

Noordbrabants Museum (Verwersstraat 41): Provincial history museums in Holland tend to be mixed-bag repositories not only of paintings, but a range of artifacts, clothes to crystal. By and large, they are first-rate, none more so than North Barbant's. It was organized in 1837 and moved a century and a half later, in 1987, into its third home—a superb late-eighteenth-century palace, originally the official residence of royal-appointed provincial governors—designed by the same architect, Pieter de Swart, responsible for the Royal Palace on Lange Voorhout in The Hague (Chapter 10). Alas, there are no paintings within by Den Bosch-born Hieronymus Bosch, but that master's studio is represented. There are several fine works by another Den Bosch native, Theodor van Thulden—allegories in the style of Rubens, to whom he was an assistant. There's a Peter Brueghel the Younger village scene, a group of a dozen paintings—one representing each of the months—by a follower of Peter Brueghel the Elder; a painting celebrating each of the seasons, by David Teniers; and two Van Goghs—dark-hued works of the early Potato Eaters' period preceding his departure for France. Take your time as you proceed: Roman glass and Roman busts, superb medieval sculpture, silver and pewter, tiles and brass, not to mention numerous painted views of Den Bosch over the centuries.

Stadhuis (Markt): City Hall is seventeenth century—a Baroque beauty as much for its neoclassic facade (look up at the gilded crown under the pediment) as for its recently restored main hall—very formal and very spiffy, and visit the up-a-flight Council Chamber, whose walls are surfaced with paintings of sovereigns, right up to and including Queen Beatrix.

Zwanenbroedershuis (Hinthamerstraat 94) is, to be sure, a mouthful. It's the seat of an unusual Middle Ages-founded religious society, and it's chockablock with mostly medieval memorabilia—the range, paintings through pewter. Hitch is open-hours, traditionally Friday only and then from but 11:00 A.M. to 3:00 P.M.

Heusden (12 miles northwest of Den Bosch) is a venerable village—it has Roman roots—that has in recent years been meticulously restored at considerable government expense and with apparently unlimited professional expertise. It may be argued that the result is more museumlike than spontaneous. Withal, a half-day's outing beginning with lunch or terminating with dinner (see *Daily Bread*, below) can be agreeable. And it should be made clear that although Heusden is today a tranquil village devoid of international consequence, it was not always so. For centuries, as much fortress as town—it is situated on the southern bank of the Meuse River—it has known such visitors as Holy Roman Emperor Charles V (1539), his son King Philip IV of Spain (1549), and Napoleon (in company with his second Empress, Maria Louisa, in 1811). World War II saw heavy destruction, and the elaborate government-aided restoration begun in 1968 continues apace, with well over a hundred (of some 400) landmark houses and a host of bastions, ramparts, moats, and windmills rehabilitated. Pick up a map on arrival at the tourist office (address below). Tour *Vismarkt*, the central square flanking the harbor, just off the attractive main street, *Breestraat*. Then take in *Het Gouverneurshuis* (Putterstraat 14), residence of eighteenth-century governors, now a museum of Heusden history with a vast scale model of the town as it appeared during its Golden Age (1400–1570); the fortified walls and bastions, *Noord Bolwerk* through *Verpoort Bolwerk*, on whose summits you may walk, the better for bird's-eye views;

the three restored (and neighboring) *windmills; St. Catherine's Church*—Gothic in a walled park; and streets with restored houses, including *Kerkstraat, Putterstraat,* and *Serrestraat.*

SETTLING IN

Central Hotel (Loeffplein 98; Phone 12-51-51) is nondescript modern. But it has pluses: Location—just around the corner, behind Markt, the main square—is one. Its big superior-category, higher-up rooms with views of Markt constitute the second. And a restaurant with a generous breakfast buffet and bar comprise the third. Service, though cooly impersonal, is nonetheless efficient. *First Class.*

Euro Hotel (Hinthamerstraat 63; Phone 13-77-77) is nicely situated on the pedestrian thoroughfare joining Markt and Parade, the cathedral square. The small but welcoming lobby is on the main floor; the 42 rooms (those I have inspected are modern, albeit with only hand showers connected to tubs), satisfactory. There's a bar-lounge, buffet breakfasts, and a restaurant that's available only to groups. *Moderate.*

In Den Verdwaalde Koogel Hotel (Vismarkt 1, Heusden; Phone 1933)—as much restaurant (below) as hotel—occupies quarters in a looker of a landmark seventeenth-century house, with a gabled brick facade and a super situation, center of the Heusden action. The bridal chamber is good sized, but other rooms I have inspected (there are but ten) are small though attractive, blending contemporary furnishings with original ceiling beams. Congenial. *Moderate.*

DAILY BREAD

Auberge de Koets (Korte Putstraat 21; Phone 132-779): Two key words here—smart and delicious. Owner Joop van Zantvoort has taken an old gabled house, core of town, and turned it into a handsome, two-story restaurant, illuminated by antique brass coach lanterns, with aged prints of coaches on the walls and chairs upholstered in linen to complement draperies of the same material. Tables are centered by brass candlesticks, with octagonal place plates, also of brass. The *amuse-*

gueule, or house appetizer, will be *nouvelle*—a *purée* of avocado and carrot, perhaps. Otherwise, De Koet's fare is at least as traditional (praise be) as it is contemporary. Choose from either of a pair of prix-fixe menus or order à la carte, opening with half a dozen oysters on the half-shell, Parma ham and melon, or—heartily counseled—mushroom-flecked beef *bouillon*. The chef does interesting things with seafood—combination platters, *nouvelle* accented, or classic filet of sole *meunière*. Not often encountered poultry is available: filet of guinea hen deliciously roasted and sauced. And *carré d'agneau*—roast lamb seasoned with mustard, parsley, and garlic—is quite as mouthwatering as it would be in France. There's a good-sized wine list and a fair-sized dessert choice. And service is as expert as it is cheerful. Dinner only. In my experience, one of Holland's best restaurants. *First Class.*

Chalet Royal (Wilhelminaplein 1; Phone 135-771)—a rambling white pavilion enclosing a cocktail lounge and a series of connected dining rooms, furnished in white wicker—appears, at first glance, more glitzy than substantial, but it delivers. Waiters—in maroon jackets atop long white aprons—are swift and chatty, but, more to the point, the chef is skilled. The dinner that will be brought to your table, illuminated by silver candlesticks—on Art Nouveau-patterned Bauscher-Weiden china—should please. The five-course, prix-fixe menu is a good buy and might include pigeon salad, the day's hearty soup, perfectly sautéed trout, steak *au poivre* expertly sauced as the main course, and a sweet. Dinner only. *Luxury.*

De Raadskelder (in the separately entered basement of the Raadhuis, or town hall [above], on Markt; Phone 136-919): The tradition of restaurants in cellars of city halls, prevalent throughout Germany, is not nearly so widespread in Holland. Be glad of this exception to the rule. You like the environment—venerable vaulted ceilings hung with wrought-iron chandeliers, brick walls, flower-centered tables—and you like the well-prepared fare. Open, for example, with the house's reputed onion soup, and follow with a beef or lamb entrée, or the simply but expertly grilled sole. And bear in mind that you may pop in for coffee or a drink in the bar-lounge. Delightful service. *First Class.*

Dekivorsch (Parade 6; Phone 141-619) is at once attractive and tasty, with well-priced prix-fixe menus and an à la carte with Alsatian-style snails, grilled salmon, and veal steak, among options; and super ice-cream desserts. *Moderate.*

Taormina (Verwersstraat 46; Phone 147-036): The Dutch clientele favor Taormina's pizzas (the choice is wide) but assorted *antipasti* (with imported-from-Italy salamis featured) and the pastas with authentic sauces are good, too. Your hosts are Salvatore (he's from Taormina) and Aranka (she's from Budapest) Pollino. *Moderate.*

Brasserie de Paris (Kerkstraat 49, just off Markt; Phone 14-16-97) features stick-to-the-ribs, Gallic-origin specialties: mussels *marinière* and *entrecôte-frites*, among them. Spare ribs, too. Good value. *Moderate.*

Delifrance (Hinthamerstraat 47) is indicated for coffee-cum-croissants at an outdoor table on this popular central artery. *Moderate.*

Pumpke (Parade 37): Take a table on the square if it's a sunny day, so that you can steep yourself in the beauty of the cathedral's lacy Gothic facade. Have coffee, a drink, or a casual lunch. *Moderate.*

In Den Verdwaalde Koogel (Vismarkt 1, Heusden; Phone 1933) is brought to your attention as a hotel (above). But it is a commendable restaurant, as well, with beamed ceilings and ladderback chairs at tables set in pale pink linen. The three-course lunch menu can be good value, but at dinner you might want to select from the à la carte—opening with seafood bisque or the house's own *pâté*, selecting grilled porkchops, tarragon accented, or marjoram-seasoned lamb steak, as an entrée. There's always a pastry and a platter of Dutch cheese among desserts. *First Class.*

De Pannekoekenbakker (Vismarkt 4, Heusden; Phone 2559): Talk about choices: There are 95 species of pancakes herein available. Take your time selecting, perhaps opening with a savory (like ham and cheese or bacon and tomato) and concluding with a sweet—the range, apple with whipped cream through banana with ice cream. *Moderate.*

Bertels (Breestraat, Heusden) is a main-street café; have pastry with your coffee and watch the crowds pass in review. *Moderate.*

SOUND OF MUSIC
Schoubourg Casino (Parade 23) is Den Bosch's ever-so-contemporary municipal theater; concerts, both classical and pop, ballet, opera. The tourist office (below) has schedules.

INCIDENTAL INTELLIGENCE

Breda (Chapter 5) is but 30 miles distant; fast and frequent trains link the two cities. *Further information:* VVV Den Bosch, Markt 77; VVV Heusden, Engstraat 4.

8

Deventer
Detour to the East

BACKGROUND BRIEFING

Think Hanseatic League and you think of the medieval maritime prowess of such northern ports as Hamburg, Lübeck, and Bergen. But before this rich and powerful northern European trading consortium lost its clout in the sixteenth century, well over a hundred towns—including a number situated in the Dutch interior—had become affiliated with it, prospering from their association. Deventer, fronting the oddly spelled IJssel River, in the east-central OverIJssell Province, was one of these.

Wisely locating factories and foundries—which, with tourism, contribute to its contemporary prosperity—away from its historic center, this handsome town appears smaller than a population approaching 70,000 might indicate. And therein lies its charm. Walk its historic core, today with landmarks essentially what they were in a 1578 painting that hangs in its museum, and you have no difficulty understanding that Deventer was where the Augustinian monk, Thomas à Kempis, studied in the fifteenth century, to be followed by the Rotterdam-born humanist, Erasmus, in the sixteenth, and the elegant portraitist, Gerard Terborch, as well as France's René Descartes—philosopher as well as scientist—in the seventeenth.

Distances in Holland being what they are—by no means great—Deventer's easterly situation should not deter the contemporary traveler. This is a charming city with an enviable patina. Tarry overnight.

ON SCENE
Lay of the Land: Sensible. The railway station is at the northern edge of the core on *Stationsplein*, while the *IJssel River* delineates the southern flank of the central area. And a splendid, sprawling café-, shop-, and landmark-bordered square—*Brink* by name—lies amidships, anchoring Korte *Bisschopstraat* and other pedestrians-only shopping streets. Keizerstraat leads directly north to the station from Brink, while *Bergstraat, Maansteeg,* and *Roggestraat*—three arteries paralleling each other—lead past meticulously restored Middle Ages houses to the also restored *Bergkerk*, a principal church, along with the large *Grote Kerk* on the square called *Grote Kerkhof* and with a high octagonal tower that pierces the Deventer skyline. *Stadhuis*, the town hall, is just opposite, and another square, *Grote Markt*, is adjacent. *Onder de Linden* is a Dutch-language variation of the famous Berlin thoroughfare, Unter den Linden; it flanks the IJssel River. From its ferry terminal, boats depart regularly for the opposite bank of the river—and memorable views of the town.

Grote Kerk (a.k.a. Lebuinuskerk, Grote Kerkhof) went up in the early decades of the tenth century, in the Romanesque style of that long-ago era. All that remains from then is an unadorned crypt. Above ground, the church is fifteenth-century Gothic, with an immense interior highlighted by fine frescoes and with the square tower—topped by an octagonal bell enclosure—that is Deventer's principal landmark.

Stadhuis and Landhuis (Grote Kerkhof), Grote Kerk's neighbors, are impressively aged municipal buildings. The former—parts of it as old as the thirteenth century, most of it later Baroque—is the City Hall; you want to go inside and ask to see not only the upstairs Council Chamber, but the painting of the town fathers in session, created by the cele-

brated artist Terborch while he served as mayor, four centuries back. The latter, the seventeenth-century Landhuis, is
where civil marriages take place; have a look at the wedding
chamber.

Bergkerk (Berkkerplein): This Romanesque church was completed in the second decade of the thirteenth century and was
paid relatively little attention until the sixth decade of the
twentieth, when it was designated focal point of a Dutch Gov-
ernment-funded neighborhood restoration, in which Queen
Beatrix participated. The severity of the red-brick facade—
beneath a pair of slim steeples—contrasts with an interior
brightened by lavish frescoes, a fine Baroque organ, and brass
chandeliers of the same period. Hope that your visit will co-
incide with a concert or an art exhibition. And take your time
as you wander streets of the quarter, noting restored medieval
facades of *Bergstraat, Kerksteeg,* and *Maansteeg.*

Museum de Waag (Brink): The building first. The Waag went
up in the early sixteenth century—style is detailed Gothic-
Renaissance—as the municipal weigh house. Surmounted by
a graceful clock tower that is itself topped by a gilded cock of
a weathervane and with minitowers at each of the corners, it
is impressive enough to have served as the City Hall. Today
its two floors of beamed-ceiling galleries house the town's
Historical Museum. I am partial to the paintings—the earlier-
mentioned sixteenth-century illustrated map of the town; a
seventeenth-century view of the De Waag and surrounding
Brink houses; a mid-nineteenth-century perspective of Deventer, painted from across the river; and, star of the show,
a likeness of a Deventer mayor by Terborch, who created portraits of a number of prominent locals. But there is much else:
pewter and pottery through to an unexpected cache of antique bicycles—a hit with Dutch viewers, virtually all of
whom regularly ride latter-day models.

Spielgoed en Blikmuseum (Brink) is an amusing repository of
aged toys, meticulously furnished dollhouses of earlier eras,
model ships, and marvelous miniature trains. It occupies a

late-sixteenth-century merchant's mansion next door to Museum de Waag. You'll have a good time.

SETTLING IN
Royal Hotel (Brink 94; Phone 11880) is at once convenient to the railway station and heart of town, on the principal square. This is an updated traditional house with an attractive paneled restaurant, bar that draws locals as well as hotel guests, outdoor café for warm-weather months, and just under 20 contemporarily furnished rooms, all with bath. *Moderate.*

Postiljon Hotel (Deventerweg 121; Phone 14022), though not central—it is one in the chain whose name it takes, all links of which are situated on highways just beyond the town they serve—has the virtures of modern accommodations (there are just a hundred up-to-the-minute rooms with good baths, even including glass doors protecting showers over tubs), reasonably priced restaurant, welcoming bar, and a staff at once friendly and efficient. *Moderate.*

DAILY BREAD
't Arsenaal (Nieuwe Markt 33; Phone 16495) is not your everyday restaurant environment. By that I mean it is based on a fifteenth-century chapel of the ruined Mariakerk and extends into an adjacent building, only a century newer, with tables spilling onto the square called Nieuwe Markt in summer. Choose from four prix-fixe menus—entrées include *médaillons* of pork, the day's fish in Sauterne sauce, and veal casserole— or order à la carte, perhaps commencing with smoked salmon, the house *pâté,* or cream of spinach soup garnished with hard-cooked quails' eggs; continuing with roast duck *tournedos* with crayfish sauce or estragon-flavored lamb chops. Service? I don't know of a friendlier restaurant in Holland. *First Class.*

Het Hoeckhuys (Brink 38; Phone 19595) is a veritable symphony (a modern symphony at that) in green—the range, palmlike plants, thick carpeting, upholstery on the chairs, and even the color of the ink on their menus. You are welcomed by a smiling staff and do well to order either of the prix-fixe menus (fillets of beef and pork are among entrées). Desserts include pastry, not often the case in the Netherlands, and both wine and beer choices are extensive. *First Class.*

Pizzeria Romano (Grote Overstraat 61; Phone 15373), well located on a busy street just off Brink, is indicated for a satisfying Italian lunch built around pizza or pasta. *Moderate.*

Bussinks Koekhuisjke (Brink 84) is long established. In the front, it's a source of the Deventer spice cake specialty called *bijtje;* out back is a café where a coffee and cake pause is in order. *Moderate.*

Hansen Grietje (Brink 79) is especially attractive in summer, thanks to a clutch of tables on the square. Casual café sustenance. *Moderate.*

SOUND OF MUSIC
Deventer Schouwburg (Grote Kerkhof), the municipal theater, runs the entertainment gamut, pop singers through classical concerts. The tourist office (below) has schedules.

INCIDENTAL INTELLIGENCE ══════════════════

Deventer is not far east of Apeldoorn (Chapter 11) and not far south of Zwolle (Chapter 20); consider working it in with visits to those towns. *Further information:* VVV Deventer, Brink 55.

9

Giethoorn

The North's Curiosity Village

BACKGROUND BRIEFING

If the horns of thousands of goats—wild goats, at that—and a concentrated mass of peat bogs appear as unlikely ingredients for the establishment of a thriving village that reportedly lures a million curiosity seekers every summer, well, so be it.

Even Giethoorn's founders, a pious and persecuted group of flagellants who found their way north from the shore of the Mediterranean in the late thirteenth century, were hardly run-of-the-mill.

Nor was their vocation. When the seigneur, the ruling noble, of nearby Vollenhove accepted them as refugees, they set to work developing bogs of peat—the partly decomposed turf, still used as fuel today in Ireland—to earn a living. Two things happened as a consequence. First, in the course of digging, they excavated countless horns of wild goats that had perished in the region before their arrival (thus giving the village its name, a derivation of the Dutch for goathorns). Second, their ever-intensive cultivation—incessant digging for peat—eventually resulted in the tranformation of these low-altitude bogs (not far east of what had been the Zuider Zee) into bodies of water, some of them quite large lakes, some considerably smaller, the lot necessitating the creation of a network of canals for local transport.

And, although Holland is hardly a country where the canal is an eye-opener, Giethoorn evolved as a village with waterways in abundance—but nary a road.

This odd state of affairs—requiring that you approach by boat, on foot, or on a bicycle, there being absolutely no provision for four-wheeled vehicles—has, to be sure, served as an impediment to growth or, at least, population; Giethoorn's is a scant 2,000. (Of humans, that is. There must be many times that number of resident ducks in the canals, not to mention cows, the lot of which are transported by *punter*, Giethoorn's variation on the pole-propelled gondola of Venice.)

To say, though, that short-term visitors compensate is to understate. They come in force, during the warm-weather months. Ideally, your visit should be in uncrowded spring or autumn (when kids, who flock in summer with their parents, on camping vacations, are in school). Not that winter is to be avoided. In really cold weather, the canals are frozen, with transport by sleigh and residents on ice-skates, and the scene is a veritable latter-day Hendrik Avercamp painting.

ON SCENE
Lay of the Land: Arrive by car, via nearby *Beulaker Wijde*, and you find the principal hotel (below) and parking lots edging the village's main canal, from which *punters* (the very same vessels used for livestock and whatever freight enters or leaves the village) are available for guided, hour-long excursions, with gossipy commentary by the boatmen in a choice of languages, English always among them. Alternately, you may walk or cycle; paths line the canals, fronting houses— the lot of them thatch roofed, in accordance with village tradition—and immaculately maintained by village residents, not a few of whom have become prosperous through the lucrative summer tourist business. It is householders who maintain not only their spick-and-span houses and elaborate gardens but, with some government funding, the 150 picturesque bridges traversing the network of canals. Surrounding lakes draw bird watchers, fishermen, and water skiers; aquatic diversions, including sailing and windsurfing, are or-

ganized by local firms operating out of waterfront café-restaurants.

De Speelman Museum (Binnenpad 123) occupies a thatched Giethoorn house and amuses visitors—the youngsters love it—with a diverting collection of venerable street organs and other aged musical instruments.

De Oude Aarde Museum (Binnenpad 43) displays crystallized rocks and fluorescent minerals to good advantage, with ultraviolet and other catchy types of lighting to show them off.

Vollenhove, taking the name of the centuries-old fiefdom that welcomed the original settlers of Giethoorn, is a charming village, but ten miles distant, around whose central square, Kerkplein, are to be found St. Nicolaaskerk (a.k.a. Bovenkerk)—lovely Gothic and with a free-standing bell tower and the Baroque-era Stadhuis, or town hall, now seeing service as a restaurant (below), which serves well as an excursion lunch-stop.

SETTLING IN
Giethoorn Hotel (Beulakerweg 128; Phone 1216)—a single-level motel edging the village—has 20 identical up-to-the-minute double rooms-cum-terraces (those facing the motel's own yacht harbor have the nicest views), pair of restaurants (the more formal [*First Class*] is centered with a typical Giethoorn *punter*; the second [*Moderate*] is an adequate café), and a cordial staff. *Moderate.*

DAILY BREAD
Giethoorn Hotel Restaurant (Beulakerweg 128; Phone 1216) is indicated for a nicely served dinner—ask for a table overlooking the yacht harbor—built around an entrée of fresh lake fish. There's a fairish selection of French white wines and elaborate ice-cream desserts. *First Class.*

Hollands Venetië (Beulakerweg 167; Phone 1231)—like the Giethoorn Hotel (above) edging the village and with a big parking lot—makes a specialty of groups, but small parties are welcome (there's a terrace-café that's pleasant in summer) for a meal based on, say, *Wiener schnitzel* or beef stew. Snacks, too. *Moderate/First Class*.

Paviljoen 't Wiede (Bovenwiede; Phone 1312) typifies the lakefront establishments in that it is at once a restaurant/café (barbecues are a specialty) with outdoor tables and a water sports center. Congenial Klass Koen and his family are your hosts. *Moderate/First Class*.

Smit's Paviljoen (Bovenwidje; Phone 1215) features lunch on its sprawling lakeside dock and offers boating and other aquatic activity. *Moderate*.

De Otterskooi (Dwarsgracht 4; Phone 1474) is canalside, heart of the village, in typically thatch-roofed quarters (and with an alfresco terrace). Fish lunches and dinners. *Moderate*.

Seidel (Kerkplein 3, Vollenhove; Phone 1262) occupies the former town hall, atmospherically seventeenth century, on little Vollenhove's main square; go for lunch—fish is favored, but there are meat entrées, too—on an excursion from Giethoorn. *First Class*.

INCIDENTAL INTELLIGENCE ═══════════════════

Giethoorn is nicely combined with Zwolle (Chapter 20), from which it is but 14 miles distant. *Further information:* VVV Giethoorn, on its own boat moored alongside Beulakerweg; VVV Volenhove, Kerkplein 15.

10

The Hague/ Den Haag/ 's Gravenhaage
Seat of Crown and Government

BACKGROUND BRIEFING
Cities whose names are preceded by a definite article are rarities. But the North Sea city of The Hague—between Amsterdam and Rotterdam, albeit closer to the latter—is otherwise anomalous. Despite eminence as seat of both the Netherlands' Crown and Government, is not designated the capital (that honor is Amsterdam's), has never been awarded official rights as a city (there is a certain pride in being Europe's largest village, population 450,000, excluding suburbs), is not cut through by canals (a commonplace of urban Holland), has never been walled (it's largely built on *polders*, the Dutch term for land reclaimed from the sea), and uses its seafront not as a commercial harbor, but primarily as a beach resort.

The cosmopolitan influence of 64 foreign embassies—it is to The Hague that ambassadors are accredited—and the august eminence of the Andrew Carnegie-endowed Peace Palace housing the International Court of Justice have no doubt contributed to the decidedly likeable ambience of The Hague; it is smart, sophisticated, often elegant. And there is no question that, given the virtual absence of canals, its architects have built more in the style of neighboring European countries than of neighboring Dutch cities.

But give pedigree its due. The Hague's roots are, if not regal, noble. By that I mean it began not so much when it was a Roman colony or even later as a little fishing port, but rather when, in the thirteenth century, it became a residence (at first a hunting lodge, later a proper palace) of the Counts of Holland. The name—'s Gravenhaage, meaning the Count's Hedge, Wood, or Park—suggests provenance from the country house of Count Floris IV in 1222 to the more substantial palace of his successor, William II. Succeeding counts—Floris V, Jan I, Albrecht, and, in the early fifteenth century, William VI—extended and enlarged what had come to be called the Binnenhof, the while impelling settlement of merchants and tradespeople anxious to do business with the Counts and their courtiers to the point where the periphery of the Binnenhof came to constitute the beginnings of a proper town.

The die had been cast. Counts of Holland were followed in the late sixteenth century by the States General, or Parliament, of the United Provinces of the Netherlands and in the seventeenth by stadholders who settled in as leaders of the then-new Dutch Republic. Louis Bonaparte, appointed king by his brother Napoleon, headquartered in The Hague before moving on to Utrecht and Amsterdam. Later, for a decade and a half, starting in 1815, The Hague was, with Brussels, seat of the parliament of the short-lived United Netherlands.

As the nineteenth century became the twentieth, The Hague became a favored venue for peace conferences, with what history books term the First (1899) and Second (1907) Hague conferences. At the latter, the Permanent Court of Arbitration was established; it, together with the International Court of Justice or World Court, meets in the Carnegie-financed Peace Palace. But there are other palaces—a trio of royal residences, the city having been seat of the Crown from 1815 all the way through the reign of Queen Wilhelmina in 1948. Wilhelmina's successor, Juliana, selected Soestdijk Palace, outside Utrecht, as her principal home, overnighting annually in The Hague to open Parliament.

But Juliana's daughter, Queen Beatrix, returned the Royal Family to the city. They live in Paleis den Bosch, at the edge of town, and the Queen and Prince Claus maintain offices at

Paleis Nordend, in the heart of town. Will you see Queen Beatrix, her husband, or Princes Willem Alexander, Johan Priso, or Constantijn in the course of your visit? It is possible. And if not the royals, their automobiles: vehicles with an "AA" license plate are Crown cars.

ON SCENE
Lay of the Land: The Hague is not compact. This is a sprawling city, most attractive and monument filled in and around its venerable core, immediately to the north and west of *Centraal Station* (Julianaplein), the principal, but not the only, rail terminal. A few worth-visiting destinations are a bus/tram or taxi ride to the north, mostly edging the western side of a park called *Zorgvliet*. Farther north, at the terminus of *Scheviningsweg*—a long, north-south thoroughfare—is the beach resort *Scheviningen*, with *Strandweg* the promenade separating it from the sands and varied amusements of *De Pier*, tower tipped and jutting into the *North Sea*. Where to headquarter? My suggestion—unless your stay coincides with *really* hot and sunny summer weather, when a dunk or two from Scheviningen beach into the waters of the rarely warm *Nordzee* might appeal—is a central Hague hotel, where you can catch the flavor of the city as you walk about, conveniently close to most of the places you'll want to explore.

The lake called *Hofvijver*, fronting the historic *Binnenhof* complex, including *Museum Mauritshuis* (below), marks the center of The Hague's central area. Three utterly beautiful thoroughfares, lined by the Baroque palaces and townhouses that are this city at its most representative, are *Lange Voorhout*, enclosing a broad green and site of *Koninklijke Paleis Voorhaut* (mid-eighteenth century, smallest of the three royal palaces, and used for state receptions), *Koninklijke Bibliothek* (the million-volume Royal Library designed in 1734 by the same French-born Daniel Marot who created Paleis Het Loo [Chapter 11] for King-Stadholder William III and with a superb interior that's visitable), *Kloosterkerk* (handsomely Gothic and used for concerts), and the history-rich, nineteenth-century *Des Indes Hotel* (below); *Lange Vijverberg*, which fronts the *Hofvijver* lake; and *Korte Vorhorhout*, wherein is jarringly

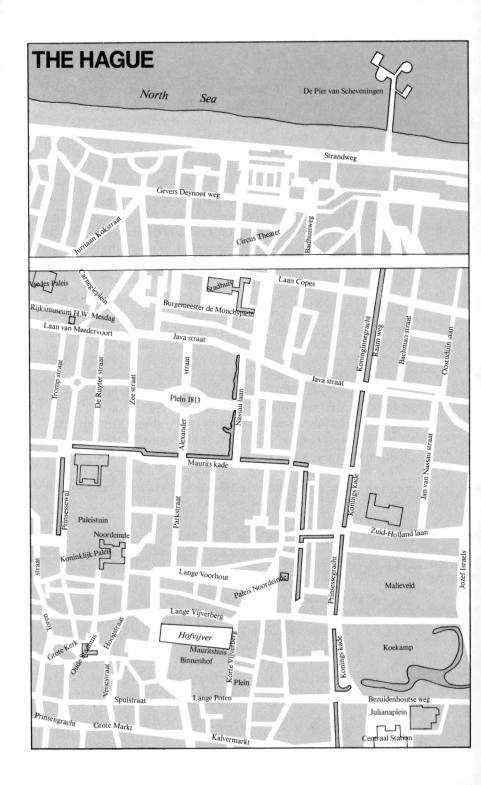

located the gracelessly contemporary *United States Embassy*, its facade laced with narrow, slitlike windows, not uncommon in 1960s buildings.

The café- and restaurant-lined square called *Plein*, just east of the Binnenhof, marks the western end of a good-sized shopping district that extends west along *Lange Poten*, as it becomes *Spuistraat*. A couple of blocks west, *Venestraat*—core of the pedestrian area—is linked at its northern tip with *Groenmarkt's* department stores (see Shopper's The Hague, below), *Oude Stadhuis* (the Old Town Hall), and neighboring, essentially fifteenth-century *Grote Kerk*, an important landmark Gothic church transformed, alas, into a congress hall. Boutiques are due north—on *Hoogstraat*, which becomes *Noordeinde* (taking the name of *Koninklijke Paleis Noordeinde*, the recently restored seventeenth-century palace that houses Queen Beatrix's and other Crown offices and with open-to-the-public gardens out back), changing its name for the last time to *Paleispromenade*. The third—and most impressive—of the royal palaces, *Koninklijke Paleis Huis Ten Bosch*, flanks eastern precincts of the park called *Haagse Bos*; its cupola-topped central pavilion is seventeenth century, with wings to either side added in the eighteenth century by the same Daniel Marot who designed Paleis Lange Voorhout in town and Paleis Het Loo. Before the Royal Family moved in, after Queen Beatrix ascended the throne, Ten Bosch was open to the public, when not in official use; its kicker is an octagonal central hall, lavishly frescoed. Even now, though, you may drive up to the main gate in the park, as I have done, and sentries—unlike stern-visaged counterparts you may have encountered guarding royal palaces in Britain—will reply in kind when you say hello, as you peer through the wrought-iron grilles.

The Binnenhof complex is not, truth be told, as old as it may appear—which is not to say you don't want to pay your respects at this cluster of historic buildings wherein The Hague had its beginnings. It now serves as seat of the States General (the Dutch Parliament), opened officially the third Tuesday of every September by the Queen, riding the opulent Golden Coach—led by a team of eight horses, in the company of as many resplendently liveried royal grooms, along with military escorts and marching bands—from Paleis Noordeinde (above) into the vast courtyard fronting the *Ridderzaal*, or Knights' Hall. With the look of a Romanesque church, the Ridderzaal was built by Count Floris V more than seven centuries ago, restored at the turn of the present century, and is where both the First and Second Chambers of the States General join forces, at each Official Opening, to hear the Speech from the Throne. Indeed, the Throne is a permanent fixture of the barrel-vaulted room, as are flags of the twelve Dutch provinces, and stained-glass coats-of-arms of major cities. Inspection is undertaken on frequently departing guided tours, which open with a slide show as orientation and usually include a peek at one of the houses of the States General.

Mauritshaus Museum (a.k.a. Koninklijk Kabinet van Schildernijen, or Royal Cabinet of Paintings, part of the Binnenhof complex and entered opposite the Hofvijver) occupies an absolute treasure of a Baroque palace—originally home to the *bon vivant*, seventeenth-century count whose name it takes, and was reopened in 1987 by Queen Beatrix after an extensive five-year restoration, during which some of the paintings were on view in Washington's National Gallery of Art and Fort Worth's Kimball Art Museum. On display is one of the choicer of the smaller European collections. You find, when you return to The Hague, that priority is accorded to a revisit to the Mauritshaus. How could it be otherwise? This house, built during Holland's Golden Age, is the perfect environment for a presentation celebrating that era. There are just 15 galleries divided evenly between two floors. The proportion of paintings in the Mauritshuis that you will have seen reproduced is surely one of the highest such of any museum. By that I mean Vermeer's *Head of a Girl*, blue turbaned, with a dangling pearl earring; that same artist's serene *View of Delft*; Hals's *Head of a Child*—smiling happily, long haired, and white collared; Avercamp's *Skaters* enjoying themselves on a frozen village pond; Salomon van Ruysdael's *River Landscape*; Gerard Terborch's *Mother and Daughter*, the former combing the latter's hair; Jan Steen's *A Merry Company*—typically

Steen-convivial—and that same master's ermine-robed *Girl Eating Oysters*; a near-geometric De Hooch courtyard; and a representative Emanuel de Witte church interior. And Rembrandts! There are no less than 16—*The Two Negroes, Dr. Tulp's Anatomy Lesson, David and Saul*, among them, as are three incisive self-portraits—youthful, middle years (wearing a big hat and an earring), and older. Flemings—a grand gent and an equally grand lady as portrayed by Van Dyck; Ruben's *Ascension* and an extraordinary Rubens-Brueghel collaboration, *Adam and Eve*; and a Teniers country-inn interior—are on view, too. Earlier Flemish Primitives leave indelible impressions—Memling's *Head of a Man* and Van der Weyden's *Descent From the Cross*, among them. There are likenesses of Queen Jane Seymour and other riveting portraits painted in England by Holbein, not to mention works by Dutchmen whose names may not be so familiar but whose art is sublime—Pieter Saenredam, Thomas de Keyser, Pieter Claesz, Adriaen van Ostade, and Gerard Dou—to name a handful.

Gemeentemuseum (Stadhouderslaan 41, a tram or taxi ride from the center) is The Hague's superlative Municipal Museum, quartered in a smashing Art Deco building to designs of architect H. P. Berlage, completed in 1935, with the careful brickwork of its asymmetrical exterior quite as noteworthy as the three-story-high entrance hall, dramatically scaled and lighted by its original fixtures, with both walls and floors tile accented. The collection is a marvelously mixed bag. If you enthuse over Dutch artist Piet Mondriaan's geometric compositions, you are in for a treat: The Gemeente has the biggest collection of his works extant. But the Dutch Impressionist Jongkind and the French Impressionist Monet are on hand, too, as are the Spaniard Picasso, the German Kirchner, and the Austrian Egon Schiele. Decorative arts are at their best in period rooms—an eighteenth-century salon, with superb stuccowork: Art Nouveau dining room; and clean-lined and color-drenched 1917 bedroom. The costume collection opens, not inappropriately, with Rococo underwear and continues on a chronological survey, through the oft-cumbersome nineteenth century, beyond to the amusing twenties, and into our own era, concluding with an exhibit labeled *Boy and Girl in Punk Gear 1981–1984* that is nothing if not a crowd-stopper. There's a restaurant, an interesting shop, and two adjacent museums—relatively recently opened—that may or may not interest you: one, called *Museon*, is a survey of world cultures and customs, presented World's Fair style in a Buck Rogers setting, and the other, also up to the minute, is called *Omniversum*; it presents planetarium-type programs, focusing on space travel and astronomy.

Prins Willem V Gallery (a.k.a. Schilderijengalerij Prins Willem V, Buitenhof 35) is a delightful throwback to the eighteenth century. The public museum was a rarity then, and in those instances when paintings were collected and displayed, usually by royalty in family palaces, every bit of wall space was utilized; the more paintings, the merrier. The Prins Willem Gallery, named for its Rococo-era founder, exhibits his collection quite as he must have, in an up-a-flight salon of an eighteenth-century mansion. You must look carefully to locate such standouts as Rembrandt's *A Bearded Man*; Rubens's portraits of both Helene Fourment and Isabella Brant, Jan Steen's *The Doctor's Visit*, as well as *As the Old Sing, So Twitter the Young*, Gerard Dou's *Young Woman Holding a Lamp*, Van Dyck's *Portrait of Quintijn Simons*, Adriaen van Ostade's *The Scholar*, and Paulus Potter's *A Bearhunt*.

Historisch Museum (Korte Vijverberg, at the square called Tournooiveld) is housed in the striking Baroque palace, St. Sabastiaandoelen by name, that had been home to the Gemeentemuseum (above) before it moved to its current building half a century back. In late 1986, the History Department of the Gemeente—to gain breathing space—was moved to a smartly refurbished and restored St. Sabastiaandoelen, the better to do justice to its extensive holdings. You want to see this landmark building, as well as its exhibits—paintings and silver, ceremonial crystal and weathered documents, maps and memorials. Special.

Rijksmuseum H. W. Mesdag (Laan van Meerdervoort 7) is an underappreciated gallery of nineteenth-century painting, some of it by the local painter whose name it takes and by fellow artists of The Hague school. But there's a kicker: work by their French contemporaries, as well. By that I mean such stellar masters as Delacroix, Millet, Rousseau, and my favorites of this period—Corot, Courbet, and Daubigny.

Rijksmuseum Meermanno-Westreenianum (Princessegracht 30, and, like the Mesdag, above, nationally operated) constitutes the collection of a local baron, amassed in the late eighteenth and early nineteenth centuries, with the setting a substantial seventeenth-century mansion. To see are antiquities—mostly Greek, Roman, and Egyptian and a brilliant cache of illuminated manuscripts going back as far as fifteen centuries. Special.

Rijksmuseum Gevangenpoort (Buitenhof 33): Instruments of torture are not everyone's idea of diversion. But the Gevangenpoort—housed, as its name indicates, in a city gatehouse that served as medieval jail—has architecture (a step-gabled Renaissance structure) in its favor, as well as paintings and prints whose subject matter is the dispensation of justice in centuries past; these complement the gruesome tools of torture.

Panorama Mesdag (Zeestraat 65) was painted in 1881 by the same H. W. Mesdag whose name is given to the Mesdag Museum (above). It's one of the last surviving panorama paintings (there's another in Lucerne—see *Switzerland At Its Best*), has Scheveningen—its beach, fishing boats, sand dunes and the sea beyond as its subject—is 394 feet in circumference and 46 feet high, with a surface of 18,000 square feet, and, withal, is not incapable of inducing yawns among viewers.

Scheveningen Museum (Neptunusstraat 92) leads at least one visitor to believe that the Scheveningen of yore might have been more appealing than that of today. The old fishing village comes to life by means of paintings and antique photos, fishing gear and model boats, villagers' costumes, and a slide show.

Vredespaleis (a.k.a. Peace Palace, Carnegieplein). One need
not enthuse over the esthetics of this heavy-handed, mock
Renaissance pile—its many-turreted clock tower is a landmark of The Hague—to appreciate that benefactor Andrew
Carnegie could not have subsidized a comparable building
today for the one and a half million dollars the Peace Palace
cost, when it went up in the early years of this century to
designs, at once ostentatious and overblown, of a French architect who won an international competition. Not unlike interiors of the UN headquarters in New York, art and artifacts
are contributions of various nations (a meeting room with
Japanese embroidered silk surfacing walls is possibly the most
successful). Judges of the International Court of Justice—15
from as many countries, with terms of nine years—deliberate
in the Grote Zaal, or Great Hall of Justice, its walls part
paneled and with massive stained-glass windows. There are
satellite courtrooms and meeting rooms, a ceremonial staircase that could be out of a Graustarkia movie filmed in the
forties, and ballroom-size corridors vaulted in the manner of
Romanesque cloisters that are a veritable quarry of marble.

Madurodam (Haringkade 175): Time was, not so many years
back, when KLM Royal Dutch Airlines had a spacious New
York ticket office at the corner of Fifth Avenue and Forty-ninth
Street, and powers that be at Madurodam—an animated scale
model of a Dutch town that packs in 1.2 million visitors per
year—would fly sections of their exhibit (via KLM, of course)
for display in the big corner window, over the Christmas season. Over a period of several years, I was able to see a fair
portion of the village on my side of the Atlantic. Alas, KLM
has moved east to another Manhattan location, and Madurodam stays put. Nowadays, you must go to *it*. The visitor's
route embraces two miles of traditional architecture and landmark buildings from throughout the Netherlands. There's action, too: Trains chug, planes taxi, ships tie up, and the
Queen's Golden Coach leads a procession to The Hague's
Binnenhof. After dark, illumination is provided by 50,000 tiny
lamps, and you may take in the scene from terraces and cafè-
restaurants. If all of this sounds too commercial, be advised

that profit after costs goes to charity and that Queen Beatrix, who opened Madurodam, as a princess in 1952—is today its patron.

SETTLING IN

Des Indes Hotel (Lange Voorhout 54; Phone 46-95-53): Location and environment should assure a hotel of success—but not necessarily. The Des Indes, occupying what was built in 1870 as a nobleman's mansion—splendid neoclassic, pedimented and with a balustrade extending the breadth of its second floor—on the most beautiful and fashionable street in town, has known downs, as well as ups, since a prince of the Royal House opened it as a hotel in 1881. Following a 1970s visit, I wrote in my *Cue* magazine column that it was "not aging nearly as gracefully as I had hoped." There were fears, at that time, that the owning Dutch Government might turn it into a ministry. It closed briefly and in 1979 was sold to Crest Hotels, a British chain whose expertise had been with first-class rather than luxury-category houses. No matter. The Crest people hired the same architect responsible for the extensive refurbishing of London's landmark Ritz, and the Des Indes was set to rights in the course of a costly restoration in the grand style of the Belle Époque era when it initially flourished. The high-ceilinged main-floor lounge—for long one of The Hague's more opulent public spaces—is again a congregating spot for locals, as well as guests, who meet over morning coffee, drinks, and afternoon tea. The cocktail lounge is at once cozy and luxurious. The first meal of the day is served in the Netherlands' handsomest breakfast room, not buffet style but by pretty waitresses who smilingly bring whatever you like—including eggs and bacon prepared to order—from an extensive, all-inclusive, one-price menu. Private party rooms—including that named in memory of prima ballerina Anna Pavlova, who died in the Des Indes after a 1931 performance—are lovely; most are on the second floor and constitute the Sunday venue for what has to be the most festive champagne brunch in the kingdom. Le Restaurant (evaluated in a later paragraph) is an all-city leader. There are just 77 bedrooms and suites, the lot of them tastefully traditional (with the exception of a smashingly modern rooftop suite) and with excellent baths. Best of all is service. Genial General Manager B. E. N. Felix greets guests, early breakfast through late evening, and his staff—reception through room service— is cordial and proficient. Along with the Keizerskroon in Apeldoorn (Chapter 11), the Des Indes is, in my experience, the best operated hotel in Holland. *Luxury.*

Corona Hotel (Buitenhof 40; Phone 63-79-30) is a gracious, heart-of-town old-timer, smartly updated, with just over two dozen rooms (those I have inspected are Louis XVI in style, pastel hued, and handsome), a competent terraced restaurant, popular sidewalk café, crackerjack management, and the same ownership as that of the excellent De l'Europe Hotel in Amsterdam (Chapter 2). *First Class.*

Sofitel Den Haag Hotel (Koningin Julianaplein 35; Phone 81-49-01) is the boldly contemporary structure, to your right, that you can't help but notice as you exit Centraal Station, with which it's connected by means of a shopping mall. Those of the 143 rooms and suites I have inspected are accented in tones of nubby brown, pastels, or plaids and have good baths. I like the convenience of ice machines on every floor, not to mention the big bar (you sink into deep leather chairs); the smart restaurant (evaluated on a later page), whose menu is the genuine French article; a kind management; and smiling staff. A link of France's Sofitel chain. *Luxury.*

Parkhotel de Zalm (Molenstraat 33; Phone 62-43-71) is at once supercentral—edging the pedestrian shopping zone—and attractively traditional in public spaces, which include a zippy bar. Those of the 143 rooms I have inspected vary in size, from a quite-small single to a generous twin, with those to aim for overlooking the park edging Paleis Nordeinde, housing the Queen's offices. Breakfast only. *First Class.*

Central Hotel (Spui; Phone 62-53-24) is up-to-date (it opened in 1987), aptly titled (it's heart of town, next to the also-recent concert hall), and full facility. There are 162 nicely equipped rooms with both bath and shower, à la carte House of Lords Restaurant, moderate price Brasserie, cocktail lounge, terraced café, and sauna-gym. A link of the French-origin PLM-Etap chain. *First Class.*

Paleis Hotel (Molenstraat 26; Phone 62-46-21), not unlike Parkhotel de Zalm (above), has rooms overlooking Paleis Nordeinde and its park; of the 26 in this house, they're the ones to aim for—contemporary and with good baths. Breakfast only. *Moderate.*

Promenade Hotel (Van Stolkweg 1; Phone 52-51-61—away from the center, edging a park about midway between the Netherlands Congress Center and Madurodam): The Promenade is convenient for travelers with cars or attending conventions nearby. And it is popular, management advises me, with foreign delegations on missions to The Hague, in part because, given its isolated situation, security arrangements can be tight. The look—in the rambling lobby and adjacent lounge (for coffee, tea, and drinks)—is clean-lined contemporary, with considerable work (paintings and graphics) by modern Dutch artists. Those of the 101 terraced rooms and suites I have inspected are thoughtfully equipped; rear rooms, facing the wooded park, are the preferred ones. There are three restaurants: elaborately decorated, à la carte La Cigogne, with French-inspired *nouvelle* cuisine, and moderate-tab Panorama Room—both off the lobby; and basement Bistro Flaneur. Member, Leading Hotels of the World. *Luxury.*

Bel Air Hotel (Johan de Wittlaan 30; Phone 50-20-21) is, like the Promenade (above), away from the core of town, near the Netherlands Congress Center and overlooking the Gemeentemuseum (above). This is a biggie, with 350 rooms (ask for one of the relatively recently renovated ones, beige toned and attractive), à la carte and casual restaurants, bar, indoor pool, welcome ice machines on alternate floors, and stationery in help-yourself racks—a novel touch, this—alongside elevators (of which there are four, more than in any other hotel in the Netherlands of which I'm aware and, for which, Bravo!). *First Class.*

Europa Crest Hotel (Zwolestraat 2, Scheveningen; Phone 51-26-51), though not in the same league as its sister-Crest, the Des Indes (above), is congenial, nicely located for a Scheveningen layover, and well equipped. This is a modern house with 174 rooms (including some set aside for nonsmokers and some snazzy, premium-rate Executive Rooms), indoor pool, sauna, gym, lively bar, and a restaurant later evaluated. Friendly. *First Class.*

Flora Beach Hotel (Gevers Deynootweg 63, Scheveningen; Phone 54-33-00) takes its name seriously; a packet of flower seeds is stapled to each copy of its brochure, and bowls of fresh flowers grace public spaces. There are 88 inviting rooms-cum-terrace—in tones of pink, yellow, and white— as well as a pair of restaurants and a bar. Staff is cordial, and you're near the beach. *First Class.*

Kurhaus Hotel (Gevers Deynootplein 30, Scheveningen; Phone 52-00-52), dating back a century, was relatively recently (albeit not entirely felicitously) restored. Elaborate brickwork of the massively domed facade happily remains, and the immense, up-a-flight Kursaal—the best part of the restoration with its delicately decorated, frescoed ceilings back to their original state—is the only requisite interior to be inspected in Scheveningen and an appropriate venue for frequent public concerts. Alas, the stadium-size Kursaal does not work well as the hotel's main restaurant (you help yourself to buffet breakfasts, lunches, and dinners from uncovered containers and, in my experience, the food has cooled by the time you get it to your table). The reception area, at street level, is low ceilinged and drab, the reception-concierge staff is unsmiling, and—a handful of deluxe suites excepted—the 254 rooms (at least those I have inspected or inhabited) are, though full-facility, hardly handsome, with small baths and (again, in my experience) with worn carpeting and upholstery. Gamblers will find the on-premises casino convenient. There's a costly à la carte restaurant and a pair of bars, the beach is out back and groups are a specialty. Operated by the German-origin Steigenberger chain. *Luxury.*

Badhotel (Gevers Deynootweg 15, Scheveningen; Phone 51-22-21) is a worth-knowing-about budget house, with 78 okay rooms with bath, dinner-only restaurant, bar, and near-the-beach location. Affiliated with Best Western. *Moderate.*

Carlton Beach Hotel (Gevers Deynootweg 201, Scheveningen; Phone 54-14-14) lures with a bold, futuristic facade and beachfront situation. But my inspection disappointed. Public spaces wanted sprucing up and smelled—as did corridors—of cooking. Although the hotel opened as recently as 1986, furniture in those of the 95 rooms I looked at was already showing signs of wear. Restaurants, bars, pool, sauna. *First Class.*

DAILY BREAD
Le Restaurant (Des Indes Hotel, Lange Voorhout 54; Phone 46-95-53): I enthuse, in an earlier paragraph, about Sunday champagne brunch at the Des Indes, grandly served by tail-coated and white-gloved waiters in the hotel's connected private-party salons, up a flight from the lobby. Le Restaurant, down a flight, has, to be sure, lower ceilings but is hardly less stylish. Nor is it without a skilled chef whose bent is classical French fare, albeit with surprise accents. The menu des gourmets—cheaper of two prix-fixe formulas presented daily—is good value and might open with a treat, cockaleekie soup out of Scotland; proceed with beef *médaillons*, lobster sauced; follow with nothing less than deep-fried *beignet d'ananas*, pineapple fritters, Gallic style; and end with coffee and a miniplatter of *petits-fours*. Fine wines. *First Class/Luxury.*

Le Relais (Sofitel Den Haag, Koningin Julianaplein 35; Phone 81-49-01): You're seated in plush, mauve armchairs in a flower-filled room, where, chances are good, the captain who takes your order will be French, as are the chefs. The à la carte is no-nonsense Gallic—*foie gras frais* and *soupe de poisson*, among openers; rosemary-scented lamb filets and *escalope de* *saumon* in a Noilly Prat sauce, among entrées; and a chariot of pastries, among desserts. With good-value prix-fixe menus, too. Well-selected French wines. And such tempters as smoked salmon, the house's *pâté*, seafood stew, and grilled lamb chops available in the bar-lounge. *Luxury/First Class*.

Saur (Lange Voorhaut 47; Phone 46-33-44) is a two-story proposition. The so-called Oesterbar (actually a sit-down eatery-cum-counter, with an abstract mural covering an entire wall) is on Main; the pricier, more formal restaurant proper is upstairs. The restaurant's prix-fixe might embrace lobster soup, sole specialties, sherbet, and coffee, with *bouillabaisse* available à la carte. The Oesterbar's prix-fixe, though cheaper, is tasty enough, perhaps opening with Lady Curzon soup or Ardennes ham, followed by an entrée of grilled salmon nicely garnished, with the day's dessert to conclude. Service is not memorably cordial. *First Class/Luxury*.

De Verliefde Kreeft (Bleijenburg 11; Phone 64-45-22), conveniently central and inviting, offers a quartet of prix-fixe menus and an extensive à la carte, with the thrust seafood. Cheapest of the menus—lobster bisque, trout amandine, and coffee—is supervalue. And no seafood à la carte is more tempting: Crab cocktail, lobster thermidor, oysters on the half-shell, and grilled sardines are among openers; Italy's *fritto misto* (a mixed seafood deep fry), France's mussels *à la marinière*, and Spain's *zarzuela de pescado* are among entrées. Friendly. *First Class*.

Royal (Lange Voorhout 44; Phone 60-07-72), with magnificently paneled quarters on the street level of a landmark Lange Voorhout mansion, is long on scene. Staff is sprightly and welcoming, but the kitchen appears tired. One has the feeling that when the present patrician clientele retires the Royal may follow suit. Stick to simpler entrées like roast chicken and plain ice cream for dessert. The Royal's version of the classic pear Belle Hélène, for example, is not worthy of that name. *First Class*.

Garoeda (Kneuterdijk 18; Phone 46-53-19): Book a window table (the view is agreeable) in the upstairs dining room and tuck into a multicourse *rijsttafel*. You will no doubt have sampled Indonesian fare before arriving in The Hague; if not, be advised that this Indonesian-inspired extravaganza consists of easily a score of piquant dishes, brought to the table *in toto*. You and your companions divvy them up. Waiters, Indonesian or of Indonesian origin at Garoeda, as at most such restaurants, will explain what's what; suffice to say here that you'll be served the skewered pork and chicken cubes known as *saté*, mussels, meatballs, fish preparations, warm and cold vegetable platters, and a selection of hot dunking sauces. Beer or white wine make ideal accompaniments. *First Class.*

Julien (Vos in Tuinstraat 2, with an entrance also on Jagerstraat, near the Des Indes Hotel; Phone 65-86-02), engagingly Art Nouveau in look, presents a prix-fixe at midday that includes three courses—soup or the house *pâté*, grilled fish or veal filet, and dessert, with bonuses: *two* glasses of wine, plus coffee. *First Class.*

't Goude Hooft (Groenmarkt 13; Phone 46-97-13) is at its best in warm weather when you have a table on the square, for coffee, ice cream, or a casual lunch. Inside, there's a café on main and a restaurant upstairs. Caveat: Stick to simple things; nothing complex or sauced. *Moderate.*

Pizzeria Biffi (Passage 17; Phone 46-06-05): For many Dutch diners, Italian cuisine means pizza—and pizza only. Biffi satisfies locals with no less than 24 species. *Moderate.*

Le Perroquet (Plein 12; Phone 63-97-86) is worth knowing about for a budget lunch any day. On Saturday—when the entire population of Dutch cities, The Hague included, appear to go shopping en masse—it is strategically enough located, particularly if you take a table facing the square to take in the frenetic scene. The low-tab prix-fixe menu—tomato soup (at which the Dutch invariably excel), *entrecôte/frites*, and ice cream—is tasty. Snappy service. *Moderate.*

Prins Taverne (Noordeinde at Stille Verkade) is seventeenth century, brimming with atmosphere, in a lovely part of town. Have a beer. *Moderate.*

Vroom & Dreesmann (Grotemarktstraat): The third floor of this leading department store is where you'll find a cafeteria whose specialties are American—ribeye steak and chicken pot pie, among them. *Moderate.*

La Galleria (Gevers Deynootplein 120, Scheveningen; Phone 52-11-56) is one of a number of restaurants lining the unattractive modern square fronting the Kurhaus Hotel (above) and marring the perspective of its facade. It's agreeable enough within, however, and a dinner—*antipasto misto* (with imported Italian sausages), the eggdrop soup called *straciatella* or *spaghetti alla vongole,* followed by *veal scaloppine* or *bistecca Fiorentina*—can be satisfactory, if hardly distinguished. *First Class.*

Ducdalf (Dr. Lelykade 5, Scheveningen; Phone 55-76-92), on the harbor, is indicated when you crave a no-nonsense seafood repast, opening with Zeeland oysters or shrimp cocktail, preparatory to filet of sole, simply grilled, or a whole lobster. *First Class.*

New Orleans Ribhouse (Europa Crest Hotel, Zwolsestraat 7, Scheveningen; Phone 51-26-51): In their well-meaning attempt to create a southern-style restaurant with a nineteenth-century flavor, designers of this otherwise exemplary eatery positioned a life-size statue of a subservient-appearing, bowing black man—a racially stereotypical Uncle Tom—at the entrance. My complaint to management brought a reply of surprise, and I was advised that a representative of the U.S. Embassy, attending the official opening, made no comment at all on the offensive statue. Withal, I hope my objection herewith will lead to its removal. All of this is by way of introduction to a restaurant whose specialty is U.S.-imported prime beef and whose desserts include a trolley full of fruit tarts and cakes, not easily come by in Dutch restaurants. Pleasant service. *First Class.*

SOUND OF MUSIC
Het Muziektheater (Spui)—The Hague's answer to Amsterdam's similarly named, also-modern performing arts center— opened in 1987 and shelters a pair of auditoriums: one, with a capacity of a thousand, that's home base for the esteemed Netherlands Dance Theater, and the other, with a capacity of 1,500, for concerts of The Hague's celebrated symphony, Het Residentie Orkest. Programs are listed in Den Haag Info, a monthly what's-on giveaway obtainable from your hotel concierge or the tourist office (below).

Nederlands Congresgebouw (Churchillplein, north of the center), besides serving primarily as a convention hall, is home to performances of the Nederlands Kamerorkest—a leading chamber orchestra—and of other musical groups.

Koninklijke Schouburg (Koorte Voorhout) translates as Royal Theater, and it's a jewel out of the eighteenth century— among Holland's loveliest—with its stock in trade plays, performed of course in Dutch, but with other attractions as well, including opera.

Theater Diligentia (Lange Voorhout) is still another handsome house out of the eighteenth century; drama, mostly, but other presentations, too.

SHOPPER'S THE HAGUE
This is a super shopping city. The No. 1 department store, *Bijenkorf*, which you no doubt know from Amsterdam and possibly Rotterdam, occupies an uncommonly handsome Bauhaus-era building of red brick and glass, on Grotemarktstraat. You'll find an excellent chocolate department on Main, along with a casual café and men's clothing on One, women's duds on Two, La Ruche Restaurant—self-service and reliable—on Three, and housewares and china on Four. *Vroom Dreesmann*, part of a ubiquitous department store chain, is

just opposite, in a two-building complex, with a super supermarket in the basement; men's clothing, chocolates, and
a bakery on Main, women's clothing on Two, and a restaurant
(recommended above) on Three. *Hema*, another chain neighbor, has a budget-priced cafeteria and excellent packaged
cookies, crackers, and chocolates, as well as clothing, toiletries, and the like.

Specialty Shops: Maison de Bonneterie, quite the most elegant
of the specialty chains and with shops in Amsterdam and
Rotterdam, is on Gravenstraat; as in the other cities, the main
floor is illuminated by crystal chandeliers, and both men's
and women's clothing departments are smartly conservative.
Also on Gravenstraat is a nineteenth-century shopping ar-
cade, on the order of the Galleria in Milan (see *Italy At Its
Best*) that warrants a walk-through. Paleispromenade, an ex-
tension of the street called Noordeinde—lined with Art Nouveau and Art Deco buildings—has such leading stores as *Focke
& Meltzer* (a chain with porcelain and crystal specialties), *Max
Mara* (women's clothes), *Van Gils* (men's clothes), and *Van
Weilik* (jewelry, watches, and the decorations the Queen
awards). Venestraat, off Groenmarkt, is the site of *Heinrich*
(china—Delft and imported), *Zumpolle* (leatherwear and luggage), *Bally* (shoes), *Douglas* (perfumes), and *Peek & Cloppenburg* (a mid-category clothing chain). *Denneweg* is Antiques
Row, with such shops as *M. M. Antiquities* (furniture and
silver), *Persepolis* (small objects), *Het Hollandsche Huisje* (tiles,
copper), and *Wennekes* (prints and engravings). Look also at
shops on Spuistraat, Kortepoten, Hoogstraat, and Oude Mol-
straat, bearing in mind also that *Babylon* is the name of a two-
level, 60-store shopping center adjacent to Centraal Station,
with its *Drugstore* complex (fancy groceries, restaurants, boutiques) star of the show and a *Mister Minit*, for repairs to your
shoes.

INCIDENTAL INTELLIGENCE

Schiphol Line is an express rail service linking Centraal Station
with Schiphol International Airport in 30 minutes; frequent

departures. *Hoek van Holland*, from which ships sail to Harwich in England, is 45 minutes by train. *Further information*: VVV The Hague-Scheveningen, Centraal Station and Zwolsestraat in Scheveningen.

11

Het Loo Palace
Jewel of Apeldoorn

BACKGROUND BRIEFING

European monarchies have never lacked the ability to project images of grandeur and majesty. The Baroque era's Versailles was the model for counterparts ranging from Madrid's Palacio Real to Munich's Schloss Nymphenburg, the style invariably classic and the design based on a central pavilion with flanking wings enclosing stylized gardens.

The palace vogue spread even to the Netherlands which, in the seventeenth century, still was not a proper kingdom, but rather a federation of provinces ruled by more egalitarian heads of state called stadholders. What happened, though, was that a mid-seventeenth century stadholder—Prince William III of Orange, whose mother (Mary, eldest daughter of the beheaded Charles I) and wife (another Mary, elder daughter of the deposed James II) were both English princesses—was, in 1689, offered the English crown, to rule jointly with his queen, who became Mary II.

The new sovereign—reigning north of the Channel and remaining stadholder in his homeland, as well—was a keen hunter, in the fashion of the period. By the time he assumed the crown, he had begun building a hunting lodge near a twin-turreted, fifteenth-century castle called Oude Loo (still, incidentally, a royal retreat) at the northern edge of the east-central city of Apeldoorn. Indeed, by 1686, burgeoning Het Loo's central portion, or *corps de logis*, and its wings were completed, and its fountain- and sculpture-embellished gardens—based on the rigid symmetry of the era—had been planned, initially by a Dutch architect, Jacob Roman. Roman was succeeded by French Huguenot Daniel Marot, who immigrated to Holland with many other Protestants, after Louis XIV's revocation of the Edict of Nantes, and also designed the palatial Royal Library in The Hague (Chapter 10) and other buildings in that city and, it is believed, in Amsterdam. When Stadholder William became King William, achieving a kind of international celebrity, Het Loo became the subject of more attention. The king-stadholder and Queen Mary came to regard it as their favorite country residence, and for as long as William lived—until 1702—it was continuously embellished and refurbished.

Succeeding eighteenth-century stadholders, William IV and William V, retained Het Loo as a country seat, and so did nineteenth-century kings who followed them—another trio of Williams, designated the First, the Second, and the Third (this last not to be confused with the *original* William III, whom the Dutch, for clarity's sake, always refer to as King *Stadholder* William III).

The final King William's successor was the doughty, universally admired, long-reigning Queen Wilhelmina, who retired to Het Loo after abdicating in 1948; she was to be the last sovereign of the House of Orange-Nassau to inhabit Het Loo. Her daughter, Queen Juliana, preferred another country palace, Soesdijk, and Juliana's successor, Queen Beatrix, lives with Prince Claus and their sons at Ten Bosch Palace in The Hague. Beatrix's younger sister, Princess Margriet, followed her late grandmother at Het Loo from 1967 to 1975, before moving with her husband and children to a new house built on the grounds of the vast Het Loo estate.

Margriet's departure left the palace unoccupied for the first time in its long history. And so the Dutch Government, not without opposition—Holland is a country that, though genuinely fond of its royal family, still remains egalitarian—embarked on a long (seven years), costly (reportedly $40 million), and painstaking restoration. The goal was a national museum—the official designation today is Rijksmuseum Paleis Het Loo—which would delineate the history of the House of Orange-Nassau and its relationship with the nation. What it accomplishes, concurrently, is a celebration of the genius of seventeenth- and eighteenth-century art and architecture—the range, building and garden design through furniture and textiles, ceramics and glass, weaving and woodcarving, stuccowork and sculpture.

With the nineteenth and early twentieth centuries as well represented, Het Loo's interiors embrace the living quarters of the Dutch ruling house, William and Mary through Wilhelmina. No restoration of which I am aware, in any country, has been more meticulous or more authentic. Het Loo is a world-class achievement, of which the Netherlands may be proud.

ON SCENE
Lay of the Land: The palace is at the northern precincts of Apeldoorn, a substantial city (population is around 140,000) whose core is centered by *Deventerstraat* and an adjacent clutch of busy pedestrian streets, north of the train station on *Stationsplein.* You might want to pop inside the red-brick, cupola-topped *Raadhuis,* or city hall *(Raadhuisplein),* whose restoration, following World War II bombing, was completed in 1977, to see the main-floor wedding rooms and upstairs Council Chamber. *Historisch Museum Marialust* (in Verzetsstriidersпark) occupies a lovely early nineteenth-century house, with period rooms and a range of exhibits relating to the city's past; and *Apenheul* (J. C. Wilsonlaan 21, west of the center) is a zoolike compound chuckablock with resident monkeys, in the company of myriad Dutch youngsters befriending—or attempting to befriend—them.

Exploring the Palace: But all of the foregoing is incidental to the primary motivation for your visit: Rijksmuseum Paleis Het Loo, whose official address—Koninklijk (or Royal) Park—indicates its location in splendid grounds alongside a vast open-to-the-public nature reserve, eminently visitable, but only if you've time to spare after taking in exhibits of the detached royal stables, the palace proper, and the formal gardens entered from the rear of the palace. Plan a lunch pause either in the palace complex or at an Apeldoorn restaurant (see Daily Bread, below). Het Loo rates a full day of your itinerary. And note that you take yourself through the palace via self-guided tour, unless you opt to engage one of the corps of 150 specially trained volunteer guides—which I counsel; but you must reserve a guide in advance: phone 055-21-22-44.

The Royal Stables —gained by a walk from the main entrance, through a pretty and fairly long, tree-bordered *allée*—make for appropriate orientation. Rambling, turn-of-century, and with two spacious, high-ceilinged wings, the stable exhibits are at their best in the case of perfectly preserved royal coaches and carriages, even more romantic sleighs used by the reigning family, and, most amusing of the lot, wonderfully oversized automobiles, some a half-century old, which conveyed passengers from the palace on royal rambles through the countryside.

The Palace: Even the facade—plastered over in white as long ago as 1806 by Napoleon's brother Louis Napoleon, who was, for a period, Holland's king—has been restored; the original brick had remained in excellent condition. Within, as many as ten layers of paint were carefully removed from walls and ceilings to reveal, almost miraculously, centuries-old frescoes. But some of the interior has been left quite as it was, the better to reveal tastes and lifestyles of members of the house of Orange-Nassau during the period of their occupancy. Where actual contents, room by room, are not original or Crown-owned, they are appropriately aged and of the period.

Begin your visit with an introductory videofilm (it lasts 15 minutes, and there are English, French, German, and Dutch versions); take in courtyard exhibits—art and artifacts, paintings and porcelain, prints and pewter—associated with the palace; peep into the Netherlands Knighthood Museum, concentrating, then, on state rooms and the quarters of a succession of monarchs and their consorts, in the central pavilion—the so-called *corps de logis*—as well as both east and west wings.

There is an absolute smasher of a view of the gardens from the *Voorhuis,* or entrance hall—you peer through a gilded wrought-iron gate created by architect Daniel Marot (above) in the seventeenth century. The *Old Dining Room*—centered by a Delft-decorated mantel, its walls hung with Brussels tapestries—is lovely but not as grand as the *New Dining Room,* with its orginal Marot-coffered ceiling and gilt-capital columns, a dozen blue-damask-seated, seventeenth-century chairs, and William and Mary's coats of arms woven in tapestries.

The *chapel* is historically interesting in that it once had a special altar, properly Anglican, for the Anglican-reared Queen Mary, and it was—three centuries later—where Queen Wilhelmina, the last monarch to live in Het Loo, lay in state.

Grotezaal (a.k.a. Audientiezaal) translates as Great (or Audience) Hall. Call it what you will, this is Het Loo's grandest interior, designed by Marot, splendidly gilded, sculpted, mirrored, and frescoed, an appropriate environment for royal audiences, and, it turned out, for an abdication—that of King William I in 1840. Pause at the Resistance Table, to the left as you enter; Queen Wilhelmina arranged it—with moving mementoes of the valiant Dutch Resistance Movement of World War II. And it adjoins a grand staircase that will put London visitors in mind of that in St. James's Palace (see *Britain At Its Best*).

In the *Library,* Marot's sumptuous ceiling, a mix of mirrors and Baroque stuccowork, frames walls lined with reproductions of his original bookcases. The *Gallery*—not unlike long, narrow repositories of family paintings in many mansions of the period in a number of countries—is illuminated by immense crystal chandeliers; green damask walls are hung with superb portraits of Orange-Nassaus, particularly those of William and Mary by German-born, Dutch-trained Sir Godfrey Kneller, well known for his likenesses of English royals.

There is little doubt that for English-speaking visitors familiar enough with the history of the period (which led to the downfall in England of Catholic King James II and the ascent to the throne of the Dutch Protestant Prince Stadholder William and his wife, James II's elder Protestant daughter), the most significant Het Loo interiors are suites of the palace's builder and his wife. The *King Stadholder's Apartment* embraces a so-called Passage, with leather-surfaced walls, William's so-called Closet—intimate and where William relaxed in private—with walls of purple and scarlet damask, and his bedroom, centered by a spectacular blue-damask-covered state bed that is enclosed by a canopy of the same material, with walls of orange damask accented in blue (the Orange-Nassau colors). Complementing the bed are a smasher of a gilt-trimmed marble fireplace, a suite of rare, German-made silver furniture, and companion portraits of William and Mary, each resplendent in state robes, by Jean-Henri Brandon. *Queen Mary's* suite comprises a tapestried dressing room; a charming closet, or boudoir—a felicitous mix of red-and-green damask, gilded marble fireplace, and English-imported accessories; and a bedroom—in my view, the No. 1 interior of the palace. Its state bed, framed by a canopy whose patterned brown-and-green damask is the ideal foil for similar-hued fabric surfacing the walls, one of which is punctuated by a splendid marble mantel, flanked with portraits of Mary and her co-ruler, William, by Dutch-born Sir Peter Lely, who made his mark as a painter of voluptuous English ladies.

But there's more: Prince William IV's porcelain and painting-filled closet; Prince William V's bedroom, with a family portrait by Tischbein and a chandelier that was a gift of Prussia's Frederick the Great; nineteenth-century King William I's Empire-style bedroom, with chairs from the reign of King Louis Napoleon; King William II's room, heavily Gothic Revival; Queen Sophie's Room (highlighted by a portrait of her by the same Winterhalter who painted France's Empress Eugénie and Britain's Victoria); the sitting room of Queen Emma (second wife of King William III and delightfully cluttered late-Victorian style); the hunting room of Queen Wilhelmina's consort, Prince Hendrick, its walls busy with trophies and photos of royal hunting parties; and, surely the most moving of the later rooms, Wilhelmina's sitting room-study, with a bust of her sixteenth-century ancestor, William the Silent, and portraits of King Stadholder William III by German-born Casper Netscher (noted for his Dutch work and a portraitist, as well, of William's wife, Queen Mary) and of King William II by America's John Singleton Copley, long resident in England.

The Garden: You have only to buy an aerial-view postcard of the Het Loo complex to appreciate the strikingly detailed symmetry of the palace gardens—contemporarily—and then to look at engravings of the garden, circa 1700, to marvel at how closely the new resembles the old. King Louis Napoleon altered not only the facade of the palace during his reign, but the look of the garden, changing its French-origin formal design to that of a landscaped park more common to Britain than the Continent. Het Loo's restorers put things to rights, thanks to fortuitous finds that occurred in the course of excavations preparatory to refurbishing the palace, including fragments of decorative vases and sculptures and bits of original pipes through which water—to power the garden's fountains—had flowed. And archives contained prints, watercolors, and other documentation.

The gardens—*De Tuinen*, in Dutch—are planted with more than 200 species of plants that were contemporary with the original garden. Their organization follows the crystal-clear logic of Baroque-era designers. Edging the rear wall of the palace are the King's Gardens (on the west side) and the Queen's Gardens (on the east). These plots, with the monumental Dolphin fountain separating them, give onto the Upper Garden, with four intricately designed beds to the west (entered by the spherical fountain of the Celestial Sphere and edged by the monumental Narcissus Fountain) and another four to the east (based on the also-spherical Fountain of the Terrestrial Globe and edged by the monumental Arion Fountain). The Lower Garden, most distant from the Palace, is based on the King's Fountain (flanked by a pair of Roman emperors' busts and backed by a semicircular colonnade). I cite only the principal landmarks; the fun of a garden stroll is to make relatively minor discoveries—man-made, as well as natural—as you amble about.

ON SCENE

De Keizerskroon Hotel (Konigstraat 7; Phone 21-77-44) is a relatively recent successor to a much older Keizerskroon, proud of a long association with the occupants of Het Loo, its near neighbor. Princess Margriet, the last royal resident of the palace, dedicated the new Keizerskroon in 1980. Owner-general manager Hans van Eenennaam-Beck, invariably on scene from breakfast through nightcaps at the convivial bar, runs a lovely house. Those of the 67 rooms and suites that I have either inhabited or inspected are good sized and well equipped. Public spaces extend from a fabulous, top-floor swimming pool (with a glass wall facing toward the palace and an adjacent sauna) to a capacious lobby, with a pair of restaurants (one later evaluated) and the bar, where guests and locals invariably chat each other up. The look throughout agreeably mixes traditional with contemporary, and the staff, again throughout, is skilled and smiling. In my view—along with The Hague's Des Indes—this is the best operated hotel in the Netherlands. *Luxury.*

Nieland Hotel (Soerenseweg 73; Phone 55-73-12) comprises a pair of rambling, turn-of-century houses that, within, have been competently modernized. There are 40 neat, clean-lined rooms, with either tubs or showers in their baths, comfortable lobby, good-sized bar, convenient restaurant, and, if you please, a bowling alley. Not far from the palace. *Moderate.*

Hotel Apeldoorn (J. C. Wilslaan 200; Phone 55-08-55) is a 50-room-cum-bath house, low slung and functional-modern, with a restaurant, bar, and terrace that's pleasant in warm weather. Location is just out of town, edging the palace's park. *Moderate.*

Bloemink Hotel (Loolaan 56; Phone 21-41-41) is convenient to the palace, with a main building (preferred) and annex and close to 90 rooms, as well as an indoor pool/sauna, terraced café-bar, and a restaurant whose food odors pervaded the lobby, which appeared shabby and in need of renovation when I inspected. *Moderate/First Class.*

DAILY BREAD
De Echoput (Amersfoortseweg 86; Phone 05749-248): The setting, at first glance, is unexceptional: a contemporary, two-story brick building, with a steep pitch to the red-tiled roof. In the nonsummer months, you might open with an aperitif before the open fire in the brick-walled lounge, moving over a low partition to lunch or dine in a space that is not overly large and anything but pretentious, but with tables nicely set and accessorized and lighted by hurricane lamps. In warm weather, you may reserve alongside the carp pond in the garden. Chances are the host Peter Klosse will have greeted you, suggested that you order *champignons Dordogne*—an utterly irresistible beer-batter mushroom dip that may well be the single most habit-forming dish in the Netherlands—to accompany your drink, and taken your order. There are four prix-fixe menus, the four-course Alliance the best bet. And there is an extensive à la carte. The thrust of Echoput's kitchen is—as Mr. Klosse puts it, and with accuracy—*"nouvelle* with a solid French classical base." You might commence with a prune marmalade-accented veal terrine and continue with *consommé* on which tiny stuffed *crêpes* float; have, as your fish course, *escalope* of salmon, expertly sauced, before tackling roast veal, tarragon flavored and deliciously garnished; or, if it's the season, try one of Echoput's celebrated game dishes, perhaps a sampler embracing teal, duck, watersnipe, and baby venison. Desserts appear in variety, but you want to select pastry. Satisfactory as this last may be, I wager you will gobble up the tiny *petits-fours* that accompany coffee. As for wine, well, the cellar is an all-Holland leader; ask Mr. Klosse or the captain for suggestions, bearing in mind the rich store of Bordeaux. In my view, one of Holland's best restaurants. Member Relais et Châteaux. *Luxury.*

Le Petit Prince (De Keizerskroon Hotel, Konigstraat 7; Phone 21-77-44): Chippendale-style armchairs surround tables illuminated by black candles in this small, smart restaurant, expertly staffed, chef to captains. Soups are either delicate (a bracing *consommé*) or rich (superb lobster bisque), but salads—with *nouvelle* twists—make nice openers, too. The *carré d'agneau*, French-style roast lamb, is first rate; ditto *canard sauvage*, wild duck, during the game season. Filet of beef is as tasty as you'll find in Holland; ditto, for that matter, filet of sole. French wines are among the most reasonably priced of any restaurant I know in Holland—and well selected. *Luxury*. (And bear in mind that the Keizerskroon's second restaurant, *Keizersgrill*, is a good bet for a casual meal—an omelet or a burger, perhaps—and is *Moderate*.)

De Raadskelder (Raadhuisplein; Phone 22-18-22): If it is not as atmospheric as some city-hall cellar-restaurants (there are, to be sure, beamed ceilings and ladderback chairs), Apeldoorn's entry in this league is agreeable for a meal built around fish, its specialty: sole, of course, but the catch of the day, as well. And while you're on scene, have a look at the seat of municipal government, upstairs. *First Class*.

Poppe (Paslaan 7; Phone 22-32-86) is a heart-of-town favorite with locals. Non-Gallic name notwithstanding, this pert and pretty mod-look spot makes a point of French-accented fare. Order from the prix-fixe or from blackboard-listed *plats du jour*, with onion soup and *coq au vin* tasty possibilities. *First Class*.

Hema (Hoofdstraat 77): Eateries in this all-Holland department-store chain are invariably reliable for on-the-run lunches, morning coffee, or a tea break mid-afternoon. This one's big, bright, and self-service. *Moderate*.

Rijksmuseum Paleis Het Loo Restaurants (Koninklijk Park): Take your choice of the attractive *Café* in the Royal Stables complex, detached from the palace proper, or, my preference, the *Restaurant* proper in what was originally the theater of the palace—vast and splendidly scaled, with leather-surfaced walls, a ceiling punctuated by a trio of huge crystal chandeliers, and a terrace whose tables give onto the King's Garden. Both are self-service (soups, sandwiches, salads, sweets, as well as hot dishes midday) and *Moderate*.

De Klepperman (Oosterdorpstraat 11, in Hoevelaken, 21 miles northwest of Apeldoorn; Phone 34120) is as much posh hotel (those of the 37 contemporary-decor rooms I have inspected are attractive, albeit with the smallest bars of soap in their baths of any non-Moderate category hotel I know in Holland) as trendy restaurant. The dining room occupies a deftly restyled A-frame barn out of the last century. You sit at tables dressed in pink linen, ordering from a prix-fixe menu or the tempting à la carte, with the range warm mussel salad, goose liver *pâté* laced with Port, or velvety shrimp bisque. Grilled salmon is served with a delicate champagne sauce. If game is in season, consider roast pheasant or shoulder of hare in a piquant sauce. Beef is reliable; ditto, desserts which can even include rare-in-Holland pastries. And the staff is swift and cordial. Both the hotel and the restaurant are *Luxury*.

SOUND OF MUSIC
Cultureel Centrum Orpheus (Churchillplein) is Apeldoorn's municipal theater complex; the tourist office (below) will apprise you of the schedules of concerts, opera, and dance.

INCIDENTAL INTELLIGENCE

Deventer (Chapter 8), Arnhem (Chapter 4), and Nijmegen (Chapter 17) are nearby. *Further information:* VVV Apeldoorn; Stationsplein 6.

12

Kampen
A Pause on the IJssel

BACKGROUND BRIEFING
Small, in the case of certain Dutch towns, can mean charming. In the case of placid Kampen, a grid-shaped rectangle alongside the IJssel River—just east of IJsselmeer, the vast lake created from the old Zuider Zee by the construction of a dam, half a century back—roots with the past are hardly tenuous.

This is a community with a seven-century history, which grew rich as a member of the aggressively mercantile Hanseatic League in the fifteenth century and stayed so as a Zuider Zee port until the creation of IJsselmeer. Remaining today are just enough monuments of its prosperous past to make a brief visit enjoyable.

ON SCENE
Lay of the Land: Weathered maps of long-ago Kampen in its municipal museum make clear that the town's contours, with principal thoroughfares paralleling the *IJssel River*, have not changed over long centuries. A fortress on the right bank—now, as then, connected with the town proper by a solitary bridge, *IJssel Brug*—has long since been succeeded by the railway station, on *Stationsplein*. Cross the bridge, and the first street you encounter is hotel-edged *IJsselkade*, straddling the

river. A network of streets running perpendicular to it—*Vis-poort*, *Melksteeg*, and *Dwarsteeg*, the most central—lead to *Oudestraat*, the town's monument-, shop-, and restaurant-lined main street.

Oude Raadhuis (Oudestraat 133): Kampen's mid-sixteenth century Old Town Hall is not, to be sure, very large. Up you go, though, to the second floor, to feast your eyes on its richly Renaissance-era Schepenzaal, surely the definitive Dutch courtroom; I defy you to come across another in the kingdom quite so lavishly decorated. The stone fireplace with caryatids supporting no less than four sculpted tiers, under a likeness of Holy Roman Emperor Charles V, is unparalleled in the Netherlands and the work of an underappreciated Utrecht-origin artist named Colijn de Nole. Observe, as well, the pair of carved wood magistrates' benches, richly Baroque cupboards in which the town's treasures were stored, and at the end of the room—a screen that divides the space into two sections, one of them the stunning area that was for long the chamber of the Kampen Town Council. Move along to the Raadzaal of the adjacent Nieuwe Raddhuis, the new Town Hall, to inspect a series of royal portraits. Standout, hands down, is a Tischbein of William IV, but there are, as well, a stirring likeness of the stadholder who became England's King William III and paintings of four recent queens: Emma, her daughter Wilhelmina, Wilhelmina's daughter Juliana, and Juliana's daughter—the reigning Beatrix.

Stedelijk Museum (Oudestraat 158): Kampen's museum of history and art makes its home in Gotische Huis, a gabled medieval masterwork. I would like to be able to report to you that there are works on display by the Baroque-era painter Hendrik Avercamp—born a deaf-mute in Amsterdam, but raised and buried in Kampen—of bourgeois Hollanders in scenes of daily life, ice-skating, most notably. Alas, there are not. You will, however, find a skating scene, with Kampen the locale, by Barents Avercamp, Hendrik's nephew. There are a number of other paintings with local motifs, a lovely *Gezicht*—or view—of the town executed in 1654 by an artist called Bellekin, among them. And there's a collection of coins—minted several centuries back not only in Kampen, but in nearby Zwollen and Deventer—and silver from area churches.

A trio of gates are Kampen standouts; few towns so small are so well represented in this regard. *Koornmarktspoort's* steep-roofed central portion is flanked by a pair of conical towers; it is thirteenth century. *Broederpoort*, with an elaborately embellished, red-brick facade, rises half a dozen stories and is graced by a quartet of towers; it's a veritable minipalace, mostly seventeenth century, big enough to have housed the Stedelijk Museum until as recently as 1984. And turreted *Cellebroederspoort* is of Gothic origin with Renaissance restyling.

Bovenkerk and Buitenkerk, Kampen's principal historic churches, are so similarly named that they are often mistaken for each other by visitors. *Bovenkerk*, a.k.a. St. Nicholaas, is gigantic Gothic (it dates to the mid-fourteenth century). It contains a memorial to the painter Hendrik Avercamp and superb choir and pulpit, with its especial glory a dozen-plus chapels tucked into its apse. *Buitenkerk*—a.k.a. Onze Lieve Vrouwe, or Our Lady—is Gothic, as well, with the elongated windows of its nave and tower creating a pleasantly patterned facade. Do go in; the interior was restored in 1976.

SETTLING IN
Van Dijk Hotel (IJsselkade 30; Phone 14925) comprises a pair of contiguous riverfront houses, whose spanking white facades attract. Public spaces are elderly but cozy, and there are 30 rooms with bath; those I have inspected are satisfactory. The Van Dijk serves breakfast only, but its management owns *d'Oude Vismarkt Restaurant*, down the street at 45 IJsselkade (Phone 13490) and with traditional Dutch specialties. Both are *Moderate*.

d'Oude Brugge Hotel (IJsselkade 48; Phone 12645) occupies an aged brick house, with its restaurant (below) in glass-fronted riverside quarters. There are just 16 bath-equipped rooms and a bar-lounge. *Moderate.*

DAILY BREAD

Bottermarck (Broederstraat 23—a street perpendicular with Oudestraat, core of town; Phone 19542) is long on scene and welcoming, with hearty Dutch standbys—soups are good—on occasion, French accented. *First Class.*

d'Oude Brugge (IJsselkade 48; Phone 12645): The look is light and bright; you're in a glass-walled porch elevated enough to afford agreeable river views. Fish is the specialty. Order the day's catch à la carte or as part of a prix-fixe menu. *First Class.*

De IJssel (IJsselkade 59; Phone 12809) features a three-course menu—soup (hope that it's pea), entrée (hope that it's fish), and dessert (don't worry—it will be ice cream). *Moderate.*

INCIDENTAL INTELLIGENCE

The *MS Insula* makes river excursions in summer. *Further information:* VVV Kampen (alas, its brochures are in the Dutch language only, unless a translator has come aboard since my last visit), Oudestraat 85.

13

Leeuwarden
And a Friesland Sampler

BACKGROUND BRIEFING
Leeuwarden's location—and indeed that of the Province of Friesland, of which it is the capital and sole city of consequence—is at once its blessing and its bane. Tucked away in the remote northwest corner of the kingdom, with Amsterdam a three hours' train ride (a long distance in Holland) to the south, it is not always comfortable with strangers. And there are relatively few good places to stay and dine; you have the feeling that Frisians, by and large, are stay-at-homes and eat-at-homes.

Still, there are compensations. The countryside is placid and pretty, chockablock with cows (some 600,000—considerably more than there are Frisians), dotted with lakes, punctuated with villages in virtually any one of which you half expect to run into Hans Brinker, and with a craft tradition that is arguably the richest in Holland. The same isolation that has been a factor in the bucolic ambience of the province (Leeuwarden, though undeniably urban and architecturally distinguished, is hardly in competition with, say, Rotterdam) was responsible for the retention of a bona fide local language.

Though similar to Dutch, it is not a dialect; Frisian, if I may be technical, is a part of the West Germanic group of the

Germanic subfamily of the Indo-European cluster of languages. And a good number of Frisians—easily a couple of hundred thousand—speak it alongside of Dutch (they are both official languages). Like fellow Dutchmen, they are, as well, fluent in English (to which Frisian is said to be closer than any other tongue).

Apart geographically and linguistically, Friesland's early politics also bore a Frisian stamp. When, in 1579, it joined with the other Dutch provinces in the anti-Spanish Union of Utrecht, it insisted on continuing to appoint its own stadholders, or heads of state. This was the case well into the mid-eighteenth century when, in 1748, its stadholder, Prince William IV of Orange—as descendant of a long line of Oranges, starting with William the Silent in the sixteenth century—became sole and hereditary stadholder of the United Provinces, forerunner of the present monarchy. His descendants, upon establishment of the Kingdom of the Netherlands in the nineteenth century, came to constitute the Dutch Royal Family.

ON SCENE
Lay of the Land: A proper city since as long ago as 1435, when it was officially chartered, long-prosperous Leeuwarden (called *Ljouwert* in Frisian) may well be proud of a core as noteworthy for lovely townhouses as for felicitous public buildings, as well as impressive squares. Its historic center, enclosed by canals, is edged on the south by the railway terminal on *Stationsweg*, which gives onto *Zuiderplein*, a broad square with a statue of a Frisian cow dubbed *Us Mem* (Our Mother)—in recognition of the significance of dairying in the Leeuwarden economy. *Wirdumerdijk* leads into the heart of town: *Waagplein*, the square dominated by the sixteenth-century *Waag*, or weigh house. *Nieuwestad*—the main shopping street, with *Vroom & Dreesmann* and *Hema* department stores—runs west of Waagplein. *Weerd*, a short but smart thoroughfare dotted with antique shops, runs north from Waagplein to a trio of contiguous squares—*Raadhuisplein* (named for the early-eighteenth-century town hall, a Baroque beauty with a visitable Council Chamber), *Hofplein*, and *Gouverneursplein*. *Wilhelminasplein*, to the south, is the site each

Friday and Monday of a big public market. But even more worthwhile is the every-Friday (6:00 A.M.–noon) cattle market—one of Europe's largest—in *Frieslandhal* on *Heliconweg*.

Fries Museum (Turfmarkt): Provincial art and history museums rarely disappoint in the Netherlands, but Friesland's is exceptional, one of the superlative cultural surprises beyond the major cities. It spreads itself over four levels in a pair of superb buildings—one, a Baroque mansion; the other, a step-gabled Renaissance-style townhouse adjacent. There is, to be sure, the work of but one superpainter: a portrait of Saskia, the Leeuwarden-born wife (her father was mayor) of Rembrandt, as interpreted by her husband shortly after they married in 1633. A pair of portraits of Renaissance couples elegantly garbed in black, attributed to Adriaan van Cronenburg, are standouts, too. Another portrait from the same era, of a child holding an elaborate silver rattle, is memorable, as is Anton Melling's nineteenth-century view of Leeuwarden. There is early work—Roman coins from the neighborhood, ancient pottery, medieval sculpture. Go on, then, to Baroque silver, Leeuwarden crafted; painted furniture out of the village of Hindeloopen (below); objects of carved and gilded wood; caches of Frisian pottery and tiles; eighteenth-century Chinese export porcelain made from the Dutch market; a collection of costumes—from Hindeloopen and elsewhere in Friesland—in wool, linen, silk and chintz, some of them exquisitely embroidered; and a splendid series of seventeenth-century living- and bedrooms, with walls of tile made at nearby Makkum (below): cozy nineteenth-century kitchen, tobacco shop (its jars Delft blue). Baroque sitting room, rococo dining room.

Museum Het Princessehof (Grote Kerkstraat 1): Take in the carved-stone embellishment of this seventeenth-century mansion's brick facade. You are entering the onetime residence of a princess who had been married to William IV of Orange, who became Stadholder of the United Provinces. Indeed, the building's single period room has been retained as a memento of the princess's occupancy. Otherwise, this is a sleeper of a museum of ceramics—one of the finest such in Europe. There is a heavy and quite marvelous concentration of Chinese work: T'ang horses, Celadon ware, both green and gray; the various schools of Ming—in yellow, brown, green, and blue; later Famille Rose; striking jet-black Encre de Chine; and a cache of Chinese Export ware. Tile galleries take up the better part of two big floors, with the provenance not only Dutch, but Spanish, Italian, and Flemish, as well. And Art Nouveau buffs will be delighted with treasures of that late nineteenth-century period.

Grote Kerk (a.k.a. Jacobijner Kerk; Grote Kerkstraat) keeps such absurdly minimal summer-only hours (traditionally Tuesday and Friday 10:00–11:00 A.M.; 2:00–4:00 P.M.) that I hesitate calling it to your attention. It was originally built by the Dominicans in the thirteenth century—the style Gothic, the walls red brick—but there have been reconstructions over the centuries; you'll note the Baroque additions. Have a look, too—if you gain entrance—at the tombs of Friesland's stadholders.

Oldehove (Oldehoofsterkerhof): It's not in every town that you find a 120-foot leaning tower. Oldehove is all that was built of a planned, but never realized, cathedral. (They ran out of money.) Substantial Gothic, it has been restored, and there's a stairway to the summit, open in summer.

Mata Hari Huis (Grote Kerkstraat at Beijerstraat): The Netherlands was neutral during World War I; still, given its occupation by the Germans during World War II, one can wonder why Leeuwarden remains so apparently proud of native-daughter Mata Hari, the dancer who was executed as a German spy by the French in 1917. There is a statue of her a few blocks distant, a leading restaurant named for her, and this turreted mansion was, for a period, her home; it serves now as a museum celebrating Frisian literature and the Frisian language.

Makkum (a coastal village about 20 miles southwest of Leeuwarden) draws summer crowds for two reasons: a first-rate

museum of the pottery for which Makkum is celebrated—
Fries Aardewerkmuseum de Waag, by name—and, you guessed
it, the Tichelaer factory where it's made, with an attached
shop and additional retail outlets, as well. The museum is
deftly housed on two floors of the compact seventeenth-century Waag, or weigh house of the village, on the street called
Fruikmakershoek. Exhibits extend over three centuries—seventeenth through nineteenth. There's a spectacular rococo-
era tiled fireplace and overmantel, a chocolate pot on its own
warmer from the same period, composite paintings com-
prised of a cluster of joined tiles, delicate candelabra, multi-
colored Majolica from other areas of Holland, and traditional
faience from Harlingen. The ever-so-commercial and ever-so-
expensive factory is at Turfmarkt 61, and there are shops both
on Kerkstraat and the square called Plein, in the center of
town—at its best when you wander about, taking in fishing
boats at the harbor, facades of weathered houses on central
streets, and the plethora of churches, half a dozen of them
scattered about. Have a proper lunch at *De Waag Hotel's* restaurant (Markt 13; Phone 1301; *First Class*), pancakes at *Schip-
pers Welvaren* (Waagsteeg 3; Phone 1273; *Moderate*); or move
along to the neighboring village of *Piaam* (a couple of miles
south and with a museum in a onetime church celebrating
Friesland's bird life), for a meal at *Nijnke Pleats*, an eighteenth-
century farmhouse turned restaurant, at Buren 25 (Phone
1707; *First Class*).

Continue seven miles south along the coast to *Workum*,
around whose central square, *Markt*, you want to take in the
seventeenth-century *Waag*, or weigh house, with Workum's
historical museum within; the *Raadhuis*, or town hall, from
the same era; and—loveliest of the lot—*Sint Gertrudis Kerk*,
sixteenth century and with unusual signs for mourners of
families connected with the village's nine guilds.

Hindeloopen (in Frisian, *Hynlippen*, and a few miles south of
Workum) achieved Middle Ages wealth as a member of the
mercantile Hanseatic League. No. 1 of two museums—*Hidde
Nijland*—makes its home in the onetime town hall, dating to
the seventeenth century. Its theme is the decorative arts, Hindeloopen style. By that I mean exquisitely tiled walls, the

village's famed painted furniture (much of it as old as the seventeenth century), typical Hindeloopen "front" and "back" rooms, and a range of delightful exhibits, paintings through pottery. Take in the ice-skating museum, too, and the leaning tower, Westertoren, of the seventeenth-century Reformed church.

SETTLING IN

Oranje Hotel (Stationsweg 4; Phone 12-62-41): Forget about the Oranje Hotel you may have known before 1986. That was the year it reopened, after a complete and thorough rebuilding. Location is just opposite the train station, a seven- or eight-minute walk to the center of town. Public spaces are bright and tasteful, and there are 78 ever-so-modern rooms and suites, a paneled bar-lounge that is the No. 1 Leeuwarden congregating spot at day's end, the Taverne for informal meals, and a restaurant—L'Orangerie—worthy of evaluation in a later paragraph, as the No. 1 eating spot in town. *First Class.*

Eurotel (Europaplein; Phone 13-11-13) is away from the center (you need a car), with 55 functional rooms, restaurant, and bar. *Moderate.*

DAILY BREAD

L'Orangerie (Oranje Hotel, Stationsweg 4; Phone 12-62-41): A captain seats you in a rattan armchair at a candlelit, flower-centered table and offers a choice of two prix-fixe menus or an extensive à la carte. Endive soup is no better in Belgium, its country of origin. Shrimp cocktail, smoked salmon, and a warm *nouvelle*-style quail salad are other first courses of note. Fish is, not surprisingly, reliable, but the big surprise is beef; you won't find a finer *entrecôte* in the Netherlands. Veal steak is exemplary, as well. And roast duck, appearing as *canard à l'orange*—is on the menu, rarely the case in Holland. Excellent wines. Dinner only. *First Class.*

Mata Hari (Weerd 7; Phone 12-01-21) is quartered in a looker of an aged house on a smart shopping street. It's small and predominantly white in decor, with modern chairs enclosing tables set in pink linen. Open with seafood *mousse* or Ardennes ham-cum-melon. Sole is the favored fish, and tournedos are among the meat entrées, with Parfait Mata Hari the house sweet. Dinner only. *First Class.*

Onder de Luifel (Stationsweg 6: Phone 12-90-03) is big and busy, and if you stick to simpler dishes you'll be okay—but just—in the course of a casual lunch. A plain omelet is a safe bet, as is the traditional *uitsmijter*—bread topped with ham or roast beef and fried eggs. *Moderate.*

Likkepot (Nieuwesteeg 45), opposite the Weigh House; Phone 34-36-87) is all white tables and white bentwood chairs, with a sidewalk terrace in warm weather. Go for coffee and cake, afternoon tea, or a soup and salad or sandwich lunch. The last mentioned—sandwiches on French *baguettes*—are good. *Moderate.*

't Schellinkje (Nieuwesteeg 3; Phone 12-84-09) has a cozy traditional ambience and is reliable for *entrecôte* and T-bone steaks and grilled lamb chops, served with french fries. *Moderate.*

Pannekoekschip (Willemskade; Phone 12-45-67) translates as Pancake Ship—and is precisely that, a vessel moored in a canal wherein are served up a variety of pancakes, savory and sweet. *Moderate.*

SOUND OF MUSIC
Schouburg de Harmonie (Ruiterskwartier 4) is the municipal theater—pop and classical concerts, ballet, opera. The tourist office (below) should have schedules.

INCIDENTAL INTELLIGENCE

Further information: VVV Friesland/Leeuwarden, Stationsplein 1, adjacent to the station; VVV Makkum, Waagebouw; VVV Workum, Merk 4; VVV Hindeloopen, Weide 1.

14

Leiden

Rembrandt and the Pilgrims

BACKGROUND BRIEFING
Painting enthusiasts think of it as the birthplace of Rembrandt
(his dad was a local miller), Lucas van Leyden, Jan van Goyen,
and Jan Steen (who, incidentally, married van Goyen's daughter). Americans regard it as an interregnum—albeit a decade-
long interregnum—in the Pilgrims' long journey to the
Massachusetts shore. And the Dutch are proud of its distinguished university (Queen Beatrix is an alumna, and Rembrandt was a student, too) and its museums—exceptional out
of all proportion to its relatively modest size (a hundred thousand population).

West-central Leiden—midway between Amsterdam to the
north and Rotterdam due south and with a network of canals
lined by substantially the same buildings as when Baroque
masters committed them to canvas—is a town to be reckoned
with. Roman-settled but with a name derived from the Dutch
leede, meaning waterway, of which it has its full share, Leiden
achieved wealth during the Renaissance, when a substantial
community of weavers migrated north from Flanders and developed a thriving textile industry.

The city's economic clout was to put it in good stead in the
course of the late-sixteenth-century revolt against the de-
tested ruling Spaniards. Indeed, it was close to being taken

by them when, in 1574, William the Silent—the Prince of Orange who is the Netherlands' all-time national hero—not only saved it from the Spanish enemy, but only a year thereafter founded its university.

The Pilgrims, with their leader, John Robinson (he was trained as an Anglican minister), received permission to settle in Leiden (then the second largest Dutch city after Amsterdam) on February 12, 1609, in a document quoted in a publication of the Leiden Pilgrim Documents Center, which indicated that the town would refuse "no honest people free entry to come live . . . as long as they . . . obey all the laws and ordinances. . . ." And so the Pilgrims settled down to work, primarily in the textiles trades, as "hatters, woolcombers, twiners, tailors, weavers and glovers. . . ."

Still, despite gainful employment and official acceptance, these English expatriates remained foreigners in Holland. As early as 1617, according to another of the Pilgrim Documents Center's booklets, they contemplated a New World colony "to lay a foundation for the expansion of the true Kingdom of Christ in distant lands." Three years later, in 1620, "probably Friday July 31st," the "youngest and strongest" members of the congregation departed from Delfshaven (now part of Rotterdam, Chapter 18) on the *Speedwell* for Southampton, ultimately sailing for the New World from Plymouth, aboard the *Mayflower*, on September 16, 1620.

Although the Pilgrims' Leiden leader, John Robinson, did not sail with them, he is not forgotten. In 1891, the National Council of the Congregational Churches of the U.S. placed a bronze plaque on a wall of the leading church, Pieterskerk (below), which reads, in part:

In memory of
Rev. John Robinson, M. A.
Pastor of the English Church, worshiping over
against this spot A. D. 1609–1625, whence at
his prompting went forth
the Pilgrim Fathers
to settle New England
in 1620.

ON SCENE

Lay of the Land: Central Leiden is delightfully walkable, but not as compact as the cores of other Dutch cities of comparable size. And the places you will want to visit are not component parts of a solitary cluster; they're spread out. A striking medieval circle of a castle called simply *Burcht*—its facade embedded with coats of arms—straddles a central hill, guarding the city as it has these many centuries. Canals enclose the core. *Oude Rijn*, or Old Rhine, more or less bisects the town, west to east. It is paralleled by the northerly *Oude Vest*, with *Kapenburg'* the principal north-south canal. Arrive by train and you exit the station on *Stationsplein*, in the northwest, walking south along *Stationsweg* as it becomes *Steenstraat* and thence, as it turns east, *Harlemeerstraat*, one of two leading shopping streets, along with *Breestraat* to the south, with the *Stadhuis*, or City Hall—distinguished by a superb, triple-gabled Renaissance facade—its principal landmark and the Baroque-era *Waag*, or weigh house, nearby on *Aalmarkt*. *Pieterskerk*, the No. 1 church, is a couple of blocks west of the Stadhuis on *Pieterskerkstraat*, while *Houglandsekerk*, another important church, is to the east, on *Nieuwstraat*. Leiden's celebrated museums are scattered, mostly in the western half of the city.

Stedelijk Museum de Lakenhal (Oude Singel 28): No Dutch museum achieves what it sets out to do—portray with a sense of style the history and art of the city in which it is situated—more successfully than the Lakenhal. Its home is a walled Baroque masterwork—neoclassic, with a quartet of pilasters supporting an elegant pediment beneath a steeply pitched roof topping a central pavilion flanked by lower wings. The name—Lakenhal, which translates as Cloth Hall—indicates the original function, as indeed do five sculpted plaques of the facade, whose subjects are spinning, weaving, dyeing, clothworking, and shearing.

Go inside, then, to see period rooms that delineate Leiden's wealthy past, noting, as you move about, the antique furniture—some of the finest-quality such on public view in Holland. There's a seventeenth-century salon in dark-green velvet, its chairs leather covered, its ceiling frescoed; a pale-green, eighteenth-century reception room; a chamber celebrating the nineteenth-century Biedermeier era; the so-called Grote Pers, an ever-so-formal repository of civic guards' paintings and their banners, with caches of ceremonial pewter and silver and stained-glass portraits of medieval Counts of Holland executed in the sixteenth century. There are gem-like small rooms, too, a corner one with sublime canal views; still another, honoring the town's brewers, with murals surfacing its walls.

Paintings are more a case of quality than quantity. Although Lucas van Leyden undoubtedly spent much more time and effort on *The Last Judgment*, a triptych painted in oil, it is his black and white drawing of a debonair Leiden blade, *Mansportret*, that is the Lakenhal's trademark work of art. But the other Leiden-born painters of note are on hand, too: Rembrandt, with an early *Palamades Before Agamemnon*; Jan Steen, with *Amorous Couple*; Jan van Goyen, with *View of Leyden*; and the less well-known Gerard Dou, with *Astronomer Lit By Candlelight*.

Rijksmuseum van Oudheden (Rapenburg 28)—housed in an originally early-nineteenth-century building that has been several times expanded—is Holland's preeminent repository of antiquities. I can appreciate your reacting to this statement with little interest, opining that you are more interested, while in Holland, in seeing Dutch art. Well and good. But the Van Oudheden warrants your attention. Not unlike museums of the caliber of the Metropolitan in New York and the Egyptian in West Berlin, it was the recipient in the late 1960s of an entire Nubian temple transplanted, as a gift from the Egyptian Government, from Aswan, preparatory to construction of a dam at that point. Taffeh by name, the temple was built 1,900 years ago and rates space in a specially created hall that takes its name, complementing a range of Egyptian objects: mummies and masks, jewelry and games, statues and steles. Still another exhibit, Tribunezaal, embraces a 25-yard-long display that is a veritable sampler of the cultures and civilizations alloted departments elsewhere in the museum. Take it in before you branch out to ancient gold, ivory, bronze, and pottery from the Near East, Greek terracotta, Roman busts, and Etruscan artifacts in the Classical department; revealing finds from home territory, the Netherlands, with prehistoric weapons and tombs, as well as remnants of Roman colonies, altars through armor; and, my favorite section, the Dutch Middle Ages: gold and glass through shields and spears.

Rijksmuseum voor Volkenkunde (Steenstraat 1): There is, to be sure, no dearth of ethnology museums in Holland, nor, for that matter, across the Atlantic. Still, Leiden's—which catches your attention, upon entering, in a dramatic three-story atrium—is of high quality. You will want to see the North American Indian exhibits—there's a lifelike Plains chief in deerskin garb that's a standout—as well as exceptional Indonesian displays (including instruments of a typical Gamelan orchestra, arranged as if for a concert), artifacts from Sri Lanka, Siberian costumes, Japanese screens, Indian paintings, African sculpture, and South American crafts.

Academisch Historisch Museum (Rapenburg 73) brims with historical lore, prints and paintings especially, that bring to life this institution's long relationship with the city whose name it takes. (And note that Rapenburg 65 is the entrance to the university's *Prentenkabinet*, a collection of drawings, prints, and photographs; if it's open, have a look.)

Pilgrim Fathers Documents Center (Vliet 45): I quote two publications of this worthy organization in Background Briefing (above). The center publishes still other material relating to the Pilgrims' 11-year residence in Leiden. And there are copies of records on display—fascinating, some of them—relating to their life here. Most New World visitors, with good reasons, make a pilgrimage (no pun intended).

Stedelijk Molenmuseum de Valk (a.k.a. Windmill Museum, Lammermarkt): You've always wanted to see the inside of a windmill; here's your chance. This one, built in 1743 and a municipal museum since 1966, is a veritable skyscraper of eight stories. The miller's living quarters are on the street floor. You climb two flights to the museum floors, with displays of millrights' tools. Higher up—in the top four stories— is the mill machinery and a balcony from which there are nice views of town.

Pieterskerk (Pieterskerkhof) is Leiden's oldest (it went up more than 500 years ago) and, I suspect, largest church—a Gothic red-brick mass, with a delicate spire, corner turrets, marvelously high nave, and lovely choir—as well as the tomb of Pilgrim leader John Robinson and a plaque (partially quoted in Background Briefing, above) commemorating the Pilgrims' stay in Leiden.

Hooglandsekerk (a.k.a. St. Pancratiuskerk, Hooglandsekerkgracht) rivals Pieterskerk with respect to gargantuan dimensions. Protestant since the Reformation, its splendid, red-brick Gothic interior (dating to the fifteenth century) is whitewashed, and its enormous windows are fitted with clear— not stained—glass.

The Hofjes —35 all told—are variations on the theme of almshouse. In most cases, they constitute a complex of little houses arranged, horseshoe shape, around a pretty garden, usually with a chapel, often with a gatehouse wherein their trustees meet. Some Hofjes are for single women, some are for couples, some are church sponsored, and others are lay organized. The most interesting, certainly for transatlantic visitors, is *Jan Pesijnshofje* (Kloksteeg 21, near Pieterskerk, above). It went up in the seventeenth century on the site of the house where the Pilgrim preacher John Robinson lived and where he died in 1623; a plaque makes note of this. Try also to take in *St. Elisabethsgasthuis* (with its visitors' entrance on Lijdsbethsteeg), a restored fifteenth-century home for the aged, with a notable chapel; and *St. Annanof* (Hooigracht 9, with the entrance on Middelstegrach), late fifteenth century, again with its restored chapel a highlight.

SETTLING IN

De Doelen Hotel (Rapenburg 2; Phone 12-05-27) has the virtues of situation (Leiden's most beautiful canal) and environment (an imposing seventeenth-century house that has kept
pace with the times). There are nine no-two-alike rooms with
showers (rather than tubs) in their baths and contemporary
furnishings beneath original ceiling beams. The restaurant is
later evaluated. Friendly. *Moderate.*

Mayflower Hotel (St. Aagtenstraat 5; Phone 14-26-41), though
behind an unprepossessing facade, is conveniently central. It
has 14 doubles, all of which, I am reliably informed by management, are as big and as comfortable and with as good
baths as those I have inspected. Breakfast only. *Moderate.*

Holiday Inn (Haagse Schouwweg 10; Phone 76-93-10) is not,
alas, anything like central—it's on Highway A14, west of
town—but it's modern and diversely equipped: 200 well-ap-
pointed doubles with typically reliable Holiday Inn baths;
both restaurant and café-bar in a high-ceilinged, glass-enclosed central space; and swimming pool and sauna. You
need a car. *First Class.*

Bastion Hotel (Voorschoterweg 8; Phone 76-88-00) is, like Holiday Inn (above), west of town and detached from it. A sleekly
designed, two-story pavilion, it comprises 40 severe-looking
but comfortable rooms and baths (with showers rather than
tubs), inviting restaurant, and congenial bar. *Moderate.*

DAILY BREAD

Rotisserie Oudt Leyden (Steenstraat 51; Phone 13-31-44): This
is a handsome restaurant complex behind the aged facades of
a trio of contiguous centrally situated houses. I say complex
because if you take the entrance at the left you're in a pancake
house, with a menu built around that traditional Dutch specialty, and the tabs are *Moderate.* Enter on the right, and you're
in a proper restaurant, properly atmospheric, and with a

choice of three prix-fixe menus. The look is agreeable; the service, charming; the fare, *nouvelle* influenced; and, in my experience, more ambitious than distinguished. A lunch from the least pricey menu might include leek soup or a not especially tasty duck-liver *pâté* and entrées of veal (a chop, Armagnac-sauced) or trout *meunière*, with the desert specialty—*trois mousses au chocolat*—distinctly disappointing. *First Class*.

La Cloche (Kloksteeg 3; Phone 12-30-53): The key word here is trendy, but in the nicest sense. La Cloche's cordial management has brightened up venerable quarters with style and wit. White-painted rattan chairs encircle tables set with pale-blue linen. Fare is French accented. Order from the prix-fixe, which might consist of a duck-liver *mousse* to open, tossed salad following; roast pork, substantially garnished, as an entrée; with Cassis ice cream and *petits-fours* as dessert. Dinner only. *First Class*.

De Bisschop (Kloksteeg 7) is winning, paneled walls enclosing an inviting room, whose tables, in pink linen, are centered by bowls of artfully arranged flowers. The prix-fixe menu is indicated. It might well open with shrimp salad, a prelude to tomato *consommé*, followed by filet of sole, with *profiteroles au chocolat* for dessert. Pleasant. *First Class*.

De Doelen Hotel Restaurant (Rapenburg 2: Phone 12-05-27), a high-ceilinged salon giving onto the city's most picturesque canal, is an old, reliable eatery in an old, reliable hotel. Best deal is the prix-fixe: vegetable soup or *consommé* as starters; roast pork or the day's fish, prepared as you prefer, as entrées; and a pudding or ice-cream dessert and coffee, to conclude. Friendly. *Moderate*.

Snijers (Botermarkt 42) is a delightfully old-fashioned bakery-cum-"lunchroom," which means that you may select pastry (or order a sandwich), consuming your snack or lunch at one of the rear tables. Central. *Moderate*.

SOUND OF MUSIC

Leidse Schouburg (Oude Vest 33) is the municipal theater—horseshoe-shaped in the style of past centuries, with a pair of balconies and a great central chandelier. Go for pop programs, opera, dance; the tourist office (below) has schedules.

Stadsgehoorzaal (Breestraat 60) is the city's concert space, a looker of a nineteenth-century auditorium, with symphonic and rock both presented. Ask the tourist office (below) what's on.

INCIDENTAL INTELLIGENCE

I try to make clear on foregoing pages of this chapter how much Leiden has to offer—more than can be properly taken in in the course of a day's excursion. Do plan to stay at least overnight. *Further information:* VVV Leiden, Stationsplein 210.

15

Maastricht
And the Limburg Hills

BACKGROUND BRIEFING

If it is hardly the *ville exotique* exclaimed over by Dutchmen from the largely gastronomically uninspired, terrain-flat north (who admire its Franco-Belgian-accented cuisine and the gently rolling hills of its countryside), southerly Maastricht is hardly a city to be despised—or, for that matter, passed by.

Situated at the southern tip of the finger of Dutch territory that brushes Belgium to both west and south, with Germany due east, Maastricht—whose government-protected historic core blessedly escaped World War II bombs—is a proud survivor of more than a score of major military sieges over the past half-millennium. French invaders, in the course of one of these, were led personally by no less august a commander than King Louis XIV, positioned atop a royal horse, on St. Pietersberg hill, overlooking the city.

That was in 1673, by which time Maastricht was nothing if not cosmopolitan. It was founded by Romans (the name evolved from the Latin *Mosae Trajectum* (indicating its location at a fording point on the Maas, or Meuse, River), served as a seat of Catholic bishops for a three-and-half-century span beginning as long ago as the year 382, was enriched by largesse from Charlemagne (from his northern base at nearby

Aachen) in the late eighth and early ninth centuries, and was peculiarly co-governed by Dukes of Brabant and Prince Bishops of neighboring Liège for a sustained period beginning in the late thirteenth century.

Maastricht thrived as a religious, cultural, and mercantile center in the sixteenth century—which saw it rise against Spanish domination in a number of battles, though it was ultimately defeated by the Duke of Farnese's troops in a bloody 1579 siege. It became Dutch again half a century later, only to be conquered by French troops in several seventeenth- and eighteenth-century battles. In the early nineteenth century, at the Congress of Vienna in 1815, what is now Belgium joined the Dutch United Provinces to become the Kingdom of the Netherlands, with the House of Orange's William I its first—and only—monarch. Alas, that arrangement was short-lived; only 15 years later, the dissatisfied Belgians revolted, declaring themselves independent. If geographical logic had prevailed, Maastricht would no doubt have become part of the new Belgium. But enough of its citizens were pro-Dutch to have impelled petition of Limburg Province, part of which became Belgian, the rest (including Maastricht) remaining in Holland.

And so, more than a century later, on September 14, 1944, Maastricht found itself the first city in the Netherlands to be liberated (by America's "Old Hickory" Division) from World War II Nazi occupation.

ON SCENE
Lay of the Land: Given its advanced age, this is a well-planned city, relatively easy to get about, so long as you appreciate that it's a two-part proposition, with Maastricht proper to the west of the Maas River and the district called *Wijk* to the river's east, with a quintet of bridges linking them. Of these, *St. Servaas Brug*—itself an historic monument originally built in the late thirteenth century and named for the city's sainted first bishop—is the most central and the most important. It leads east to Wijk's *Wyckerbrugstraat*, which soon becomes *Stationstraat* and terminates at the *Railway Station*, passing several hotels en route. The thoroughfare called

M. *Brugstraat* takes you westward from St. Servaas Brug into the historic heart of Maastricht. After a short block, aptly named *Kleinestraat* ("Little Street") appears, joining M. *Brugstraat* with *Grotestraat*, the main pedestrian shopping street and in the center of a network of such. *Muntstraat*, one of these, leads north a block to *Markt*, venue of Maastricht's multinational, multilingual, multicurrency open market (below), and one of Holland's most lavishly decorated city halls. The other major square, enormous *Vrijthof*, lined with cafés and landmarks—St. *Servaasbasiliek* and next-door St. *Janskerk*, most significantly—is at the western terminus of *Grotestraat*. Nary a central Maastricht street is without venerable facades, but there is a clutch of streets, comprising the so-called *Stokstraat Kwartier* directly south of St. Servaas Brug, whose Baroque houses were relatively recently restored and cry out for a walk past them. Ideally, it would conclude in the quarter's southwest corner, at historic *Onze Lieve Vrouwe Basiliek*, on the square taking its name. If you are a hardy explorer, with a bent for military history, note that both Maastricht's *Kazematen*, or Casemates—stone shelters in *Waldeckpark*, through whose openings cannon were fired in seventeenth-century battles—and a formidable network of bastions-cum-subterranean passages, dating to the eighteenth century and centered on *Hoge Fronten*, guard the southwest and northwest corners of town, respectively, and are visitable on guided tours.

St. Servaasbasiliek and its Treasury (Vrijthof): Approached from the broad expanse of the square called Vrijthof, the Gothic tower and nave of St. Jankerk (below) and the great apse, flanked by twin Romanesque-style towers of St. Servaasbasiliek, blend one into the other, creating the single most dazzling of Maastricht facades. St. Servaas—called after the fourth-century priest who was Maastricht's first bishop (alas, the bishop's see was moved to nearby Liège, now in Belgium, in 722 A.D., and there it remains)—is a Romanesque beauty, the bulk of which was constructed at the start of the eleventh century, but with even older—and eminently visitable— crypts, among whose tombs are those of the sainted Servaas.

The church itself—subject to a long-range, meticulous, and costly restoration in the mid-1980s—is based on one of the superlative Romanesque naves of the Netherlands and is notable, as well, for the exquisitely detailed sculpture framing its Bergpoortal, the south entrance. But it's St. Servaas's *Schatkamer,* or Treasury, which constitutes Maastricht's single most requisite destination. Smartly presented in contemporary glass vitrines, which are lighted from also-contemporary ceiling spots, are such Servaas relics as an ivory crucifix edged in precious stones, gold embedded; an extraordinarily beautiful gold and silver key: and even fragments of saintly vestments. But the most spectacular of the Treasury's treasures are a gilded bust of the saint, dating to the sixteenth century, and an altar, Brabant-made in 1500, whose mass of tiny gilt-accented figures recount the Crucifixion.

St. Janskerk (Vrijhof), anticlimactic after a visit to its next-door neighbor, is younger (fourteenth-fifteenth century Gothic) and Protestant (rather than Catholic), with very limited open hours and at its best without, given a tower soaring some 210 feet.

Onze Lieve Vrouwebasiliek (Onze Lieve Vrouweplein)—not unlike St. Servaasbasiliek (above), the other principal Maastricht church—stuns with its facade. In front, it is severe, broad, and fortresslike, with a pair of slim towers. Out back, its two-level apse is felicitously overscaled. Essentially Romanesque—again, like St. Servaas—the interior is memorable for the capitals of its columns and a *Schatkamer,* or Treasury, which, though not as brilliant as that of Servaas, warrants inspection if only for a tapestry illustrating the martyrdom of St. Lambertus, one of the early Maastricht bishops, as well as a collection of reliquaries and ecclesiastical silver.

St. Mattiaskerk (Boschstraat) went up in the thirteenth century, became Protestant in the course of the Reformation, and reverted to Catholicism in the early nineteenth century. It is one of Maastricht's loveliest houses of worship, with modern—or relatively modern—stained glass in its marvelously massive windows, but otherwise it is quite the same Gothic structure it was eight hundred years ago, with a long nave that leads to a high altar centered by a dazzler of a shrine that is, in effect, a multipinnacled mini-Gothic church.

Bonnefantenmuseum (named for a convent in which it had been housed, but now occupying the two sprawling floors above the Entre Deux shopping center at Dominikanerplein 5): If it is by no means the most impressive of the provincial art and history museums (to this inspector, those of such cities as Leeuwarden, Den Bosch, and Middelburg—to name three—make a stronger impact), Maastricht's Bonnefanten is not without distinctive exhibits. You find bits and pieces of prehistoric Maastricht—flints and tools and pottery, coins and sculpture fragments from Roman Maastricht, and a scale model of medieval Maastricht. But for me, the museum, Holland's southernmost, is at its best with paintings from neighboring Flanders. These include five by Pieter Brueghel the Younger (including a brilliant village snow scene), a luminous Bernard Van Orly *Pietà*, a David Teniers interior, Rubens's portrait of red-bearded Peter Jan Neyen, and Van Dyck's study of a pensive monk. There are Dutch works, as well (a Jacob Ruysdael landscape stands out), and some French canvases with a lavishly garbed Largillière nobleman exceptional. And the polychrome medieval sculpture—a likeness of St. Rémy, companion standing pieces of Sts. John and Mary, and a group of thirteen embracing Christ and the twelve Apostles—stays with you.

Stadhuis (Markt): Maastricht's city hall stands out in a country where such buildings are frequently of high caliber. Set off by the broad expanse of Markt and topped by a slim tower, it shelters an art-rich interior, highlighted by a ballroom-size entrance hall with a beautifully frescoed ceiling; a Louis XV-era room, with eighteenth-century Brussels tapestries covering its walls and a splendidly stuccoed ceiling; and the room reserved for the mayor and his cabinet, illuminated by a pair of rococo crystal chandeliers.

Spaans Gouvernement (Vrijthof 18) is the odd appelation of a sixteenth-century mansion whose name suggests its original function. Maastricht headquarters of long-ago Spanish officials, it was the seat, as well, of Dukes of Brabant. The arcaded courtyard, Flemish Renaissance and striking, aptly suggests the caliber of the interior, which comprises a series of period rooms, rich with antique furniture and furnishings, Dutch and Flemish, French and Italian—the range, paintings and bronzes, silver and porcelain, tapestries and chandeliers. Caveat: Open hours are limited; ask the tourist office (address below) for help in securing admission.

The Limburg countryside: Northerly Dutch visitors, who equate their homeland with Flat, adore the rolling hills of provincial Limburg. To the rest of us, from countries whose terrains are not so consistently horizontal, Limburg makes for an agreeable enough excursion from Maastricht; indeed, I suggest sojourns at any (or all, if you like) of several selected Limburg hotels, the better to experience meals in their outstanding restaurants (see Settling In and Daily Bread, below).

Leading Limburg points include *Valkenburg*, chockablock with hotels and restaurants of all categories, a pretty core, grottoes from which the Romans quarried stone and which were used as World War II bomb shelters, a museum of regional lore in its Oud Stadhuis, or Old Town Hall, and a casino (foreigners need passports: men wear jackets and ties or turtlenecks) with roulette and blackjack the lures; *Vaals*, whose Dreilandenpunt accurately translates as Three Country Point, and is not only where the Dutch, Belgian, and German frontiers converge, but is—at 961 feet –the most elevated terrain in the Netherlands; *Epen*, a village of centuries-old, half-timbered houses; *Thorn*, whose draw is one of Holland's handsomest village churches—originally the chapel of an Abbey, a Romanesque-Gothic-Renaissance-Baroque meld, as visitable for its somber crypts as for its art-embellished chapel and ebullient, crown-topped high altar; *Hoensbroek*, where the draw is nearby Kasteel Hoensbroek— a moated fourteenth-century complex whose architecture, scale, and courtyard are more impressive than its visitable interiors; the U.S. Government-operated *Netherlands American*

Cemetery, on a 65.5-acre plot in an area liberated in World War II by the U.S. 30th Infantry Division on September 13, 1944, with marble headstones marking the graves of 8,301 American soldiers, and a chapel (whose crown-shaped lighting fixture is a gift of the Dutch people), with this inscription: "In proud remembrance of the achievements of her sons and in humble tribute to their sacrifices, this memorial has been erected by the United States of America" (and with framed letters signed by Queen Juliana and President Eisenhower). And last, but hardly least, *Roermond,* exceeded in Limburg only by several times larger Maastricht, for historic interest, with its Gothic-era, high-towered Catholic Kathedraal, twin-steepled Romanesque Munsterkerk, step-gabled Gemeentemuseum (paintings of some caliber and area historical lore), and squares—busy Markt, broad Munsterplein—its standouts.

SETTLING IN
De l'Empereur Hotel (Stationstraat 2; Phone 21-38-38)—grandly mock-Renaissance of facade—went up at the turn of the century just opposite the Station and is now, as then, well located and welcoming. Public spaces—inviting lobby, bar as popular with locals as with visitors, restaurant evaluated in a later paragraph—are traditional in style, but accommodations—35 no-two-alike on-premises rooms (those I have inspected are good sized, good looking, and with good baths) and 13 kitchen-equipped suites in a neighboring building—are contemporary. And both management and staff are friendly and proficient. Very nice, indeed. *First Class.*

Du Casque Hotel (Vrijthof 52 at Helmstraat; Phone 21-43-43) begins with location as a plus; it edges a broad, central landmark-rich square. All 40 rooms (with either tubs or showers in their baths) are mod-look, the restaurant is worthy of comment on a later page, and there's a café with tables spilling out onto Vrijthof that's a pleasure in warm weather. I like. *Moderate.*

Derlon Hotel (Onze Lieve Vrouweplein 66; Phone 21-67-77) appears at its best on upper floors, where there are 42 well-equipped rooms, in contemporary style. The little lobby has a combination reception/concierge desk with but one attendant (at least in the course of my inspection), and there is a casual restaurant adjacent. *Luxury.*

Stijne Hotel (Stationstraat 40; Phone 25-16-51): Proprietor H. J. Rinkens is invariably on hand to welcome guests to this charming 15-room house, near the bridge connecting Wijk with central Maastricht. Most, but not all of the rooms, are bath equipped; those I have inspected are bright and spacious. And an attractive restaurant is adjacent to the lobby-lounge. Very pleasant. *Moderate.*

Maastricht Hotel (De Ruiterij 1; Phone 25-41-71) is a sprawling 112-room house that specializes in groups. Location is several blocks south of Servaas Brug in the Wijk section—a quarter-hour trek from central Maastricht, far enough to make you feel isolated from the city. Rooms are spacious and comfortable enough, but staffing appears minimal: Reception-concierge desk, when I have called at it, has been attended by but one person, as has the cramped breakfast room, so that obtaining coffee (not part of the help-yourself buffet) can be time-consuming. Restaurant, bar. Disappointing. *Luxury.*

Kasteel Wittem Hotel (Wittemer Allee 3, in Wittem, Limburg; Phone 1208): A hotel whose guests have included Holy Roman Emperor Charles V (in 1520) and Prince William the Silent (in 1568), was founded as long ago as 1100, and was for long in the hands of a dynasty of knights, and at a later period of a succession of counts, is not your ordinary hostelry. Not by a long shot. Kasteel Wittem—backed by a swan-populated lake in its own park, its facade largely surfaced by centuries-old stones—has been a hotel only since 1958. And current owners, the Pieter Ritzens, senior and junior, have been on hand only since 1972, during which time they have deftly refurbished the castle, to the point where it is one of the finest hotels in the Netherlands. There are precisely a dozen rooms—the range, a fabulous suite atop the tower, with a circular bedroom, to a capacious single, with twins and doubles—no two alike, the lot of them traditionally handsome and with exceptionally well-designed baths. Little touches at Kasteel Wittem are a joy. Bed-turndown in the evening brings fresh towels in the bath, and in every room fresh fruit and and made-on-premises cake appear on bedside tables, along with arrangements of fresh flowers. The lounge, paneled, with brass chandeliers and easy chairs surrounding tables, is fun at cocktails and for after-meal coffee and drinks, and it is supplemented by a terrace edging the garden. And the restaurant warrants extended comment on a later page. Member, Relais et Châteaux. *Luxury.*

Prinses Juliana Hotel (Broekhem 11, in Valkenburg, Limburg; Phone 12-244) is a long-on-scene hostelry that owner-manager Paul P. M. Stevens inherited from his family. Stevens and his wife, Doris, one of Holland's top hotel-management teams, retaining the original facade, have transformed the Prinses Juliana into an uncommonly handsome contemporary house. Most of the 17 rooms are doubles, no two of them quite alike, but the lot smartly luxurious in restful pastels complemented by good art on the walls, brass lamps, baskets of fruit on tables, alongside easy chairs, and good baths that lack only proper overhead showers. The bar-lounge off the lobby is complemented by a covered terrace-café and white wrought-iron tables edging the garden. There remains the restaurant; it is reviewed on a later page. Member, Relais et Châteaux. *Luxury.*

Winseler Hof Hotel (Tunnelweg 99, in Landgraaf, Limburg; Phone 464-343) is arguably the most imaginatively conceived of the Netherlands' newer hotels: an early sixteenth-century estate (for long, the seat of a family of gentlemen farmers), converted with wit and panache into a refreshingly offbeat luxury resort. By offbeat, I mean just under 50 rooms and suites retaining original paneling, albeit otherwise smartly contemporary (and in some instances duplex); cocktail lounge occupying quarters in what had been the wine cellar, still with original Gothic brick vaults; ballroom in what had been the barn—three-story-high, a beamed A-frame space unlike any other serving this function that I know of; and a restaurant as trendy looking as it is otherwise trendy—the first of any top-category hotel in the kingdom to specialize in Italian cuisine. This is a highly professional operation, and a congenial one at that, thanks to direction by skilled General Manager Toine Scheerens, ex-Hotel des Indes, The Hague. *Luxury.*

Kasteel Erenstein Hotel (Oud Erensteinerweg 6; Phone 46-13-33) makes its home in what once was a country estate dating to the early eighteenth century. It is owned by the firm that operates the Winseler Hof (above), which it preceded. And although it is full facility—with 45 rooms and split-level suites, glass-roofed café, bar in what was the farm's bakery, and a restaurant (later reviewed) in a detached, originally fourteenth-century, still-moated château—it does not come off nearly as well, for me at least, as its Winseler Hof offspring, than which, I must add, it is less expensive. *First Class.*

DAILY BREAD
't Klääske (Plankstraat 20, just off Onze Lieve Vrouplein; Phone 21-81-18) represents Dutch spelling at its most difficult for English speakers, opening with an apostrophe *t*, and with umlaut accents over both the *a* and the *o*. Pronounce it as best you can, but do pop in for a meal. This centrally located restaurant is intimate (there are but nine tables) and attractive (the look is restrained Art Nouveau). Waitresses are at once professional and pretty, and fare is sensibly *nouvelle* accented and delicious. Best buys are weekday business lunches, which might include fennel-flavored mussel soup or a terrine based on guinea hen, veal steak or filet mignon, with house-made sherbet or the classically French *poire au vin rouge*—a whole pear poached in wine—to conclude. Prix-fixe menus at dinner are costlier. *Luxury.*

Sagittarius (Bredestraat 7; Phone 21-14-92) puts you at ease as you enter. Owner-manager J. W. van Werven is invariably at the door with a disarming smile, and aromas waft your way from the open-to-view kitchen, to the left. You take a table at either of the split levels (or in the garden out back if it's summer) and indulge yourself in seafood—Sagittarius's specialty, the house's own *bouillabaisse* (and very good it is), a seafood salad, and smoked salmon are favored openers. Grilled *scampi*, lobster mayonnaise, sole as you prefer it, and the same *bouillabaisse* earlier offered as an appetizer are favored entrées. They are complemented by meat dishes—an authentically Gallic *gigot d'agneau*, roast lamb—among them. Service is swift and super; wine list, excellent. In my experience, one of Holland's best restaurants. *First Class.*

't Plenkske (Plankstraat 6; Phone 21-84-56)—no more euphonious to the ears of English speakers with its two separated *k*s, than is 't Klääöske (above)—fills the bill in other respects. Take a table in the glass-roofed rear dining room and prepare yourself to enjoy a traditionally French meal, either from prix-fixe menu (cheaper at lunch than in the evening) or a broad-ranging à la carte. Appetizers include *salade Niçoise*, whiskey-sauced shrimp cocktail, the house's own *pâté*, snails Burgundy style, and a hearty onion soup. *Boeuf Bourguignon* can disappoint, but other beef entrées—*tournedos* and *entrecôte*, especially—may satisfy. And pastry, rarely found as a dessert in northern Holland, is always among sweets. Friendly and fun. *First Class.*

Le Vigneron (Haverstraat 19; Phone 21-33-64), sharing a building with *'t Escale*, (a reliable seafood restaurant) is what the French would term a *bistrot à vin*, with its kicker a substantial choice of wines—ten reds and seven whites, mostly Bordeaux and Burgundies—by the glass, served in tandem with nononsense French fare. By that I mean *quiche Lorraine* or leek soup, among starters; *entrecôte à la Bordelaise* (in a red wine sauce), rabbit in mustard sauce, braised shoulder of lamb, among entrées; and *île flottante* (floating island) and *mousse au chocolat*, among desserts. *First Class.*

Frans Schreurs (Achter het Vleehuis 13; Phone 21-58-79)—unpretentious, in a setting half brick walled, half knotty-pine—pleases with well-prepared, smilingly served fare, prix-fixe or from a Gallic-influenced à la carte based on hearty favorites like *daube d'agneau provencale* (a rich lamb stew), *pintade à l'estragon* (roast guinea hen, tarragon scented), and *escalope de veau aux morilles* (cream-sauced veal). *First Class.*

De l'Empereur Hotel Restaurant (Stationstraat 2; Phone 21-38-38): Flower-centered tables in a traditional-look environment complement reliable cuisine—served professionally and smilingly—in the Empereur's dining room. Begin with smoked trout accompanied by a piquant *mousse* or a smoked salmon-stuffed *crêpe*. *Ragoût d'homard*—the house's lobster stew—and filet of pork Esterhazy are typical entrées. And wines are carefully selected. *First Class.*

Du Casque Hotel Restaurant (Vrijthof 52, at Helmstraat; Phone 21-43-43), given its heart-of-town situation, is worth knowing about for its sound-value prix-fixe menus. The less pricey of the two might open with the day's soup, offer as entrées *truite amandine* or breast of chicken, and terminate with the day's dessert. And the costlier menu has Belgian Ardennes ham served with melon and a made-on-premises *pâté*, among appetizers; with *tournedos* in tandem with *sauce Béarnaise*, and *mignonettes de veau*, among entrées. *Moderate/First Class.*

In Den Ouden Vogelstruys (Vrijthof 42; Phone 21-48-88): The decibel count is high here at lunchtime; locals fill the Vogelstruys for a hearty meal, ideally centered on *choucroute garnie*—a platter of juniper-berry-flavored sauerkraut piled high with sausages, smoked ham and boiled potatoes, to the accompaniment of Dijon mustard. Ham, cheese and *pâté* platters are lighter options. Accompany any of the foregoing with the excellent local beer. And if the weather is fair, take a table outside on the square. Fun. *Moderate.*

Chocolaterie de Vree (Stokstraat 31; Phone 21-19-85): Maastricht abounds in candy shops that double as pastry shops and tearooms, and the pastry—often leaden in northern Holland—is delicate, flaky, and irresistible. That at de Vree, accompanied by a cup of tea, coffee, or hot chocolate, is typically delicious. And I defy you to depart without having purchased some of the house's Belgian-style chocolates. The last mentioned are expensive; for cake and coffee, de Vree is *Moderate*.

Monopol (Vrijthof 27) is one of a number of cafés whose tables spill onto this marvelous central square. Have something to eat and/or drink and take in the scene. *Moderate*.

Royale (Wyckerbrugstraat 13, in Wick; Phone 21-50-26) is at once a *pâtisserie* and a *salon de thé*, and you are missing utterly delicious pastries—not to mention *broodje sausisse* (hot sausage enveloped in puff pastry)—if you pass Royale by. *Moderate*.

Château Neercanne (Cannerweg 800, on the Nedercanne-Kanne road, three miles south of Maastricht; Phone 25-113-39) is a walled Baroque palace ideally visited midday for lunch, so that its terraced setting—in pretty countryside with the Dutch-Belgian frontier quite literally cutting through it—can be properly appreciated. Your table, if not on the terrace, will be in one of several ground-floor rooms, pastel hued, crystal chandeliered, and furnished more in the style of late-eighteenth-century Louis XVI, than of the epoch of the house's building—the late seventeenth century. Select your meal from either of two prix-fixe menus or from the extensive à la carte, with the understanding that you will be served professionally and courteously, albeit—if my experience is typical—very slowly. Still—again, in my experience—Neercanne's food, essentially French *nouvelle*, can be very good indeed. A meal might open with a salad of *raddichio* and dandelion greens, served *tiède*, or warm, in the *nouvelle* fashion, topped with half a tiny roast partridge and *foie gras frais;* or sliced scallops over smoked salmon on a bed of spinach. The entrée might be *carré d'agneau*—roast lamb, deliciously sauced and garnished, or something more *nouvelle,* like breast of wild duck with a sauce marrying sherry vinegar and honey.

Desserts merit their own card and tend to be lavish, as, for example, *tarte d'amandes à la poire William et glace à la vanille*— a sumptuous almond tart topped with house-made vanilla ice cream, itself anointed with a dollop of pear *eau-de-vie*. This is a restaurant in which a wine splurge is in order; the cellar is one of the best stocked in the kingdom. *Luxury.*

Kasteel Wittem Hotel Restaurant (Wittemer Allée 3, in Wittem, Limburg; Phone 1208): Set in a handsome and history-laden country castle that is one of Holland's loveliest hotels (see Settling In, above), Kasteel Wittem's restaurant—half-paneled walls, beamed ceiling, leather armchairs surrounding flower-centered tables illuminated by candle in silver sticks— is a celebration of French classical cuisine, albeit with creative innovations. The *maitre d'hôtel* starts you off with an *ameuse gueule* (hope that it will be sautéed sweetbreads enveloped in gossamer pastry, appropriately sauced) as a prelude to a meal that might commence with bracing venison *consommé* afloat with duck-liver-stuffed *ravioli*, half a dozen Zeeland oysters, or a salad based on sliced roast pigeon. Entrées are special: filet of sole stuffed with shrimp *mousse* beneath a dollop of vermouth-scented cream sauce; roast rabbit with a piquant stuffing, basil-flavored; or breast of chicken prepared in tandem with superbly sauced crayfish. Kasteel Wittem's cheese tray is part Dutch, part French. There are always several pastries—apple tart with apple sherbet, warm pear tart with *crème fraîche*, meringue with pistachio ice cream—among the desserts. The wine list is exceptional. And service is nowhere in Holland more expert or more kind; you can count on either of the owner-manager Ritzens, father or son, to stop by and say hello. In my experience, one of Holland's best restaurants. Member, Relais et Châteaux. *Luxury.*

Prinses Juliana Hotel Restaurant's (Broekhem 11 in Valkenburg, Limburg; Phone 12244) soft lights are aided and abetted by elegantly footed candles on tables surrounded by contemporary upholstered armchairs. Orchids are among the flowers massed in big bouquets, complementing the floral-design carpet. Order from either of two prix-fixe menus (the less pricey is four courses and good value) or the not-overly-extensive à la carte. The thrust is *cuisine nouvelle*. Openers might include a selection of the house's terrines, a minicasserole of crayfish and sole sauced with Hollandaise, or one of any number of the house's celebrated goose- or duck-liver specialties. If you have not tried fish in a light, red-wine sauce, a platter combining filets of sole and salmon, *au fleurie*, might be in order. *Filet de boeuf Béarnaise* is an always-reliable classic. Breast of chicken in a truffled cream sauce-cum-spinach is popular. And *Symphonie des desserts et des pâtisseries Juliana* is a sampler *par excellence*. Member, Relais et Châteaux. *Luxury*.

Ristorante Pirandello (Winseler Hof Hotel, Tunnelweg 99, in Landgraaf, Limburg; Phone 46-13-33) is the innovative restaurant of an exceptional hotel (see Settling In, above). By innovative, I mean not only Italian—virtually unprecedented in Dutch hotels—but *Nuova Cucina*, the fare of the southerly peninsula with contemporary twists. There are two prix-fixe menus, but I counsel ordering from the à la carte, impressively printed in the Italian, Dutch, German, and English languages. Cold *antipasti*—*prosciutto* with candied onion in Marsala sauce, squid and tuna *pâté*, saffron sauced; the paper-thin raw beef termed *carpaccio*, truffle-cream sauced—are worthy openers; so is the lemon-chicken *zuppa al limone*. Still, nothing beats pasta as a first course; choices here include *ravioli pansotti*, *tagliatelle*, and *penne*. And beef—prepared in the style of Florence—appears on the menu, along with lamb chops and veal preparations, *saltimbocca alla Romana*, among them. Service is spirited and swift. And wines are Italian. *First Class*.

Kasteel Erenstein Hotel Restaurant (Oud Erensteinerweg 6, in Kerkrade, Limburg; Phone 46-13-33)—in a freestanding fourteenth-century château, detached from the remainder of the Kasteel Erenstein complex (Settling In, above)—is the Erenstein at its most attractive by far, with the restaurant's interior—chandelier hung, traditional of ambience, charming and intimate. Fare, selected from the prix-fixe menu or from a well-organized, four-language à la carte, is *nouvelle*-influenced but hardly meager, as, for example, an appetizer combining duck liver with duck terrine, lobster bisque, filet of sole poached in butter and presented with *fois gras* on a bed of leeks, or smoked suckling pig. Zero in on *gâteau de gingembre au chocolat au sorbet d'oranges*—ginger-chocolate cake with orange ice cream—to conclude. *First Class.*

SOUND OF MUSIC
Stadsschouwburg Achter de Comedie (Bredestraat) is a onetime Baroque church, out of the early seventeenth century, that has long since been transformed into the mock-Baroque, three-level municipal theater-cum-café. Plays are in Dutch, of course, but there are, as well, concerts, both classical (mostly chamber) and pop: musicals like *My Fair Lady*; and ballet. The tourist office (below) has programs.

Staargebouw (Hendrik van Veldekeplein) is home base for the esteemed Limburg Symphonie Orkest—which has an extensive annual season, with soloists—and for visiting symphonies and other musical groups, as well.

Organ concerts take place the summer long, traditionally on Tuesday evenings, at such leading churches (see On Scene, above) as Onze Lieve Vrou, St. Servaas, St. Matthias, and St. Jan. (Note, too, that Maastricht's 20 brass and marching bands perform on Virjthof, the big central square, Sunday mornings the summer long.)

SHOPPER'S MAASTRICHT
A good-sized link of the *Vroom & Dreesmann* department-store chain, with a supermarket in the basement, is on Grotestraat, the principal shopping street, as, indeed, is the Maastricht outlet of the national *Hema* chain. *Schoonbrood* (Spilstraat 25) has big selections of porcelain, Delft especially. *Friandises* (Wijcker Brugstraat 55) is Maastricht's—if not all of the Netherlands'—answer to the celebrated chocolatiers of neighboring Belgium, not as well known abroad perhaps, but with chocolates that are quite as delicious; ask for a sample. Then there's Maastricht's *weekly market*, an international enter-

prise—for flowers, produce, meat, and seafood principally—
with prices in Belgian francs, as well as Dutch guilders, and
customers from Germany, as well; languages of all three countries are spoken. Site is the square called Markt—with the
Stadhuis as backdrop; every Friday.

INCIDENTAL INTELLIGENCE ═══════════════════════════

You are closer to the capital of Belgium (Brussels is but 60
miles to the east) than you are to Amsterdam (125 miles
north). The lovely Belgian city of Liège—No. 1 in the French-
speaking region of Wallonia—is but 20 miles southwest,
while absorbing Aachen (see *Germany At Its Best*) is about the
same distance to the east, and Luxembourg City, capital of
the charming Grand Duchy of Luxembourg, is just over a
hundred miles south. Riderij Stiphout is a boat service offering a variety of excursions on the Maas River, including to
Liège; the tourist office (below) has schedules. *Further information:* VVV Maastricht is located in a landmark medieval
building, Het Dinghus, at Kleinestaat 1; VVV Valkenburg,
Eindhovenseweg 300; VVV Vaals, Koningen Julianaplein 47;
VVV Thorn, Wijngaard 8; VVV Roermond, Markt 24.

16

Middelburg
With Forays into Zeeland

BACKGROUND BRIEFING
They still speak of 1975 in Middelburg—as well they might. That was the year this small, introverted city in Zeeland—at the Netherlands' isolated southwest tip and with a whopping 1,100 certified landmark buildings—was designated a pilot town for European Architectural Year.

It was an accolade that accorded placid Middelburg—even in the late twentieth century, not always relaxed with strangers—a measure of international stature. And well deserved it was. World War II bombing had been severe, but post-war rebuilding and restoration has been widespread and skillful to the extent that this is arguably the most delightfully strollable of the smaller Dutch provincial cities.

You don't need to be told, as you note facades bespeaking rich medieval, wealthy Renaissance, and prosperous Baroque eras, that this is a place with a substantial past. It was chartered in the early thirteenth century, thrived as a cloth-trading center, and, as the last of the Spanish-held Zeeland points during the Dutch struggle for independence, was taken by forces of William the Silent—Holland's conquering hero—in 1574. That same year, its long-celebrated Catholic abbey (contemporarily a multipurpose visitor lure of consequence) was secularized, and, ever since, Middelburg has been predominantly Protestant, despite its situation in the substantially Catholic south.

The capital of Zeeland Province, it is, as well, a convenient takeoff point for excursions—included in this chapter—to such Zeeland points as Veere, Zierksee, and the Delta Expo, at the mouth of the Ossterschelde estuary, site of the re-markable storm-surge barrier that protects modern Zeeland from the sea.

ON SCENE
Lay of the Land: Based on a wide, almost riverlike canal called *Door Walcheren,* edging it at the southwest, Middelburg's core, surrounded by a venerable moat called *Vest,* lies immediately to the south. The geography is crystal clear if you arrive by train. The station fronts *Kanaalweg,* on the far side of *Kanaal Door Walcheren.* Assuming the canal-spanning bridge out front has not been raised to allow river barges to pass (often the case!), you proceed over it, following *Stationstraat,* to *Loskade,* just across the canal and with hotels lining it. Any of a num-ber of streets—*Segeerstraat* is the most central—will take you northeast to *Lange Delft* (the main pedestrian street; along with nearby *Nieuwe Burg,* site of *Vroom & Dreesmann* and *Hema* department stores). *Abdijplein*—named for the onetime abbey (below) dominating it—is directly north, while another im-portant square, *Markt,* site of the landmark *Stadhuis,* or City Hall, is due west, with low-slung and lovely *Domplein* the square to the east. All of this central area is eminently walk-able—head northwest from Markt along *Vlasmarkt,* and you pass the so-called *Engelse Kerk* (fifteenth century and no longer English but rather Dutch Reformed), with a windmill on *Vest* some blocks distant. Take *Lange Noordstraat* northeast from Markt, and you come upon the square called *Hofplein,* its treasure a rococo-era palace, now a courthouse. Continue east on pretty *Wagenaartstraat,* and you encounter a onetime guild-hall, originally sixteenth century, called *St. Jorisdoelen,* with scenic *Spanjaardstraat* just beyond. And still another walk takes you from Markt southwest to the contiguous *Pottermarkt,* onto the street named *Lange Viele* to its extremity, the site of

Kloveniersdoelen, a mouthful to pronounce, but one of Middelburg's esteemed Renaissance structures.

The Abbey (Abdij) complex (Abdijplein, Groenmarkt, and other surrounding streets): Middelburg citizens are so familiar with the abbey complex quite literally in their midst that they often fail to realize its ramifications can confuse newcomers. What is worth knowing, first off, is that it is the site of the important Zeeland Museum, whose Dutch-language title, *Zeeuws Museum* can be offputting; it is entered from the abbey's courtyard via Abdijplein. Additionally, the Abbey embraces not one but a *trio of churches,* entered from Groenmarkt. And its newest tenant, entered from the abbey cloister, is the *Roosevelt Study Center,* opened in 1986 to commemorate links between Zeeland and the two related Roosevelts (Theodore, 1858–1919, a Republican, and Franklin Delano, 1882–1945, a Democrat) who were Presidents of the United States, as well as a highly significant third—Eleanor, at once wife of Franklin and niece of Teddy. All three were descended from Claes Maertenszoon van Rosevelt and his wife Jannetje, who sailed to Nieuw Amsterdam (later to become New York) in the mid-seventeenth century.

We can thank the little-known Norbertine order of monks (called after the French twelfth-century St. Norbert) for beginning this splendid, multitowered Gothic complex in the early twelfth century. The Norbertines, known also as White Canons (because of their habits) and as Premonstratensians, stayed on until William the Silent's troops conquered Middelburg in 1574, when the abbey's churches became Protestant and its other spaces took on secular functions. There have been two major restorations—one, between 1885 and 1917; the other, a rebuilding, as well as a restoration, that was extraordinarily skilled and meticulous, after World War II bombing by the Nazis in 1940. Start with the Zeeuws Museum, following with the churches. (You may pop in to say hello, if you like, at the Roosevelt Center, but it's primarily for scholars of the two Roosevelt eras.)

Zeeuws Museum —quartered in a sixteenth-century section of the abbey that was used to put up the monks' guests—is at its most spectacular in a generously proportioned gallery in which are hung a series of tapestries (seven, all told, with their combined length approximately 30 yards) woven over a ten-year period at the turn of the sixteenth century by a colony of weavers come north to Middelburg from Flanders. Subject is the 1574 Dutch-Spanish Battle of Middelburg, and the weavers worked in details—architecture, arms, uniforms, weapons—masterfully. Still another room celebrates the Dutch seventeenth century, with a tiled fireplace and first-rate furniture, along with myriad accessories including lanterns, clocks, pipes, toys, glass, and ceramics. The ebullient eighteenth century rates a room, as well—with Chinese Export and Delft porcelain, Louis XVI-style furniture as interpreted with Dutch nuances by Dutch cabinetmakers, and a marvelous mantel. Still other space is given over to Stone Age and Roman artifacts and an exceptionally well-presented collection of Zeeland costumes, early nineteenth through early twentieth centuries.

The trio of contiguous Abbey churches begins with *Nieuwe Kerk,* the first entered, with its most memorable architectural feature a pair of window walls and a small sea of graceful columns, tall and slim, supporting Gothic vaults. The seventeenth-century case of the organ is special, too. Proceed, then, to *Wandelkerk,* directly under the abbey's principal tower. Its proportions are splendid, as are its tombs, especially the mausoleum of a pair of brother admirals—Evertsen, by name—who died at sea in a seventeenth-century battle against the English. End in *Koorkerk,* taking the name of its choir (*koor*) and visitable for its precious Utrecht-origin organ.

Stadhuis (Markt) positively stuns with its intricate facade, a marvel of the Renaissance—soaring clock tower, steeply pitched roof embedded with rows of tiny, shuttered windows edged by turrets, with windows of its second story framed by splendid sculptures—that was completely reconstructed over a two-decade period, following World War II bombing. Gain enough perspective from the far side of Markt to appreciate the faithfully duplicated detail before you go in, for an inspection of the wedding chamber and its Brussels

tapestries: the Council Chamber, with the city's coat of arms
covering a wall; the mayor's reception room, its ceiling beamed,
its furniture Renaissance, its fireplace tiled; and the Burgerzaal, or banquet hall, its high barrel-vault hung with massive
Baroque chandeliers, the better to illuminate walls embellished with fine portraits of long-ago city fathers. Special.

Veere (4 miles northeast of Middelburg) enriched itself by the
wool trade over a four-century period ending in the eighteenth. Impressive evidence of that wealth remains in what is
now a village that thrives on the visitor trade. A day's excursion from Middelburg can be a pleasure. Edging the big lake
called Veerse Meer, it is dwarfed by the *Grote Kerk*, a capacious
Gothic pile as old as the late fifteenth century, with a 120-
foot-high tower and a ballpark-size nave utilized today as the
site of a permanent display of hardly outstanding exhibits
(costumes, a farmhouse interior, carriages, documents) relating to village history, for which an entrance fee is charged.
And modern windows rather sadly replace the Gothic originals. Infinitely less disappointing are the *Stadhuis*, or town
hall, originally fifteenth century, with a fine Renaissance facade and elaborate rooms on two floors; and *De Schotse Hu-
izen*, or Scottish Houses, dating to the sixteenth century,
when they were seats of Scottish wool traders, first on scene
a century earlier when a Lord of Veere married a Scottish
princess. Period rooms on the main floor are evocatively furnished with seventeenth- and eighteenth-century pieces.
These Veere interiors behind you, it's time to stroll about,
taking in the harbor area and shops and cafés of Havenhoofd,
the main street, either commencing or concluding your visit
with a meal (see Daily Bread, below).

Zieriksee (16 miles northeast of Middelburg by means of the
Zeeland Bridge over Oosterschelde, an inlet of the North Sea)
is among the more charming of Dutch villages, encircled by
water, with its *Stadhuis*, or town hall, on central *Malkmarkt*,
built over several centuries, starting in the early fifteenth, and
sheltering exhibits of village history. Havenplein, the broad

green main square—bandstand centered—is nearby and the site of the village maritime museum, in the step-gabled structure called *Gravensteen*. A pair of atmospheric town gates— *Noordhavenpoort* (chockablock with turrets) and *Zuidhavenpoort* (fifteenth–seventeenth centuries)—flank either side of the waterway called Oude Haven. Plan your visit around lunch (see Daily Bread, below).

Delta Expo (on Neeltje Jans Island, just north of Zierikzee, above): A half-day excursion out of Middelburg or Zierikzee (by boat, as well as road) to this remarkable exhibition, and you've learned—effortlessly, enjoyably, and, yes, excitingly— how Dutch technology has conquered Holland's ages-old struggle against the sea, long dramatized by the building of dikes, windmills, and the reclaimed land areas called polders. You are at the very point where, in the autumn of 1986, Queen Beatrix (in the presence of France's President Mitterand, Germany's President von Weizsäcker, other foreign leaders, and 25,000 Netherlanders) set into motion the closing of gates of the mile-and-a-half-long *Oosterschelde Storm Surge Barrier,* officially marking completion of the Delta Works.

After the Queen pushed the symbolic button, the gates were raised again and they remain raised, supported by 66 concrete towers, each 125 feet high and weighing 18,000 tons, allowing the tides to prevail, thereby preserving Zeeland's excellent mussels and oysters and other marine life. A 30-year project that cost $5 billion, the Delta Works were prompted by a devastating 1953 storm that flooded all of Zeeland and parts of the neighboring province of South Holland and took more than 2,000 lives.

The extraordinary project is brought into focus at *Delta Expo,* housed in the control building of the Storm Surge Barrier on the artificial island called *Neeltje Jans.* You see first what has gone before—Roman defense works and medieval locks and dams. Four maquettes and three dikes several yards high reveal how Dutch waterway engineering has changed over the centuries. Hydraulic models are impressive, too. A large maquette explains difficulties encountered with varying tides in the construction of dams, bridges, and locks. Various "shut-off" techniques are illustrated from totally scaled dams of the 1960s to sealing-off by means of sliding valves, with close attention paid to the interests of agriculture and fishing. A diorama reproduces salt marshes and mudflats to make clear Delta Works' planners' environmental concern. And a well-made movie (with English one of its explanatory languages) provides orientation.

The works themselves? You are there. By that I mean from the top of the Expo there are views of the vast project, the Zeeland countryside, and the North Sea shipping traffic. Hydraulic engineering feats—Boulder and Hoover Dams, for example—are popular visitor destinations in the United States, but virtually unknown in Europe. The completed Delta Works and Delta Expo have changed all this. You want to have a look.

SETTLING IN

Le Beau Rivage Hotel (Loskade 19; Phone 38060): In a town where locals can be reserved with foreigners, a warm and friendly hotel like the Beau Rivage is a breath of fresh air. And it's a well-located hotel, at that—on the canal-bordering thoroughfare that's an easy walk, both from the station and from the center of town, a couple of blocks distant. Roland and Johanna Kooman welcome guests warmly, offering nine bedrooms, all with bath. No two are alike, and those I have inspected are attractive and comfortable. And there's a small but reliable restaurant and bar-lounge. *Moderate.*

Arneville Hotel (Buitenruststraat 22; Phone 38456) would be a hands-down's Middelburg winner were it only central. You are a quarter-hour's walk from the core in this ever-so-contemporary (1986) house, with a small but inviting lobby, agreeable restaurant (later evaluated), casual café, bar done up in white wicker, and 30 rooms, their furnishings white, their color accents pastels, their baths with either tubs (and handshowers) or stall showers. And the staff is cordial. *First Class.*

Nieuwe Doelen Hotel (Loskade 3; Phone 12121): There is not so much as a stool or bench to sit on in the entrance hall-reception area (separated from lounge and restaurant by an always-closed, windowless door) of this elderly house, so you're not surprised that check-in is unsmiling and hardly cordial. And mattresses (at least, the one I experienced in the course of a sleepless night, after which I checked out, prematurely) are the thinnest I have encountered anywhere in the Netherlands. Twenty-eight of the 30 rooms have showers in their baths; the other two, tubs. *Moderate.*

DAILY BREAD

Het Groot Paradijs (Damplein 13; Phone 26764) pleases with the patina of age (it occupies a venerable house on a square bordered by handsome houses) and a sure sense of style. Starched tieback curtains frame spotless windows, tables are laid with tan linen, and illumination is from brass chandeliers dropped from a beamed ceiling. As elsewhere in the south of the Netherlands, close to the frontier with Belgium, whose cuisine is right up at the top with those of France and Italy— you eat well in Middelburg, especially in a restaurant the caliber of Het Groot Paradys. Open with lobster bisque or *gratin des huitres* (a hot oyster specialty), selecting salmon *soufflé, entrecôte Charolais,* or *turbot gratinée* as entrées. Fine wines. *First Class.*

De Huifkar (Markt 19; Phone 12998)—fronting Middelburg's spectacular Stadhuis, on a busy core-of-town square—appeals with its gentrified rustic look: beamed ceilings, brick arches, ladderback chairs at candlelit tables. Seafood—filet of sole, especially—is a specialty here, and if mussels are in season don't hesitate to order a big bowl of them, steamed in their shells and served Belgian style, with a great mound of *frites.* Waitresses appear shy of strangers at first, but smile tentatively as a meal progresses. *First Class.*

De Ploeg (Markt 55; Phone 34690)—like De Huifker, its neighbor (above)—faces the Stadhuis, and offers tables out front as an option to those within, where choices run from bivalves to beef, and grilled trout is especially recommended. Friendly owner-management. *Moderate.*

Piccolo Italia (Vlasmarkt 17; Phone 34100) is at once central and cordial, with such reliable Italian standbys as pizza with a variety of toppings and pasta with a choice of sauces. *Moderate.*

Arneville Hotel Restaurant (Buitenruststraat 22; Phone 38456) is good sized and good looking, its pale gray walls complementing tables set in pale gray linen, flanked by chrome and leather chairs, and illuminated by little hurricane lamps. The à la carte is Franco-Belgian accented, with such specialties as eel soup and Ardennes ham, breast of chicken sauce Robert, and mushroom-sauced veal chops, with *crêpes* flamed at table the dessert specialty. Snappy service. *First Class.*

De Abidij (Abidijplein 5) is accurately named, within the Abbey complex, fronting its court, with outdoor tables just the place for mid-morning or mid-afternoon pick-me-ups or a casual lunch. *Moderate.*

C. F. Jespere (Nieuwe Burg 12) doubles as a *pâtisserie* and *salon de thé*, which means that you may select pastry from the counter, take a table and order coffee or tea to accompany. *Moderate.*

De Campveerse Toren (Kade 2, Veere; Phone 291) could not be more romantically—or strategically—situated, on the upper floor of a harborview tower that went up in the fifteenth century and has known, management claims in its literature, Holland's own William the Silent and England's Edward IV as clients. Order from either of two prix-fixe menus (the cheaper might run to an hors d'oeuvre platter, veal chop, sherbet or ice cream, and coffee served with tiny pastries). But seafood entrées on the à la carte—sole, salmon, and turbot, among them—might hold more appeal. Friendly. *First Class.*

D'Ouwe Werf (Bastion 2, Veere; Phone 493) looks as good after you arrive—setting is a honey of white house-cum-waterfront terrace—as it does from across the harbor, as you amble the core. This is a smart spot for lunch on a sunny day, with options a prix-fixe menu, soup through sweet, or oysters and sole as you like it, prepared from the à la carte. *First Class.*

Mondragon (Oude Haven 1, Zierikzee; Phone 2670) is long on scene, well situated on the fingerlike body of water leading into the core, and with lovely traditional decor. Open with Zeeland oysters, continuing with a seafood entrée. *First Class.*

SOUND OF MUSIC
Schouwburg Middelburg (Molenwater 99) is the town's ever-so-mod theater, conveniently restaurant/café equipped. And with a range of entertainment, specifics of which the tourist office (below) can advise upon. They'll have programs, as well, of concerts at *Gehoorzaal* (Singelstraat 13).

INCIDENTAL INTELLIGENCE

Further information: VVV Middelburg, Markt 65; VVV Veere, Markt 21; VVV Zierikzee, Havenpark 29.

17

Nijmegen
Edging the German Border

BACKGROUND BRIEFING

It is close enough to the frontier with Germany for the Germans to have their own name, *Nimwegen*, for it. But its name in Dutch—pronounced, incidentally, NYE-megen—evolved from the Latin *Noviomagus*, or New Market. That was the designation decreed by a Roman emperor some 1,900 years ago, after his legions wrested control from the resident, Germanic-origin *Batavi*, or Batavians—the very same whose name was given to Holland when it was dubbed the Batavian Republic (1795–1806) by French conquerors.

Nijmegen's situation, high above the Waal River in the east-central province of Gelderland, has attracted visitors of one sort or another over long centuries. The great Charlemagne built himself a palace in what is now a public park in the late eighth century. Still other emperors, Frederick Barbarossa and his son, Henry VI, were on scene in the twelfth century, by which time Nijmegen had become a Free Imperial City of the Holy Roman Empire; and, later, it was one of many Dutch towns that became affiliated with the mercantile Hanseatic League.

By the time the Peace of Nijmegen—ending Louis XIV's Dutch War—was signed in 1678, Nijmegen was walled, fortified, and rich, evolving in succeeding centuries as a busy industrial/trading center. World War II was a period of bravery and hardship. On February 22, 1944, the Allies bombed the city, destroying its core and killing 800 people—in error, presumably because they gauged their target to be over the nearby border in Germany. Only months later, in September, the city played a decisive role in the liberation of the Netherlands from the Nazis, when, as part of much-chronicled Operation Market Garden, America's 82nd Airborne Division and Britain's 30th Corps freed the city from the Germans, after taking control of the bridges strategically spanning the Vaal. Allied attempts to rescue airborne British troops from nearby Arnham (Chapter 4) were unsuccessful.

Postwar decades saw the core of the city carefully rebuilt, centuries-old monuments included. Each of the trio of principal Gelderland towns has its own appeal. Apeldoorn (Chapter 11) lures because of Het Loo Palace on its outskirts. Arnhem is of interest principally because of its proximity to the extraordinary Kröller-Müller Museum. But Nijmegen is a city with a rich historic core and a range of substantial attractions. Pay a call.

ON SCENE
Grote Markt, the atmospheric heart of the city square, is the site of the fifteenth-century *Lakenhal,* onetime hall of the cloth merchants that's now a restaurant (below), with an arcaded passage known as *Kerkboog,* adjacent; and, nearby, the *Waag,* built in the sixteenth century as the municipal weigh house. *St. Stevenskerk* (below) is west of the square, while *Commanderie St. Jan,* the art and history museum (below), is due north, and both the originally sixteenth-century *Stadhuis,* or city hall, and *Valkhof,* a history-laden pair (below), are to the east, near the principal bridge spanning the *Waal River.* The railway station fronts *Stationsplein,* just west of *Keizer Karelplein* (translating as Charlemagne Square and actually a circle). From the circle, *Bisschop Hamerstraat* becomes *Molenstraat* as it proceeds north to the square dubbed *Plein 1944* and *Broerstraat*—the main pedestrian street—with *Vroom & Dreesmann* and *Hema* department stores.

Valkhof: Why not begin where Nijmegen began? This river-view park is where the Romans subdued resident Batavians in the first century A.D. and where Charlemagne built a palace in the eighth century, which was reconstructed by Frederick Barbarossa in the twelfth, and remained for six hundred years. What you see today is more quality than quantity. All that remain are the perfectly beautiful apse of a Barbarossa-built church and a charming little eleventh-century chapel, octagon domed and reminiscent of the octagonal Charle-magne-built part of the Dom, or cathedral, in Aachen (see *Germany At Its Best).*

St. Stevenskerk (a.k.a. Grote Kerk, Smidstraat) was con-structed over three centuries that spanned the transition from Romanesque to Gothic—as, indeed, does its design—with still a third epoch, the Renaissance, represented in its early seventeenth-century spire, surmounting a superb square tower whose 183 steps you are welcome to climb for a modest fee. But it's the massively scaled interior that you don't want to miss. Take your time ambling about, noting the Renais-sance bishop's throne, the so-called Princes' Pews, embla-zoned with municipal and provincial coats of arms, splendid Baroque chandeliers of brass, and an exceptional organ used for concerts.

Nijmeegs Museum Commanderie van St. Jan (Franse Plaats 3)—distinguished by dramatic step-gables and a conical cor-ner tower—is a delightful mix of art and history, Niemegen themed, in an unabashedly romantic environment. Relatively recently reconstructed in the style of the Renaissance (to which it dates), the riverview Commanderie is an outgrowth of a twelfth-century hospital on the site. Of the paintings, star of the show is a Jan van Goyen portraying the city's own Valkhof Park, with the Waal River beyond. Still another pic-ture—its subject, the locally signed Peace of Nijmegen (1679)—was painted for Louis XIV, whose French forces bat-tled the Dutch. And there are others, of Nijmegen over the centuries, along with elaborate silver collars worn by officers of the city's medieval craft guilds, among much else.

Stadhuis (Burchstraat) impresses, even before you step inside, given a sublime Renaissance facade embedded with sculptures. Ask to be shown the interesting room where the Peace of Nijmegen was concluded three centuries back, noting, as you move about, the high beamed ceilings, aged furniture and paintings, and first-rank tapestries.

Rijksmuseum G. M. Kam (Kamstraat, a long walk or a short taxi ride east of the center) celebrates Nijmegen's Roman roots and takes the name of its original benefactor. I don't know of another museum in the Netherlands with a more brilliant collection of its type. The Romans worked with silver, gold, bronze, copper, and glass, and the Kam shows them all in spades, wisely relating the exhibits to their Nijmegen provenance, with main-floor galleries chronological, starting with the arrival of Romans at the turn of the first century, while the early Batavians were still on scene.

Bevrijdingsmuseum (Barbarossastraat 35) translates as Liberation Museum and strikingly documents Operation Market Garden, the combined Allied effort under the command of Britain's Field Marshall Montgomery that, in September 1944, was the impetus for the liberation of Holland. This museum's thrust—by means of films, photos, slides, maps, and other graphic material—is the role of the Nijmegen area in the historic invasion.

Velorama (Waalkade 107) is as good a reason as any to stroll Nijmegen's river promenade. The name of Velorama's game is nostalgia. This is a repository of old bikes, old cars, and, as a departure, old lanterns. With amusing antique posters, as well.

SETTLING IN
Belvoir Hotel (Graadt van Roggenstraat 101; Phone 23-23-44): I wish that the Belvoir were more central, but this is to carp. Modern, but with its decor tastefully traditional, it has 50 nicely equipped doubles (except that in the baths there are hand showers only, attached to tubs), ten so-called junior

suites (these are actually oversized twins), and 14 one-bedroom suites. Public areas are spacious and include both a barcafé (wherein casual meals are served), indoor pool-cumsauna, bowling alley, and restaurant worthy of evaluation in a later paragraph. Friendly. *First Class.*

Etap-Nijmegen Hotel (Stationsplein 29; Phone 23-88-88) is next door to the train station and, like the Belvoir (above), not as central as I would like. It is, however, a sprightly modern house with a hundred thoughtfully planned, clean-lined rooms and convenient restaurant and bar. *Moderate.*

Atlanta Hotel (Grote Markt 38; Phone 24-01-28), enviably well located on the historic main square, is an updated elderly house embracing 17 bath- or shower-equipped rooms (ask for a front one) and with a restaurant-bar whose tables spill onto Grote Markt in warm weather. *Moderate.*

Apollo Hotel (Bisschop Hamerstraat 14; Phone 22-35-94) is a small modern house on the street that leads from Keizer Karelplein into the center. There are just under 20 functional rooms with good baths. Breakfast only. *Moderate.*

DAILY BREAD
Belvoir Hotel Restaurant (Graadt van Roggenstraat 101; Phone 22-23-44) is formal—silk-shaded brass chandeliers, flecked wallpaper, velvet draperies, tuxedoed staff—and inviting, with French-accented fare. Open with a sweetbread salad served *tiède*, or warm, *nouvelle* style; a more conventional shrimp or crab cocktail; lobster bisque or Burgundy-style snails. *Sole à la meunière* is a good bet. So are such other entrées as *Wiener schnitzel*, chicken sautéed with mushrooms, or T-bone steak. Desserts include *profiteroles au chocolat*—icecream-stuffed cream puffs enveloped in hot chocolate sauce. *Luxury.* (With a three-course and coffee menu—along with burgers and salads—served in the *Moderate*-category *Café*.)

In d'Oude Laeckenhal (Grote Markt 23; Phone 22-91-13) is visitable primarily for its historical setting, the city's sixteenth-century Cloth Hall, and its location, on the main square. Soups are reliable, and fish (sole, especially) is fresh and tasty, with ice cream desserts. *First Class.*

De Belvedere (Kelfkensbos 60; Phone 22-68-61): Up a flight you go, the better for smashing views over the Waal, from a table in this sixteenth-century tower. Prix-fixe menus can be good value, or order filet of pork or a veal specialty from the à la carte. *First Class.*

De Steiger (Regulierstraat 59; Phone 22-90-77) is indicated for a hearty seafood dinner. Open with fish soup, selecting the day's catch or always-reliable grilled sole as your entrée. *Moderate/First Class.*

Station (Stationsplein 5; Phone 69-61-43) is worth knowing about if you're in the neighborhood of the rail terminal. Prix-fixe menus and snacks. *Moderate.*

SOUND OF MUSIC
Stadsschouwburg (Keizer Karelplein) is the modern city theater: plays, opera, pop entertainment.

De Vereeniging (Keizer Karelplein) is an across-the-circle neighbor of the Stadsschouwburg (above). Look for concerts of Het Gelders Orkest—the Gelderland provincial symphony; Nijmegen Bach Choir; and other groups, classical and pop. The tourist office (below) has schedules of both halls.

INCIDENTAL INTELLIGENCE

Arnhem (Chapter 4) and Het Loo Palace in Apeldoorn (Chapter 11) are Nijmegen's near neighbors. *Further information:* VVV Nijmegen, St. Joristraat 72.

18

Rotterdam
World's Largest Port

BACKGROUND BRIEFING
Not every Dutchman or Dutchwoman you meet as you travel through the Netherlands likes Rotterdam. The problem has not to do with size—its port is the planet's largest, and a population of half a million makes it No. 2 in a kingdom chockablock with cities—but rather with modernity. Rotterdam's historic core was razed in the course of a Nazi air raid on May 14, 1944—every Rotterdammer knows the precise date—and it is, as a consequence, a city with a contemporary, post-World War II center.

You must, then, be prepared to forego the Baroque mansions of Amsterdam, the rococo elegance of The Hague, the sunken canals winding through Utrecht, the medieval-origin Grote Markt-cum-Grote Kerk common to most other Dutch towns. But this is hardly difficult, even for a confirmed traditionalist like me.

I like the convenience of Rotterdam, the good sense and clear logic that went into its careful—and professional—planning, the ease in getting about, the perky populace, the abundant—and sorely underappreciated—cultural options, the first-rate shopping. And, hardly least, I like the salty maritime flavor that comes of centuries-long dominance as a wealthy, strategically sited terminus, where a tributary of the heart-of-Europe Rhine—the Nieuwe Maas—converges with the Nieuwe Waterweg, or New Waterway, linking it with Hoek van Holland, edging the North Sea/English Channel, the world's busiest seaway. Today's Port of Rotterdam, handling 240 million tons per year, is almost one and a half times as big as that of Kobe in Japan, its nearest rival, and more than twice as big as the Port of New York.

The city where the humanist Erasmus was born in the fifteenth century (and with a modern-design university that takes his name), Rotterdam was chartered as long ago as 1328 and for a considerable period lagged behind nearby Delft (Chapter 6), still smallish and tranquil, and the onetime port of Delft—Delfshaven—now, ironically, a part of Rotterdam and from where the Pilgrims, en route from Leiden (Chapter 14), sailed for the New World after laying over in Southampton and Plymouth.

The political division, in the early nineteenth century, of Holland and Belgium, gave Rotterdam a boost; it picked up harbor traffic from southerly Antwerp, suddenly a foreign city. Only decades later, beginning in the 1860s, Rotterdam's port became world-class, with the construction of the Nieuwe Waterweg between its inner harbor and the sea opening it up to the largest ships linking the continents.

ON SCENE
Lay of the Land: The city is nicely walkable in its central portions. Consider massively scaled *Centraal Station* more or less the northern frontier of the core; it fronts *Stationsplein* with both *De Doelen*, the concert hall-congress center, and *Schouburg*, the municipal theater, near neighbors. From Stationsplein, the street called *Weena* leads to *Hofplein*, a couple of blocks east. From that square, the important street called *Coolsingel* (bordered by the impressive World War I-era, mock-Renaissance *Stadhuis*, or city hall, which somehow escaped World War II bombs; towering *World Trade Center*; and cafés of contiguous *Stadhuisplein*) extends south to *Beursplein*, a big square that connects with *Hoogstraat* to its east and is the site of department stores and satellite shops (see Shopper's Rotterdam, below). Coolsingel, as it proceeds south, becomes

Schiedamse and leads to a pair of *maritime museums* (below) on *Willemsplein*, at its terminus. *Westblaak*, a broad thoroughfare heading west from Coolsingel at *Churchillplein*, continues to *Museumpark*, bordering *Museum Boymans-van Beuningen* (below) and *Erasmus University*.

Euromast and a harbor tour: First, gain a bird's-eye view of the city and the enormous area of the port—on a clear day, you can see all the way to Hoek van Holland and the North Sea, sometimes even to The Hague—from the first level (340 feet) and the higher, extra-admission Space Tower (600 feet) of the Euromast (Parkhaven 20); it was built in 1960 in the course of a remarkably swift 23-day span, and it has a pair of restaurants (Daily Bread, below). Then, proceed to the *Spido boat terminal* (Willemsplein), where you'll have a choice of harbor tours (there are five options, one as short as 75 minutes; the longest, five hours, going as far south as the Delta Works (Chapter 16). Boats are café and lounge equipped, with open decks, as well. Rotterdammers are fond of calling their town a port with a city attached to it; you see what they mean as you come to appreciate the significance of the harbor from the water. This is Rotterdam at its most animated, cosmopolitan, exciting, and beautiful—especially if the sun is bright, the water blue, and the clouds billowy. And it has virtually all been constructed since World War II. There are floating docks and dry docks, rubber tire-surfaced ferries bobbing at the hulls of mammoth freighters, some in motion, others stationary, with row after row of docked giants. And flags! If a country has a merchant marine, you're bound to see its colors in Rotterdam harbor: India and Norway, East Germany and the Philippines, China and Greece, Britain and Poland, America and France. With crews of the vessels waving as you pass them by.

Museum Boymans-van Beuningen (Mathenesserlaan 18): Museums with hyphenated appelations can be offputting; my nonfavorite in this category is Cologne's Wallraf-Richartz (See *Germany At Its Best*), which I find myself referring to as Waldorf-Richards. But Rotterdam's Boymans-van Beuningen is

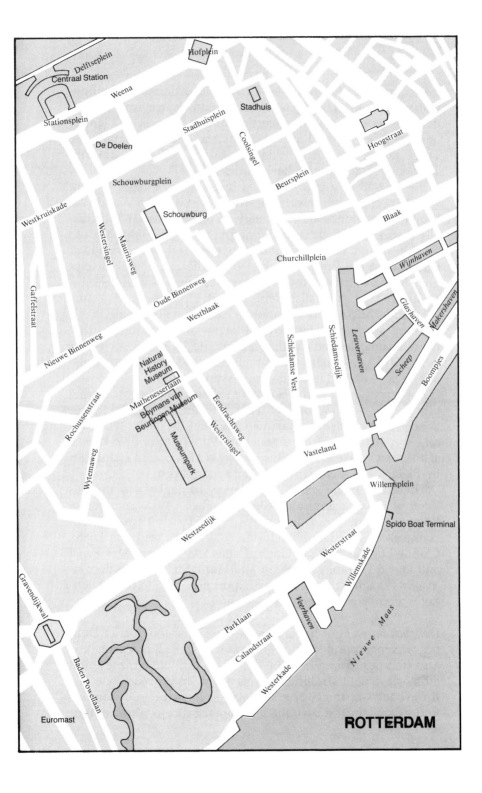

Delftseplein
Centraal Station
Weena
Stationsplein
Hofplein
Stadhuisplein
Stadhuis
Coolsingel
Hoogstraat
De Doelen
Schouwburgplein
Beursplein
Westkruiskade
Schouwburg
Blaak
Churchillplein
Wijnhaven
Westersingel
Mauritsweg
Oude Binnenweg
Glashaven
Makershaven
Gaffelstraat
Westblaak
Leuvehaven
Scheep
Nieuwe Binnenweg
Schiedamsedijk
Boompjes
Natural
History
Museum
Schiedamse Vest
Rochussenstraat
Mathenesserlaan
Boymans van
Beuningen Museum
Eendrachtsweg
Westersingel
Museumpark
Vasteland
Wytemaweg
Willemsplein
Spido Boat Terminal
Westzeedijk
Westerstraat
Willemskade
Gravendijkwal
Parklaan
Veerhaven
Calandstraat
Baden Powelllaan
Westerkade
Nieuwe Maas
Euromast

ROTTERDAM

even more of a mouthful; better refer to it simply as the Boymans, as the locals do. And allow, minimally, a couple of half-days for its contents—a collection of 250,000 objects. This is one of Europe's finest art museums and one of Holland's Big Three (along with Amsterdam's also-big Rijksmuseum and The Hague's much-smaller Mauritshuis).

It's housed in a pair of joined buildings; the older is pure Art Deco-cum-high tower, miraculously spared by World War II bombs, while the newer is early 1970s and less architecturally distinguished. It is worth noting that, very logically, old art is in the old building; modern works, in the newer. Which leads me to the Boymans' chief distinction: It is multidiscipline, Roman artifacts and Renaissance silver through Rodin sculpture and surrealist René Magritte paintings. Not surprisingly, Dutch representation is exceptionally strong.

There are not, to be sure, as many of the paintings that have become legendary throughout the kingdom, as is the case with Amsterdam's Rijksmuseum and the Mauritshuis. But there's not a Dutch Baroque painter of any caliber who is not represented at the Boymans—Rembrandt with, among others, his son *(Portrait of Titus)*, Steen *(Village Wedding)*, Bosch *(St. Christopher)*, Bartholomew van der Helst *(Abraham del Court and His Wife)*, Emanuel de Witte *(Interior with Woman at a Virginal)*, Jan de Bray *(The Finding of Moses)*, and an interior by Pieter de Hooch, who was Rotterdam-born.

There are Flemings in abundance—Brueghel's matchless *Tower of Babel*, a luminous Memling *Pietà*, and a number of Rubens's works, including his *St. Catherine*. But you will encounter, as well, Dürer and Titian, Del Sarto and Van Dyck, Claude Lorrain and Van Gogh, Degas and Picasso, Max Ernst and David Hockney, Watteau and Frank Stella. With decorative arts ranging from Chinese Export porcelain to early twentieth-century gooseneck lamps. Cafés.

Delfshaven, west of the center, was for long the port of Delft but was incorporated into Rotterdam in 1886. It is a protected area (facades cannot be altered; houses cannot be razed), and a half-day spent strolling its waterfront street, *Voorhaven*, is a throwback—in the course of a stay in late-twentieth-century Rotterdam—to the Baroque and Renaissance centuries. Your primary stop should be *De Dubbelde Palmboom,* a branch of Historisch Museum Rotterdam (below) in a deftly restored granary, with several floors of exhibits (start at the top and work your way down), at their best in the case of antique tiles, maps, prints, and paintings, with a working miniwindmill star of the show. There's a cozy café and satellite minimuseum in a nearby house. If it's open, pay your respects at the dramatically gabled, cupola-topped *Oude Kerk,* where the Pilgrim Fathers, come from Leiden, prayed before sailing on an extended journey (interrupted, of course, at the English ports of Southampton and Plymouth) to the New World. Art galleries, crafts shops, and pubby restaurant-cafés are all about.

Historisch Museum Rotterdam (Korte Hoogstraat 31)—located in a sumptuous, lavishly facaded Baroque mansion, which was the only seventeenth-century building in the city center to be spared the 1940 bombs—reopened in late 1986 after being shuttered for ten years, during which it was superbly refurbished, to the point where, in my view, it is one of the handsomest museums in the Netherlands. If you have even a passing interest in the decorative arts, you want to take in its principal period rooms—a seventeenth-century salon with carved-wood accents highlighting walls covered in blue velvet; an eighteenth-century reception room in pale green, its woodwork gilded; and a late-eighteenth/early-nineteenth-century room paneled in ivory-painted wood that contrasts with salmon-moiré-surfaced walls. There are five levels of exhibits—the range, a group of 40 paintings of seventeenth-century Rotterdam magistrates through ceremonial silver and antique tiles, porcelain and costumes, dolls and toys, embroideries and maps, and enjoyable Rotterdam-executed paintings with Rotterdam subjects: a seventeenth-century harbor scene, an eighteenth-century still life, portraits of Rotterdammers over a multicentury span. The shop is of above-average interest, and there's a rather ambitious restaurant in the high-ceilinged basement, reviewed in a later paragraph.

Maritiem Museum Prins Hendrick (Leuvehaven 1), like the Historisch Museum (above), opened in late 1986, but in a striking new building rather than a refurbished old one and has an appropriate waterfront location. Architect W. G. Quist warrants kudos for the Maritiem's quarters—pale brick and angular, with an arcaded ground floor, windows at irregular intervals on four upper levels, and an interior designed to show off an extraordinary collection, begun in the mid-nineteenth century by Prince Hendrick, a son of King William II, and befitting the world's largest port. You start with the section called Vademecum, for three-dimensional orientation on Rotterdam's maritime prowess. Then you take in the permanent collection—models and prints, maps and charts, paintings and globes, nautical instruments and ships' utensils, not to mention exemplary paintings. But the kicker of the Maritiem is its alfresco section. By that I mean the harbor out front, lined with a variety of vessels—river barges, tugboats, and the Dutch Navy ship *Buffel* (operated semi-independently as a museum on its own). You may board the lot, and, should you work up an appetite in the process, there's a terraced café.

Museumschip Buffel (Leuvehaven, just opposite Maritiem Museum Prins Hendrick, above) is a late-nineteenth-century Dutch Navy ship, open for inspection, crew's quarters and washroom (with some 30 mirrored sinks in two long rows) through comfortable officers' quarters and elaborate captain's suite. Ships' officers have been well cared for and housed at sea, at least since the seventeenth century. The surprise of the *Buffel* is the excellent facilities for the enlisted men, especially given the time slot—a century back. Bravo, Royal Dutch Navy!

Museum voor Volkenkunde (Willemskade 25): Holland, to its credit, abounds in ethnographic museums, but Rotterdam's is significant for two reasons. Its permanent collection, containing some 100,000 objects and 10,000 photos, stands out. And, not unlike the Maritiem and the Historisch museums (above), it returned to the scene in late 1986, its cupola-topped 1851 building thoroughly and drastically refurbished. Nonwestern cultures constitute the thrust. There are sections from areas throughout Asia, Africa, and the New World, with Indonesia—the former Dutch East Indies—especially well represented. And the restaurant's specialties are dishes from Third World countries.

Blijdorp Zoo (Van Aerssenlaan 49): If you're going to visit a single zoo in Holland, make it Rotterdam's, within walking distance of Centraal Station and with its specialty the breeding of animals—kapi, Père David's deer, and a horse species called Przewalski, for example—threatened with extinction. It is very big on tigers, and a boon when it's raining is the Riviera Pavilion, an enormous covered garden that's home to crocodiles and apes. There's a special building for nocturnal animals and a big café.

Kinderdijk, nine miles southeast of Rotterdam, is Windmill-ville; by that I mean 19 of them, the lot erected in 1740. Traditionally, they operate *in toto* Saturday afternoons in July and August, but one of them is open daily except Sundays, April to October. Tour groups—or at least operators of tour groups—adore Kinderdijk: do not count on being alone in the course of your visit.

SETTLING IN
Hilton International Rotterdam Hotel (Weena 10; Phone 414-4044) is the quintessential Rotterdam hotel, contemporary and trim lined, as befits a hostelry in the likewise modern city center. Location is inspired—a five-minute walk from Centraal Station, just off Coolsingel, the principal thoroughfare of the core, with De Doelen concert hall/congress center and the Municipal Theater a hop and a skip, museums and shops all within walking distance. Recent seasons have seen the interior of the Hilton smartly restyled in soft pastels. There are 246 tastefully decorated rooms and 15 generous-size suites, all with typically topnotch Hilton baths; Le Restaurant, open early breakfast through very late dinner and later evaluated; Lobby Bar, Rotterdam's No. 1 congregating place and fun for afternoon tea; Casino Rotterdam, where you may try your luck at roulette or blackjack; just off the lobby;

Le Bateau, with disco dancing into the wee hours; quick-as-a-wink room service; and a staff headed by genial, always-on-scene General Manager Rudy Rausch, than whom there is no more proficient or kindly in the kingdom. *Luxury.*

Park Hotel (Westersingel 70; Phone 36-36-11)—a fair walk to Coolsingel, but close to Museum Boymans-van Beuningen— is a two-building complex, terraced and in its own garden, with the preferred rooms, 62, all told, featuring up-to-the-minute baths. Public spaces are agreeable and include a handsome restaurant, casual grill-café and well-equipped sauna-fitness center. Management is professional, and staff is cordial. *First Class.*

Atlanta Hotel (Aert van Nesstraat 4; Phone 11-04-20) is nicely situated, just off Coolsingel. This is a modern house with traditionally furnished public spaces that include an off-lobby restaurant, bar-lounge, corridors with ice-cube machines (for which kudos), and 170 rooms. Accommodations I have inspected—including a beige twin and a pale blue single—are nice sized and comfortable. Friendly. *First Class.*

Savoy Hotel (Hoogstraat 8; Phone 13-92-80): I wish that the Savoy were central—it's a long walk or a short drive east of the core—but there is no denying its good looks. Those of the 95 rooms I have inspected are tastefully contemporary, gray and white—and with rocking chairs. There's a bar in the basement (open from 5:00 P.M.) and a restaurant in which breakfast and dinner—but not lunch—are served. *First Class.*

Scandia Hotel (Willemsplein 1; Phone 13-47-90), appropriately nautical in motif—given an enviable location overlooking the harbor, albeit an easy walk to the center—has close to 60 rooms. Almost all have baths; you want to ask for one of these, making sure it's in the front, with a view of the Nieuwe Maas. There's a pleasant bar and a restaurant featuring Scandinavian specialties (the owners are Norwegian). *Moderate.*

Rijn Hotel (Schouburgplein 1; Phone 33-38-00) shares central Schouburgplein with the Municipal Theater and occupies a modern tower with 140 rooms of varying sizes (if you're booking a double, specify a *larger* double), whose baths, in some cases, have showers rather than tubs. Restaurant, bar. Pleasant. *Moderate/First Class.*

Emma Hotel (Nieuwe Binnenweg 6; Phone 36-55-33): An engaging black dog welcomes you to the friendly Emma, whose owner-manager, Mrs. Orsini, sees to it that her 26 functional rooms are spotless and comfortable; all have shower-equipped baths. Near Museum Boymans-van Beuningen. Breakfast only. *Moderate.*

Central Hotel (Kruiskade 112) is, to be sure, central and full facility—this is an elderly, albeit updated house with some 60 bath- or shower-equipped rooms, restaurant, and bar—but I was put off by an uncordial reception, so atypical in Holland, in the course of attempting an inspection. *Moderate.*

DAILY BREAD
La Rotisserie (Euromast, Parkhaven 20; Phone 436-4811) is ideally combined with a visit to the summit of Euromast (On Scene, above) on a sparkling, sunny day, the better for clear and sharp harbor/city views. Fare is classically French accented. You order from an extensive à la carte. Open with goose liver *pâté* in Port sauce; seafood salad served *tiède,* or warm, *nouvelle* style; or snails, Burgundy style. Grilled sole is an entrée specialty, but there are half a dozen fish options, not to mention shoulder of lamb or veal *médaillons.* Desserts are mostly frozen. Lovely service. *Luxury.*

Le Restaurant (Hilton International Rotterdam Hotel, Weena 10; Phone 414-4044): Trust U.S.-based Hilton International to serve up Rotterdam's best beefsteaks, grilled just as you specify, with Yank-style baked potatoes or *frites* and a super tossed salad. Veal and lamb entrées are likewise reliable in this congenial setting, and the Hilton's *pâtissier* turns out delectable pastry. Wine list is exceptional, and service is swift. *First Class.*

Historisch Museum Restaurant (Historisch Museum Rotterdam, Korte Hoogstraat 31; Phone 433-41-88) occupies much of the high-ceilinged ground floor of the splendid—and splendidly refurbished—Baroque mansion housing the city's historical museum (On Scene, above). The look is a winning mélange of the contemporary—chrome and wicker chairs, tables centered by candles in white porcelain holders—with original, centuries-old beams overhead. Order either from a prix-fixe menu or à la carte, noting that soups are good; fish— whatever the day's specials, prepared to order—delicious; vegetables, especially good; and *mousse au chocolat,* a favored dessert. *First Class.*

Portofino (Nieuwe Binnenweg 151; Phone 36-54-42) attempts, and not without some success, to emulate the flavor of the Italian Riviera town for which it's named. A friendly Italian staff serves up authentic fare of the peninsula—with reliable openers among soups *(straciatella* and *minestrone),* decently-sauced pastas, and exemplary veal *scaloppine.* Italian wines. *First Class.*

Engels (Stationsplein 45; Phone 119-551) is a multirestaurant complex opposite Centraal Station that caters heavily to groups, but where individuals are, to be sure, welcome at a spread of specialty restaurants. Take your choice of *Viking* (Scandinavian smorgasbord), *Don Quijote* (Spanish *tapas* and *paella), Tokaj* (Hungarian, stuffed cabbage and *strudel). Chez François* (snails and frog legs), *Beefeater* (roast beef and Yorkshire pudding), and *New Yorker* (sirloin steaks and baked potatoes), with the bonus of a Dutch café, *'t Oude Engels.* I leave the authenticity of the various national dishes for you to evaluate; you're bound to be happier with some choices than with others. *First Class.*

Indonesia (Rodesgand 34; Phone 414-8588): Every major Dutch city has its share of good Indonesian restaurants; Indonesia is one such in Rotterdam; decor, staff, and of course fare, constitute the genuine article. Order *rijsttafel*, embracing a score of specialties, spectacularly presented. Your waiter will explain what's what. A tasty, enjoyable experience. *First Class.*

De Harmonie (Stationsplein 53; Phone 411-3040) is worth knowing about if you've tickets for a performance in either De Doelen or the Schouburg nearby and crave a competent, precurtain dinner, served without delay. *Moderate.*

Le Havre (Havenstraat 9, in Delfshaven; Phone 425-7172) is indicated for lunch in the course of Delfshaven exploration (On Scene, above). Build your meal around fish or, if you like, mussels variously prepared. And specify a window table. *First Class.*

De Bijenkorf (Coolsingel)—Rotterdam's ranking department store (below)—offers a variety of tasty victuals, including super pastas, from a help-yourself buffet in attractive *La Ruche* on Two, with a handy espresso bar on Three. Its *Konditerei* is a big, noisy, enjoyable street-level café, for casual lunches, snacks, or coffee-cum-crowds. All are *Moderate.*

Raoul (Coolsingel) is at its best in warm weather, when you want to take an outdoor table, order something to drink and/ or eat, and watch Rotterdammers scurry in and out of the adjacent Bijenkorf and the subway. *Moderate.*

Wall Street (Stadhuisplein): Americans, financiers or otherwise, are attracted by the name and invariably enjoy taking an outdoor table here for views of the Stadhuis, opposite, and ambulatory Rotterdammers, in tandem with a casual meal, a drink, or coffee. *Moderate.*

Marie Antoinette (Pompenburg 652, at Hofplein; Phone 433-3595): You sense that this is not the most authentically French of eateries when you recognize the celebrated painting reproduced on the menu as that of Madame de Pompadour—rather than of the consort of Louis XVI, for whom the restaurant is named. Never mind. This is an attractive spot, smallish and friendly, with a prix-fixe menu—more nourishing than tasty—that might run to house *pâté* or mushroom-flecked *consommé*, *médaillons* of pork or a beef dish, with espresso following. Central. *First Class.*

SOUND OF MUSIC

De Doelen (Kruisstraat 2)—unexceptional in appearance from without—represents exceptional contemporary design within, its ceiling high and irregular, a level of boxes tucked into wood-paneled side walls, and, when the performance is a concert, audience on all four sides, with musicians in the center. This is home base for the esteemed Rotterdam Philharmonisch Orkest, conducted in recent seasons by an American, James Conlon. But there are performances, as well, of Het Nederlands Kamerorkest, a chamber group; Nederlands Kamerkoor, a choir; and jazz and pop artists, too. Two smaller halls supplement the main one. The tourist office (below) has programs.

Schouburg (Schouburgplein) is the post-World War II municipal theater; plays are presented in the Dutch language, of course, but there's opera and dance, including the Netherlands Opera, Dutch National Ballet, and Nederlands Dance Theater. The VVV (below) has programs.

SHOPPER'S ROTTERDAM

If you are into shopping centers—really massive ones—consider a stroll through *De Linjbaan*, well over a mile long, partly covered, and replete with cafés as well as specialty shops and boutiques. I am partial, however, to *Beursplein*, leading from central Coolsingel into Hoogstraat (see Lay of the Land, above). It is dominated by *De Bijenkorf*, a branch of the department store chain you know, perhaps, from Amsterdam, except that the Rotterdam store is handsomer and more spacious, with luggage, men's accessories, and a super chocolate department on the main floor; women's and children's departments and hairdressers, along with books and La Ruche

Restaurant (above), on Two, and an impressive food department/café in the basement. *Vroom & Dreesmann*, the department store chain whose branches blanket the Netherlands is just opposite, with an eminently visitable basement that contains a coffee shop, jumbo supermarket, housewares, and souvenirs. Women's and men's clothing and luggage are on Main. *C & A*, another big chain, embraces two floors, mostly moderate-category men's, women's, and kids' clothing and a cafeteria. Still another chain, *Hema*, is at its best in toiletries, candy, and baked goods departments; packaged chocolates—especially the chocolate truffles and Belgian-style pralines—are nowhere better in the Netherlands. *Peek & Cloppenburg*, another of the apparel biggies, sells men's duds on Main, women's and children's up a flight.

INCIDENTAL INTELLIGENCE

Rotterdam has an excellent Metro, or subway, system; the tourist office (below) has multilingual flyers detailing routes, as well as those of public buses. Rotterdam has its own international airport—Zestienhoven—but two miles north of the center and with flights to London and other foreign points. Fast trains link the city with Schiphol International Airport. The most popular of the ferries to Britain is that linking Hoek van Holland with Harwich; other ferries depart from Europoort and Buitenhaven. All are nearby. *Further information:* VVV Rotterdam, Stadhuisplein 19.

Utrecht
Hart van Holland

BACKGROUND BRIEFING
Translating this chapter's subtitle comes easy to the English speaker: Heart of Holland. And it could not be more accurate. Utrecht is mid-point in the kingdom's core, an all-Holland rail and road junction and a port of consequence on the Amsterdam-Rijnkanaal—the nation's busiest. It is, as well, a place of historic import; the pact that resulted in today's independent Netherlands bears its name. And, even though a population of a quarter-million makes it Holland's fourth largest city (only Amsterdam, Rotterdam, and The Hague are bigger), its considerable charm (a center cut through by café-fringed sunken canals) and cultural prowess (medieval treasures on view in a onetime convent of that era, through a sensationally futuristic performing arts center) go oddly underappreciated. Be the first on your block: Utrecht (pronounced Oo-*trecht*) is fun.

This is the city that produced the only Dutch pope (the palace built for him still is to be seen) and whose Catholic archbishop is Primate of Holland. It is, as well, wherein were signed both the decisive Union of Utrecht (the sixteenth-century alliance of the United Provinces, which paved the way for freedom from Spain) and the Peace of Utrecht, the series of early-eighteenth-century treaties that concluded the complex, pan-European War of the Spanish Succession, braking the expansion of one principal power (France), the while triggering the expansion of another (England).

Now capital of the province taking its name—the smallest in the Netherlands—and the venue annually of an internationally significant trade fair, Utrecht goes all the way back to the Romans, who made of it a colony that developed into a town of enough substance to attract the attention of an English missionary called Willibrord. He came south in 692, used Utrecht as a base for converting the greater part of the northern Netherlands to Christianity—and was later sainted. (There's a statue of him in the little square fronting the Pays Bas Hotel.)

But the bishops who succeeded Willibrord evolved as political, as well as spiritual leaders, becoming powerful as Prince Bishops of the Holy Roman Empire and antagonists of increasingly wealthy merchants, who ultimately prevailed, in 1527, when the prince bishop of the day was pressured into surrendering sovereignty over what had become an appreciable territory to Holy Roman Emperor Charles V.

Just half a century later, in 1577, the city joined in the struggle against Charles V's son, Philip II, with the Union of Utrecht following but two years later. And for a brief period, toward the end of the brief four-year reign to which he was both appointed and removed by his brother, Napoleon, King Louis Bonaparte lived in the Utrecht palace that is now the library of its prestigious university.

ON SCENE
Lay of the Land: Central Utrecht, though hardly compact, is walkable and in its easterly historic quarter delightfully walkable, with no shortage of cafés for rest pauses, on lower terraces of the city's unique sunken canals. Start at *Centraal Station*, facing *Stationsplein* at the western edge of town. Simply cross from the station entrance to *Hoog Catharijne*, the massive shopping complex (see Shopper's Utrecht, below), exiting at *Catharijne Baan*, running north-south, until you arrive—very shortly—at *Maria Plaats*, leading eastward into the core, and a grid of pedestrian shopping streets, including

Lange Elisabethstraat, which changes its name to *Steenweg* (lined with moderate-category stores) as it veers east toward *Choorstraat*, *Vismarkt* (lined by antiques shops), and modish *Oudkerkhof*, boutique filled. These shopping arteries are just east of the square called *Domplein*, site of *Domtoren*, the detached cathedral tower and the cathedral proper (below). *Korte Nieuwstraat*, becoming *Lange Nieuwstraat*, leads south from this square to *St. Catherine's Church* and its former convent, the latter housing the city's No. 1 museum. The *Stadhuis*, or city hall, is immediately north of Domplein, just west of the idyllic sunken canal—*Oudegracht*—which curves through the heart of town quite as it has for half a millennium. Two performing arts complexes anchor eastern and western edges of the center: *Muziek Centrum* to the west, on *Vredenburg*, near Hoog Catharijne shopping center; and *Stadsschouburg* on easterly *Lucas Bolwerk*. The city's churches—architecturally among the finest such in urban Holland—are at scattered locations; so, indeed are other museums. (And, in case you are curious, the earlier-mentioned papal palace, locally termed *Paushuize*—built in the early sixteenth century for Adrian VI but never, alas, inhabited by him—is canalview, on *Nieuwe Gracht* and not open to visitors.)

ON SCENE
Rijksmuseum Het Catharijneconvent (Nieuwegracht 63): Queen Juliana—before she passed the crown to her daughter Beatrix—opened this world-class collection of medieval art in 1979, and the International Council of Museums lost little time in awarding it, in 1981, its coveted Museum of the Year prize. Catharijneconvent's theme is the history of Christianity (both Catholicism and Protestantism) in Holland. Its setting—appropriately enough—is a long-desanctified sixteenth-century convent, whose garden-centered cloister is a principal treasure of Utrecht, and wherein a selection of Baroque art beautifully complements the Middle Ages sculpture, paintings, manuscripts, and textiles. Presentation, in a pair of connected buildings, is superb. No less so are exhibits; my notes brim with exclamation points: a ninth-century ivory and silver chalice, priests' vestments embroidered in silver and gold, a Book

of Gospels whose cover is of carved bone and semiprecious stones, exquisitely illuminated manuscripts, a wood-carved *St. Paul* out of the mid-fourteenth century, a slightly younger *St. Christopher* in the same medium, processional crosses and sculpted Stations of the Cross, rosaries and Bibles, a searing Cranach study of Luther, and a portrait of Calvin—long-bearded and with a pronounced nose—by a local painter (name unknown), portraits in oil of the antagonists William the Silent and Philip II, and paintings of such seventeenth-century masters as Rembrandt (*The Eunuch's Baptism*), Hals (*Portrait of Nicolaas Stenius*), and Ferdinand Bol (*Gideon and the Angel*). Give this one time; there's a café so that you may break for coffee or a casual lunch.

Centraal Museum (Agnietenstraat 1) opened in 1838, the first of the Dutch municipal museums. If it is not in the same league as counterparts in bigger Amsterdam and The Hague, it is to be very much admired. The half-dozen period rooms of the ground floor are dazzlers—a leather-walled salon with its furniture early-eighteenth century, Dutch variations on the theme of England's Queen Anne; a seventeenth-century dining-living room with an immense tiled fireplace and an also-huge *kos*, or armoire of that era; and a Louis XV-influenced sitting room, its furnishings Chinese, as well as Dutch. Utrecht-born Jan Scorel (1495–1562) is the leading luminary of the paintings section, with a panel on which are portraits of five members of a religious-oriented brotherhood. Jacob van Claessens's *Portrait of a Knight* in black and gold stands out. On no account miss either the meticulously detailed, Baroque-era dollhouse or a witty collection of costumes, eighteenth century through late twentieth.

National Museum van Speelklok tot Pierement (Buukerkhof 10) has no more felicitous a ring in its English translation—National Museum from Musical Clocks to Street Organs—than in Dutch. But no matter. You go first for the setting, a superbly scaled, multiepoch church relatively recently restored for its present function: a repository of automatic musical instruments—the range, gilded birdcages with mechanical nightingales, turn-of-century jukeboxes, player-pianos from the 1920s, and positively enormous street organs. It is not enough, though, to simply observe these instruments. You want to be on hand when a museum volunteer plays and demonstrates them, traditionally every hour on the hour, starting an hour after opening and concluding an hour before closing. It's lots of fun and like no other that I know of—in any country.

Nederlands Spoorwegmuseum (Jan van Oldenbarneveltlaan 6): Well, if you're going to have a Railways Museum, place it in a railway station in a city that's a major train terminus and also serves as Dutch Railways' headquarters. So, at least, figured this museum's astute planners. And they have done just that. Location is the late-nineteenth-century Maliebaan Station. Out you go, onto platforms of vast covered sheds, to step aboard a fabulous mix of carriages, locomotives, and even trolley cars—some, rare antiques from early decades of the nineteenth century; others, more recent and more lavish. Requisite for rail buffs, amusing even for jet-setters.

Hedendaagse Kunst Museum (Achter de Dom 12) concentrates on contemporary art—some, part of a permanent collection; a lot of it, temporarily exhibited—with the range heavily Dutch. You are likely not to be familiar with the painters, which is not to say—if you have a propensity for the nonrepresentational—you won't like their work. And there's a congenial café.

Domkerk and Domtoren (Domplein): The church proper, first: It's a Gothic beauty (mostly fourteenth century) with a lovely, lacy facade, at its best out back, where superb flying buttresses anchor its apse; but it's eminently viewable within, as well, if only for the enormous organ, soaring vault, and massive windows. Aye, but there's a catch. The Dom's builders had not yet finished the nave when a seventeenth-century gale collapsed what there was of that area. A wall (with the organ against it) was put up to enclose the space. *Domtoren*, its tower, was separately built, and intentionally detached from the church (which is, incidentally, Protestant). The tower, completed in 1482, is—at 373 feet—the highest such in Holland and contains both chimes and bells; there are seven of the latter, weighing in at well over 12,000 pounds; there's a pair of chapels (one with an exhibit pertaining to the tower's construction); and there are precisely 465 steps to the summit, ascendable only by visitors accompanied by an authorized guide. The *Dom Cloister*, late fifteenth century, is fountain-centered and serene, with a plaque commemorating the death of St. Willibrord in 739—to complement the statue of the English-immigrant-missionary-saint in the square called *Janskerkhof*.

Pieterskerk (Pieterskerkhof 5)—Utrecht's oldest—dates to the eleventh century, and remains Romanesque in its crypt, where you'll note that designs of columns supporting the vault are no two alike, either on shafts or capitals. Upstairs, the transept is the most conspicuous feature of the remaining Romanesque area; the rest is mostly Gothic.

Jacobikerk's (St. Jacobstraat) single steeple towers over a somber, brick-Gothic facade that belies the splendor of a relatively recent interior restoration. Pulpit and baptismal are amidships, windows are of clear glass, and vaults are dramatic, with illumination from great brass chandeliers.

Slot Zeist (seven miles east of Utrecht on Zinzendorflaan in the town of Zeist) is a treat: one of the grander of the Dutch Baroque palaces, built by a Count of Nassau in the late seventeenth century with interiors designed by the same French Huguenot exile, Daniel Marot, who contributed so much to Het Loo Palace (Chapter 11). Classic-style, with a central pavilion flanked by lower wings, Slot Zeist functions contemporarily—quite sensibly, when you think about it—as a village-owned caterer/conference center. But you don't have to be a party guest or a convention delegate to have a look around; visitors are welcome to see whatever rooms are not in use. And what rooms they are: entrance hall hung with superb portraits of nobles beneath their coats of arms and

with Empire furnishings; Slotzaal, its ivory and gold panels
embedded with Renaissance tapestries and with Louis XVI-
era furniture; Blauwezaal, called after its blue damask walls,
punctuated by Baroque portraits and beautifully furnished;
and—most sumptuous of the lot—Willem Trouwzaal, its furnishings seventeenth century, its walls matchlessly mono-
chrome-muraled, its ceiling surfaced with a vast and heroic
fresco. (You may want to lunch in Zeist, after a palace visit;
see Daily Bread, below.)

Breukelen and castle country: Earmark a day of your Utrecht
stay for an excursion north of town, where, within a 15-mile
radius, are the still-charming village that gave its name to the
New York City borough of Brooklyn and a trio of landmark
castles. Route yourself to Kasteel de Haar and Slot Zuylen in
the morning, continuing to Breukelen for lunch (see Daily
Bread, below) and Kasteel Sypesteyn in the afternoon.

Kasteel de Haar (near the village of Haarzuilens and in its
own 50-acre deer park) is not only the largest of our trio of
castles but No. 1 in size in the Netherlands. Romantically
moated—you enter over a drawbridge—step-gabled, and
multiturreted, it went up over a two-year span, starting in
1892, when the owning baron and his wife (Madame was a
French Rothschild) commissioned the architect of Amsterdam's Rijksmuseum and Centraal Station, P. J. H. Cuypers,
to build them a romantic replacement, in the style of an originally medieval castle on the site. Mr. Cuypers obliged in the
flamboyant style for which he is known. De Haar is extrava-
gantly Gothic Revival. The Great Hall—which could be the
transept of a big-city cathedral—is quite the most spectacular
space. But you also inspect, in the course of a guided tour, a
paneled, beamed, and tapestried dining room, properly ba-
ronial, with a sumptuous fireplace; a ballroom complete with
minstrels' gallery, ceiling of gilded wood, exquisitely carved,
and walls partly of Gothic-style stone tracery, hung with sixteenth-century Brussels tapestries; bedrooms, including that
used by architect Cuypers, who settled in for much of the
period of construction; and kitchens, including the modern
one used to prepare meals for the current baron, who enter-

tains on a grand scale annually in late summer and early autumn, when, alas, De Haar is closed to the public.

Slot Zuylen (near the village of Maarssen): Ducks pad about Zuylen's moat and a decidedly unferocious dog guards the gate of this relatively small castle. Originally fourteenth century, its facade today weds the medieval with the Baroque. Interiors are mostly furnished with seventeenth- and eighteenth-century furniture and accessories—porcelain and crystal, paintings and sculpture. The entrance hall, antlers and other trophies sharing wall space with seventeenth-century paintings, is late Renaissance. But bedrooms, dining room, and Gobelinzaal—so named because of its memorable tapestries—are later and no less lovely.

Breukelen is something of a pilgrimage point for New Worlders resident in—or fond of—the American Brooklyn, which was a substantial city in its own right before it became one of the five boroughs of the City of New York at the turn of the present century. The original has retained not only the original spelling but its small size. It's a picture-postcard—fun to stroll, pausing for lunch or at least coffee at a café on the broad central square called *Kerkbrink* and popping into that square's originally fourteenth-century (albeit much restored) *Pieterskerk*, should it be open; *Kasteel Nijenrode*, an early-twentieth-century rebuilding of a Baroque castle-cum-tall tower that's now a school; the *Carriage Museum* at 125 Straatweg, which is open only by appointment (ask the tourist office, below, to call for you); and *Gemeentehuis*, the Baroque-era village hall. If you're a New Yorker, from either side of the East River, Brooklyn *or* Manhattan, you will want to pay your respects at the Dutch Brooklyn Bridge—*Vecht Brug*, a little white drawbridge that spans the narrow Vecht River, creating not necessarily minor traffic jams when it's raised for river traffic passing through. And all about are still-imposing mansions, most of them built by rich Amsterdammers as country retreats, as long ago as the late seventeenth century.

Kasteel Sypesteyn (in Nieuw Loosdrecht) was rebuilt at the turn of this century in the medieval style of its predecessor, itself razed some four hundred years ago. Sypesteyn functions primarily as a museum. There's a collection of paintings (sixteenth through eighteenth centuries, with heavy emphasis on the seventeenth's Golden Age, with Nicholas Maes the best known of the artists), along with sensational silver, crystal, and porcelain (including not only the expected Delft, but pieces made in the neighborhood—Loosdrecht—in the eighteenth century).

SETTLING IN
Pays Bas Hotel (Janskerkhof 10; Phone 33-33-21), Utrecht's *grande dame*, goes back a century and a quarter as a hostelry, although the facade of the building is even older. There are just under 50 rooms of varying shapes and sizes; those I have either lived in or inspected are comfortable and attractive, with motifs traditional and sizes, in some cases, overlarge. Their bathrooms, alas, tend to be tiny. But the staff is congenial and helpful, and public spaces—lobby-lounge, partially streetview, partially in a glass-roofed space that had been the carriage entrance; restaurant, later evaluated—are agreeable, and position is central, on a pretty square facing the landmark church whose name it takes. *Moderate.*

Holiday Inn (Jaarbeursplein 24; Phone 91-05-55) is at once an adjunct of Centraal Station and of massive Hoog Catharijne shopping complex, a 10- or 12-minute walk to the center. This is a big house, with close to 300 typically well-equipped Holiday Inn rooms. Even standard rooms have two double beds and real showers in their baths. There's a floor of rooms for nonsmokers and a deluxe floor—Club Europe—with upscale amenities like hairdryers and electric trouser pressers, as well as premium tabs. The glass-walled pool and adjacent saunas are on the twenty-first floor. Working model electric trains choo-choo the length of the bar in the amusing rooftop Railroad Lounge, as satisfactory for a steak-and-fries lunch as for a drink. The restaurant is worthy of evaluation in a later paragraph; it's supplemented by a coffee shop. And service-management down the line is cordial and proficient. *First Class.*

Smits Hotel (Vredenburg 14; Phone 33-12-32), in the same area as the Holiday Inn (above) is a modest, 47-room house in the course of gradually upgrading accommodations; if you book, stipulate a refurbished room. Breakfast only. *Moderate.*

Mitland Hotel (Ariënslaan 1; Phone 71-58-24), far enough north of the center so that you need a car, is a find. Thoughtfully selected modern art enlivens walls of the inviting lobby and lounge. Those of the 44 rooms I have inspected are good sized and good looking, with rattan furniture and both separate stall showers and tubs in their bathrooms. Besides the congenial bar, there are a pair of restaurants—one modern, in tones of yellow and blue; the other, traditionally Dutch. And everyone at the Mitland smiles, management through maids. *First Class.*

Ibis Hotel (Bizetlaan 1; Phone 91-03-66) is a relatively recent addition to the ranks of the French-origin Ibis chain, with uninspired public spaces that include a bar and a restaurant whose menu is more Dutch than French and 80 very plain rooms, bath equipped. It's west of the center; you'll need a car. *Moderate.*

DAILY BREAD

Lorre (Oudegracht 140; Phone 33-35-45): If you've time for but one meal in Utrecht, it should be at a restaurant housed in one of the venerable houses along Oudegracht, the medieval sunken canal that winds through the core of town. Lorre is typical in that it is two-level—you enter through the upper dining room, connected by stairs with the lower level, giving onto a canalfront terrace for warm-weather meals. Annemiek Lenders has deftly transformed an aged house (the terrace is thirteenth century) into a trendy eatery. White caned chairs surround tables set in pink linen, centered by flowers and candles in brass sticks. There's an extensive à la carte and a rather gala prix-fixe menu, with fare French *nouvelle*—in the best sense. A meal might open with a *surprise du chef* consisting of tiny filets of fish wrapped in bacon over a tiny bed of noodles. Lobster bisque or thin slices of goose breast and duck liver under a truffled sauce would follow. Entrées include grilled venison chops accompanied by apples baked with a cranberry stuffing; roast chicken seasoned with tarragon, or broiled salmon steak. Desserts—the blackberry *mousse*, most memorably—are delicious; wines, exemplary; service, super. In my experience, one of Holland's best restaurants. *Luxury*.

Stadskasteel Oudsen (Oudegracht 99; Phone 31-18-64)—with quarters in a sumptuously (and relatively recently) restored medieval mansion embracing several stories—is one of the swankiest environments in town. Go either for a drink in the bar, a snack or casual lunch in the café, or a proper meal in the upstairs dining room, beginning with the house's special beer soup, followed by the also-special *Kalfsbiefstuk*—veal filet in a beer-based mushroom sauce. Or order the four-course menu, perhaps comprising Ardennes ham and melon, leek soup, steak, and desserts selected from the trolley. And ask to be shown the restaurant's own little brewery in the basement. *First Class*.

Kromme Elleboog (Lange Nieuwstraat 7; Phone 31-97-16) conducts business in a cluster of small rooms on the ground floor of an aged townhouse. Principal accents in a severely plain decor are flora—white daisies on white linen, green plants hanging from the ceiling. Unsmiling waiters in long white aprons serve up a meal that opens nicely enough with an *ameuse-gueule* of smoked salmon on a bed of bamboo shoots. There's a pair of prix-fixe menus and an à la carte that might yield satisfactory—if hardly exciting—*nouvelle*-accented victuals. Openers include competent *consommé* and salad of smoked lotte on a bed of arugula, *vinaigrette* sauced. Roast wild duck and veal filet are among entrées. The ambience, though, is among Holland's chilliest. *Luxury*.

Le Bibelot (Oudegracht 181) offers no-nonsense French bistro fare (the proprietor is a loquacious Corsican). Open with onion soup or house *pâté*, continue with *boeuf Bourguignon* or grilled sea trout, and conclude with *pêche* Melba. Caveat: no credit cards. *First Class.*

Marie France (Catherijnesingel 81; Phone 32-26-77) is even more pristine in look than Kroome Elleboog (above)—white walls, white lighting fixtures, white chairs, white draperies, white bar. The chef's offering—an *ameuse-gueule* of the day's *mousse*, served to each guest in a teaspoon—can be delicious. Otherwise, the *nouvelle*-style fare is no more than competent, with simpler preparations—like filet of beef—the safest choices from a limited menu. Kindly service. *First Class.*

La Pizzeria (Voorstraat 23; Phone 31-60-21) takes pride in being Utrecht's oldest Italian restaurant. Besides pizza, there's a good selection of well-sauced pastas and veal entrées. Italian wines. Friendly. *First Class.*

Des Pays Bas Hotel Restaurant (Janskerkhof 10; Phone 33-33-21) evokes nineteenth-century Utrecht—gold-hued draperies at the windows, tall tapers at tables set in pristine white, tail-coated *maître d'hôtel*, and tempting hors d'oeuvres table at the entrance. Fare is traditional French, albeit with some contemporary touches. *Foie gras de canard*, shrimp cocktail in a *vinaigrette* sauce, smoked salmon marinated in dill and coriander, and a delicious watercress soup are among starters. Filet of sole, sautéed veal *médaillons*, and thyme-accented roast lamb are among favored entrées. And sweets rate their own card. *First Class.*

Café de Paris (Drieharingstraat 16; Phone 31-75-03) is the Utrecht counterpart of the Amsterdam original, one of a number of restaurants operated at various Dutch points by the enterprising—and talented—Fagel brothers. The café's menu is limited but tasty, with *entrecôte* and veal steak, deliciously sauced and served with *frites*, the favorites. Decor is appropriately Belle Époque. *First Class.*

Holiday Inn Restaurant (Jaarbeursplein 14; Phone 91-05-55) is the most formal of this hotel's public spaces. Tables are grouped around a massive floral arrangement. You order from a classically French à la carte—Burgundy-style snails or onion soup as starters and such entrées as duck *à l'orange*, poached salmon served with a delicate *mousseline* sauce, or a choice of steaks, with Béarnaise always among the sauce options. Snappy service. *First Class*.

Polman's (Corner Jansdam and Keistraat; Phone 33-21-24) occupies a desanctified seventeenth-century church, marvelous looking, with a fabulous ceiling and Art Deco accents. It's okay for a casual lunch built around an omelet, when you're not pressed for time; service can be painfully slow. *Moderate*.

Victor Consael (Neude; Phone 31-63-77) has been serving typically Dutch pancakes (in a score of varieties), waffles, the doughy sweets called *poffertjes*, and innumerable gooey sundaes (banana splits, among them) since 1850. Fun. *Moderate*.

Tapperij De Luifel (Neude; Phone 31-56-47) has been on scene, in the same quarters, since 1606. Stop in for a beer, taking it at a table on the square if it's sunny. Casual meals, too. *Moderate*.

De Hoefslag (Vossenlaan 28, in Bosch en Duin, about a mile north of Zeist, which is seven miles east of Utrecht; Phone 78-43-95): You have, perhaps, come to visit Slot Zeist (above) of a morning, and it's lunch time. De Hoefslag—among the more ambitious of the restaurants dotted about Holland, and operated by one or another of the many Fagel brothers (Gerard, in this case)—is indicated for a memorable meal. Setting is a rambling, multigabled, tile-roofed house in its own pretty garden. Look within is trendy-contemporary—good modern art on the walls, white chairs with bold plaid seats at the tables, and dramatic floral arrangements at scattered points. There's a choice of prix-fixe menus and a substantial à la carte. Gerard Fagel's cuisine pays homage to the classic fare of France, albeit with his own variations. House-smoked salmon is served with a *vinaigrette*-dressed salad. Cream of wild mushroom soup is laced with tarragon-flavored chicken liver.

Honey is a part of the thyme-based sauce accompanying roast lamb. Filet of sole is blanketed with a *cèpe*-flecked lobster sauce. But you may have a meal that gets down to basics— Zeeland oysters on the half-shell, grilled steak, and a platter of assorted cheeses to conclude. Not that desserts are to be omitted; Hoefslag's *Assiette aux Cinq Desserts de Notre Pâtissier*—a sampling of five—will give you an idea. And take time to study a wine list that simply has to be the most comprehensive in the Netherlands; by my count, the Bordeaux alone number 110. In my experience, one of Holland's best restaurants. Member, Relais et Châteaux. *Luxury*.

De Kastanjehof (Koosterlaan 1 in Lage Vuursche, 19 miles east of Utrecht, near Baarn; Phone 248) is (together with its neighbor, De Lage Vuursche, below) in Royal Family territory. Queen Beatrix lived in Lage Vuursche's octagonal manor house, Kasteel Groot Drakestein, as Crown Princess, before ascending the throne; and her mother, Princess Juliana, lives nearby at Paleis Soestdijk, with a splendidly Baroque black-and-white facade. De Kastanjehof is light and bright in pastel tones, with wicker chairs at tables, and a terrace for summer meals. The à la carte, alas, in the Dutch language only, is extensive; from it, you might compose a meal of Lady Curzon soup, veal steak served with three sauces, and another three-some—sherbets, this time—to conclude. There are guest rooms upstairs; those I have inspected are attractive, and 10 of the 13 have baths. *First Class*.

De Lage Vuursche (Dorpsstraat 2, Lage Vuursche; Phone 351), a near neighbor of De Kastanjehof, is quite as attractive in its way, beamed and white walled, on scene since 1650, and owned by the same family for five generations. Prices are somewhat lower than those of the competition, above. *First Class*.

Het Staate Wapen (Kerkbrink, in Breukelen; Phone 63-399): You can't miss this big white house at the lower end of Kerkbrink. The terrace is indicated for a warm-weather lunch. If it's cool, go inside; tables are laid in brown and tan linen, service is sprightly, and fare—à la carte or from a prix-fixe menu—runs to reliable soups, well-broiled fish (sole, especially), and frozen desserts. *First Class.*

Van Miert (Kerkbrink, Breukelen) is a long-on-scene café, with tables on the square—ideal for the writing of postcards, to friends or family in, say, Brooklyn, U.S.A. *Moderate.*

SOUND OF MUSIC

Muziekcentrum Vredenburg (Vredenburgpassage 77, near Hoog Catharijne shopping center) is an all-Europe standout, with respect to the spectacular contemporary architecture of its octagonal Main Hall: stage is dead center, and the audience—on a number of levels—surrounds it. Programming is among the Netherlands' richest—concerts by the Residentie Orkest, Nederlands Philharmonisch, Rotterdam Philharmonisch, Amsterdam's Concertgebouw, and other orchestras, as well as opera chamber concerts, recitals by celebrated soloists, pop and rock, and the circus. The center's also-octagonal small hall—glass domed—is a stunner, too. The tourist office (below) has programs.

Stadsschouwburg (Lucas Bolwerk 24)—blonde brick and striking—was completed just before World War II. The larger of the two auditoriums (1,000 seats) is the setting for opera, ballet (including the Dutch National and Nederlands Dance Theater), revues, and plays, these last, of course, in the Dutch language. And there's a No. 2 auditorium, too. Ask the VVV for programs.

SHOPPER'S UTRECHT

Hoog Catharijne —the shopping center adjacent to Centraal Station, about which I write above—is best negotiated with the aid of a directory and floor plan, obtainable at one of its information desks. It's the site of the city's No. 1 department store, a big link of the Hollandwide *Vroom & Dreesmann* chain, with a fabulous food department on its lower level. Infinitely less confusing—and to me more satisfying—are shopping streets in the center of town. Choorstraat and Kalverstraat are chockablock with popular-price stores, not unlike Amsterdam's Kalverstraat. A branch of the *Hema* department-store chain is on Oudegracht, as are *De Sleate*, a chain vending bargain-priced books, many in the English language; *Marie Christine Mode* (high-style women's clothes); and a branch of *Laura Ashley* (textiles and women's accessories). *Steppin' Out* on Zadelstraat has classic-style men's clothes. *Theo Blom* (Domkerkplein) is for fine chocolates. Lichte Gaard is a street with such antique shops as *G. J. Bestebreurtje* (books and prints), *A. W. J. de Groot* (glass, tiles, and small objects), and *Het Bisschopshof* (maps and globes). Still more antiques are to be found on the street called Vismarkt at such shops as *Gieling* (eighteenth-century furniture), *Lisman* (seventeenth-century furniture), and *Van der Leeuw* (medieval and Baroque objects). Oudkerkhof abounds in smart boutiques—*XYZ* (women's clothes), *House of Scotland* (woolens), *Manly* (way-out men's clothes), *Ebel* (jewelry), and *Reinders*, with extraordinary selections of porcelain—Delft, of course, but British, French, German, and Swedish imports, as well. And last but hardly least, there's Schoutenstraat, to which you repair when you're hungry, calling at *Edama Van Rijn* for bags of the cookies they've been baking since 1726 (as well as chocolate truffles) and at *Kruidnootjes* for a fix of the sweet biscuits called *speculaas*, or—especially if you're from across the Atlantic and are a bit homesick—American-style brownies.

INCIDENTAL INTELLIGENCE ══════════════════

A day's excursion from Amsterdam (trains take but 22 minutes) is the coward's way of experiencing Utrecht. Do plan to stay longer. *Further information:* VVV Utrecht, Vredenburg 90, in Muziekcentrum Vredenburg, with a branch at Stationstraverse 5 in Hoog Catharijne shopping center; VVV Breukelen, Kerkbrink.

Zwolle

Ringed by Walls and Water

BACKGROUND BRIEFING

What the city fathers of Zwolle—contemporarily capital of the east-central province of OverIJssel—quite obviously concluded during the town's formative medieval years, was that the protective function of a moat, encircling a castle, could be carried a step further. And so they surrounded their town with the very same canal—Stadsgracht—that borders it today, eight centuries after Zwolle received a municipal charter.

A town wall, punctuated by circular fortifications—and a network of well-guarded brick gates—backed the canal for double measure. They went up at the start of Zwolle's Golden Age, the epoch that saw the Middle Ages become the Renaissance, when the town thrived as a member of the mercantile Hanseatic League, growing rich as an *entrepôt* for the flow of goods between Germany and Flanders.

The vigilant guards are long-since gone, and not all of the great wall remains today. But there is enough of it—fastidiously restored—to evoke the atmosphere of an earlier Zwolle, a number of whose monuments happily remain. Zwolle today is one of the most enjoyably strollable of the smaller Dutch cities.

ON SCENE

Lay of the Land: The railway station is in a newer section—on *Stationsplein*, a bit south of the core, as is the principal hotel (below). But the Zwolle you have come to visit lies within the area flanked by *Stadsgracht*, the encircling city canal. Center of the center is *Grote Markt*, graced by a Rodin sculpture and edged by the town's monumental *Grote Kerk* and by the *Stadhuis*, or town hall (below). Shopping streets lead from this square—*Melkmarkt*, to the west; *Oude Vismarkt*, to the southeast; *Enggenstraat*, leading north to *Winkelcentrum*, a contemporary shopping complex; and—the most important—*Diezerstraat*, to the northeast, with a branch of the *Hema* department store chain. *Broerenstraat* leads north from Diezerstraat to *Broerenkerkplein*, named for a historic church overlooking it, which is backed by a segment of venerable city wall, with the northerly segment of *Stadsgracht* just beyond. *Sassenpoort*, a veritable minicastle the equivalent of nine or ten stories in height—more, perhaps, if you include the highest of its delicate pinnacles—is the only remaining city gate; there were four. This one, at the eastern terminus of *Koestraat* (alongside *Sassenpoorte Brug*, the bridge traversing Stadsgrach), dates to the fifteenth century and is one of the most beautiful such in the Netherlands.

Grote Kerk (Grote Markt): Smaller Dutch cities abound in centrally situated Gothic churches that tower over their surroundings. None, though, is more immediately overpowering than the Grote Kerk of Zwolle—early fifteenth century and massively square, its interior delineated by three equal-width aisles, backed by a superb Baroque organ, with choir stalls dating to the sixteenth century and—I save best for last—a pulpit carved from wood by an artisan who lived on the site, within the church, over a five-year period, 1617–1622. Windows of the church—Protestant since the Reformation—are immense and of clear glass, and the Zwolle-born, seventeenth-century painter Gerard Terborch (who spent many years in nearby Deventer [Chapter 8]) is buried within.

Stadhuis (Grote Markt): The town hall has both contemporary and old wings. The former is commendable; the latter—originally fifteenth century but with a facade renewed in the nineteenth century—is exceptional, thanks in large part to a ceremonial chamber, still used for weddings, dubbed *Schepenzaal*. A brass chandelier quite as old as the room itself, mid-fifteenth century, hangs from an oak-beamed ceiling, before a sumptuously framed painting of *The Last Judgment* surmounting a stone mantel, with fine paintings of House of Orange monarchs on surrounding walls, masterful carved-wood heads, and—the room's most unusual feature: a quartet of safes, gold embellished and embedded in the walls, that must be among the earliest such extant.

Provincial OverIJssels Museum (Melkmarkt 41) is a joy, embracing not one, but a pair of back-to-back—dare I say it?—museum-caliber buildings: one, severe sixteenth-century brick, with a turreted tower at its left flank; the other, exuberantly Baroque. You go as much for the period rooms—eighteenth-century kitchen, its walls diamond-patterned, floor to ceiling; seventeenth-century dining room with a giant, tiled fireplace; pair of parlors, one with Dutch-made furniture in the style of Louis XV; the other, also Dutch, albeit from the later Louis XVI era. As for paintings, standout works are by the most famous of native-son artists, Gerard Terborch (*Soldiers at Cards*), and by less well known Hendrick ten Oever (*Cows in a Meadow*). And there are exemplary collections of antique porcelains and silver.

Onze Lever Vroukerk (Ossenmarkt) translates as Our Lady Church and warrants inspection for two reasons. First is its distinctive tower, so-called pepperpot (*Peperbus*) in contour, and second is its scale—high, high Gothic, with a long and narrow nave, much of it not improved by nineteenth-century restoration.

Broerenkerk (Broerenkerkplein) was originally Dominican, is no longer consecrated, but has not lost its massive, late-

Gothic interior, whose vaults are supported by a splendid network of columns. Go for a concert.

SETTLING IN

Wientjes Hotel (Stationsweg 7; Phone 211-200) is housed in a pair of contiguous houses of some age, with some of the 47 rooms period-style but the majority compact contemporary and adequate, albeit cramped. There are a pair of restaurants—convenient coffee shop and pricier dinner-only dining room, a bar, and a separately entered casino in the basement. Location is close to the station, an agreeable ten-minute walk to the center. *Moderate.*

Postiljon Motel (Herstenbergweg 1; Phone 216-031), like other links of the Postiljon chain, is a couple of miles from the town it serves; you need a car. This is a modern house with 72 well-equipped rooms (baths are up-to-date), satisfactory restaurant-café, and bar. Friendly. *Moderate.*

DAILY BREAD

Barbara (Ossenmarkt 7; Phone 211-948) occupies a centuries-old house—inviting, cozy, and intimate, with the boss a French-trained chef and his French wife the hostess/head waitress. Fare is a successful Franco-Dutch meld, *nouvelle* influenced. There's a three-course prix-fixe lunch menu and two dinner menus, each costly, as well as an à la carte from which a meal might run to veal sweetbreads *en croute* with a currant sauce or Zeeland oysters on the half-shell as openers, beef tenderloin with chanterelle mushrooms or grilled smoked suckling pig as entrées. Fish dishes—filet of sole with fennel and white wine sauce—are reliable, and broiled Charolais steak is always available. And, although Barbara has but six tables, there are 10,000 bottles of wine—most of them French—in its cellar, as well as diverse assortments of French *eaux-de-vie* and other digestifs. In my experience, one of Holland's best restaurants. *Luxury.*

Poppe (Luttekestraat 66; Phone 213-050): Chefs have replaced the blacksmiths, but Poppe, which opened in the last century as a forge, retains the look of one, even to horses' stalls, through which you pass to gain entrance, and to horses' shoes—scores of them—surfacing the walls. This rustic ambience works well. Kitchen is open, tables invariably crowded, and menu Gallic influenced, with *pâté maison* and onion soup, among first courses; *entrecôte* with *sauce Béarnaise*, and *coq au vin*, among entrées. Order the prix-fixe or à la carte. Congenial. *First Class.*

De Librije (Broerenkerkplein 13; Phone 212-083) makes its home in the cellar—brick columns support whitewashed vaults—of a onetime Dominican monastery that was attached to Broerenkerk (above). It's handsome, with stained-glass windows and green plants accenting mauve linen on the table. The good-value five-course menu embraces salad, soup, *nouvelle*-style fish and meat courses, and ice cream, with coffee included. *First Class.*

Talamini (Grote Markt): An outdoor table at Talamini, on the town's principal square, with the grandly proportioned Grote Kerk dead ahead, is a Zwolle experience not to be missed, especially if you ask for the ice-cream menu—actually an elaborate brochure—and order one of the 19 magnificently ornamented sundaes illustrated in color therein. You will not regret either the Ital Grande or, my weakness, the Gondola Venezia. But if you're chicken, opt simply for *espresso*. *Moderate.*

SOUND OF MUSIC

Odeon (Blijmarkt)—the municipal theater—is updated mid-nineteenth century, neo-Louis XV in style, and a venue for concerts, both classical and jazz.

Buitensociëtet (Stationsweg 4), larger than the Odeon, sees performances of both the OverIJssel Philharmonic and the regional Forum Opera.

INCIDENTAL INTELLIGENCE ══════

The tourist office (below) has schedules on boat excursions in nearby waters. Zwolle is convenient to Giethoorn (Chapter 9) and Kampen (Chapter 12), both nearby. *Further information:* VVV Zwolle, Grote Kerkplein 14.

Acknowledgments

The special pleasure of scouting about the Netherlands to research a book about that remarkable country is the opportunity afforded for meeting its people. In no country of my experience has that been more stimulating, absorbing, or pleasurable. I am particularly indebted for the opening of many Dutch doors to Hank Fisher, with whom I have worked on a number of assignments over a sustained period, in his capacity as public relations director—ever helpful, knowledgable, congenial— of the Netherlands Board of Tourism in New York. Hank was enthusiastic about my tackling *Holland At Its Best* from the outset of the project, and I extend sincere thanks to him for manifold cooperation, as well as to his associates, Jean van Zuyden and Monica Depril; with my gratitude, as well, to Willem Schouten, veteran foreign press chief at NBT's head office in The Hague, whom I came to know and respect in the course of the extensive cross-Holland research trip— Leeuwarden to Limburg, Zeeland to Gelderland—which preceded this book's writing.

I am grateful, too, for the expertise of the Big Three at National Textbook/Passport Books—S. William Pattis, Leonard I. Fiddle, and Mark R. Pattis; to Senior Editor Michael Ross, ever patient, sympathetic, and skilled; to my research editor, Max Drechsler, like myself a longtime Netherlands enthusiast; to Louise Fisher, who typed the final manuscript with her usual expertise; to my agent, Anita Diamant, and her associate, Robin Rue; and—alphabetically—to the following friends and colleagues in the Netherlands and this side of the Atlantic, as well, for their personal kindness and professional cooperation:

Arnold Aarssen, Peter Andriesse, Mimi Baer, Sjoerd Barends, Rudy M. J. Bausch, Mila Beemer, Irma Berkvens, Frans Bonnema, Gerben Bonnema, Susan Boogert, Paul Borcher,

Eddie Burgers, Massimo Caredda, Mary Carroll, Jan D. Coersen, Monique Domsdoy, Mia Dwejnen, Hans van Eennennaam-Beck, Gerard A. M. Fagel, John Fagel, June Farrell, Bernard E. N. Felix, Odette M. Fodor, Hanke Gerritse. Also Wim G. M. Gloudemans, Adriaan Grandia, Karin Grielesen, Linda Gwinn, Pauline van der Heyden, Liduine Hoyinck, J. H. Jagersma, André Jansen, Ingrid M. Keizer, Mirjam R. Kleyn, Dr. Theo J. M. Kluskens, Klass Koen, Piet Kooistra, Roland and Johanna Kooman, René Klouwenberg, Piet Kuijper, Annemiek Leenders, Kathlen Louisse-Barrett, Georgetta Lordi, M. de Muynck-Hovestadt.

Also David B. Mitchell, R. Nuyens, Mariella Oostendorp, Fred Peelen, Fons Pessers, Helen Poort-Maureau, Ton Quik, Frans Reifitzhommer, Pieter Ritzen, Sr., Balth Roessingh, Frans de Rondejr, Bob Schaeffer, Toine Scheerens, Arlette Scherpel, William R. Sheppard, Anne Shield, Lenie Simons, Erik L. J. M. Slaats, Ellen de Smalen-Grolman, Joyce Snoek, H. Y. Th. van Stein.

Also Paul and Doris Stevens, J. M. Stikvoort, Marion Terborgh, Toon Toonen, Bert Verduin, G. E. P. Vrielink, H. Vroemen, Hans van Wees, Gina van der Weiden, A. A. Wenskat, Jan van Werven, Jaap A. Westerhuijs, Carla Wetzels, Mia Wijnen, Jos van de Zande, and Edith Zwart.

R.S.K.

Index

ABOUT THE AUTHOR

Robert S. Kane's initial writing stint was as editor of the [Boy Scout] *Troop Two Bugle* in his native Albany, New York. After graduation from Syracuse University's noted journalism school, he did graduate work at England's Southampton University, first making notes as he explored in the course of class field trips through the Hampshire countryside. Back in the U.S., he worked, successively, for the *Great Bend* (Kansas) *Daily Tribune, Staten Island Advance, New York Herald Tribune,* and *New York World-Telegram & Sun* before becoming travel editor of, first, *Playbill,* and later *Cue* and *50 Plus.* He writes regularly for leading magazines, such as *Travel & Leisure, Vogue, House & Garden, Atlantic, Harper's Bazaar, Family Circle, New York, Saturday Review,* and *Modern Bride;* and such newspapers as the *Newark Star-Ledger, New York Post, New York Daily News, New York Times, Los Angeles Times, Chicago Sun-Times, Boston Globe, San Diego Union, Dallas Morning News, San Francisco Examiner,* and *Toronto Globe & Mail.* And he guests frequently, with the subject travel, on TV and radio talk shows.

Africa A to Z, the first U.S.-published guide to largely independent, post-World War II Africa, was the progenitor of his acclaimed 14-book *A to Z* series, another pioneering volume of which was *Eastern Europe A to Z,* the first guide to the USSR and the Soviet Bloc countries as seen through the eyes of a candid American author. His current *World at Its Best* series includes two volumes (*Britain at Its Best* and *France at Its Best*) tapped by a pair of major book clubs, and a third (*Germany at Its Best*) that's a prize-winner.

Kane, the only American authoring an entire multi-volume travel series, has the distinction of having served as president of both the Society of American Travel Writers and the New York Travel Writers' Association, and is a member, as well, of the National Press Club (Washington), P.E.N., Authors Guild, Society of Professional Journalists, Sigma Delta Chi, and American Society of Authors & Journalists. He makes his home on the Upper East Side of Manhattan.